THE HOMEOWNER'S LEGAL BIBLE

THE HOMEOWNER'S LEGAL BIBLE
The Ultimate Guide to What Homeowners Need to Know

MARTIN M. SHENKMAN

JOHN WILEY & SONS, INC.

Published by John Wiley & Sons, Inc., New York.
Published simultaneously in Canada.

This publication is designed to provide accurate and authoritative information in regard to the subject matter covered. It is sold with the understanding that the publisher is not engaged in rendering professional services. If professional advice or other expert assistance is required, the services of a competent professional person should be sought.

Library of Congress Cataloging-in-Publication Data:

Shenkman, Martin M.
   The homeowner's legal bible : the ultimate guide to what homeowners need to know /
Martin M. Shenkman.
      p.   cm.
   Includes index.
   ISBN 0-471-21457-4 (pbk. : alk. paper)
   1. Home ownership—Law and legislation—United States—Popular works.   2. Homeowners—United States—Handbooks, manuals, etc.   I. Title.
   KF390.H53 S53 2001
   346.7304′32—dc21

                                                                        2001046974

Printed in the United States of America.

10 9 8 7 6 5 4 3 2 1

To my siblings, and to PK
for this suggestion and so much more.

Preface

WHAT YOU NEED TO KNOW ABOUT LEGAL, TAX, AND ECONOMIC ISSUES OF HOME OWNERSHIP

If you're like more than 60 million other Americans, your house is one of your most valuable assets; therefore, planning for your home is a key component in any personal, financial, estate, or related planning. Your house also provides shelter for your family and thus is often an emotional asset. Although houses are such ubiquitous assets, planning is not simple. Because the relevant real estate, tax, estate, and other laws are extremely complex and can have a dramatic impact on your property, your family net worth, and your finances, you must understand the general legal concepts and related rules that affect common transactions related to private homes. Most books written for nonprofessionals give little legal information. Books on purchasing houses address myriad issues such as finding the best home and negotiating price. They don't tell you who should buy the property (e.g., you, your spouse, both of you jointly, a trust). They really don't give you practical advice as to how to review a real estate contract so that you know what issues to raise with your lawyer (and whether your lawyer is really doing his or her job). That is the objective of this book.

The Homeowner's Legal Bible is not intended to substitute for the competent professional advice of a lawyer, and related professionals and experts. To do so not only would be impractical, but would take an encyclopedia-size work that you would be unlikely to want to read or even refer to. But this book will help you work efficiently with professionals to plan better, save money, and safeguard your home.

HOW THIS BOOK IS ORGANIZED

To accomplish the important objectives previously outlined and to make the book an easy resource for you, it is organized along the natural sequence in the ownership and use of your home:

- Typically, you arrange to buy the home first. This step includes a host of legal decisions. Who should buy the home? It's not as simple as you think. Most lawyers don't even raise the question. But this book will help you understand the options so you can bring it up with your lawyer and be sure you're protected. The next, and most important, step in buying a home is reviewing the contract. Detailed tips and a step-by-step walk through a sample contract will help you protect yourself. Can't your lawyer do it? Sure, but no lawyer can read your mind. First, you must educate yourself about the issues that are important to you and then advise your lawyer of them. Further, and in defense of the attorneys who handle house closings, consumer competition has in many areas beaten the price for handling a house closing so low that most attorneys have little choice but to let secretaries and paralegals handle much of the work. You can't expect $5,000 worth of advice when you're paying $750 for a closing. The next best thing is to prepare yourself by identifying the issues that you want your lawyer to focus on (the best thing is to hire an attorney who specializes in real estate and pay what is necessary to have him or her focus on all relevant aspects of your purchase). Once the contract has been signed, you have to "close" the purchase of the house, a legal process in which you obtain ownership of the home, pay the seller, and complete any other necessary transactions with others involved in the sale. Chapter 1 walks you through the steps to prepare for a closing, what should happen at the closing, and what to do afterward.
- Chapter 2 focuses on the financing of your home. Many books and web sites address the vital issues of negotiating the best loan and minimizing points and closing costs. However, it is also essential to understand the legal issues that can arise in a loan transaction, the different types of loan transactions, and the tax laws. Read other books, consult with a good mortgage

broker, use the Internet, contact a local bank; but you still need the legal information in this book to complete the job of protecting yourself.

- Once you own your home, you have to operate and maintain it. This can include properly insuring it and making improvements: You might need an easement to gain access to all of your property; or you may have to negotiate a contract with a builder for adding a dormer on your house. The tax laws provide many benefits for home ownership. Chapter 3 reviews these important legal operational issues for your home.

- While you own your home, you will want to protect it. Although most protective issues pertain to home security, fire safety, and the like, there is more. In Chapter 4, you can find a discussion of insurance coverage and law, protection of the home if you are disabled, different ways the home can be owned, and other issues that you should address.

- At some point, you might rent out part or all of your home or vacation home. Leasing a home raises tax and other legal issues. Chapter 5 answers such questions as, What tax deductions will you be entitled to? What type of lease agreement should the tenant sign? What provisions should be included?

- Eventually you may sell your home. Selling often begins with hiring a broker and signing a brokerage or listing agreement. Selling raises a legion of tax law issues. Chapter 6 explores these and other aspects of leasing your principal residence or vacation home.

- If you don't sell your home, you might arrange to give it to your children or other heirs, or perhaps a charity. Chapter 7 explains how you can best address giving your home to children or other heirs.

The chapters of this book follow this logical sequence. Throughout the book, planning tips, cautions, and examples help you.

Following most chapters is a "For Your Notebook" section that includes sample forms. Annotations are provided so you can get the most use out of discussing these forms with your attorney (and other professionals when appropriate).

WEB SITES THAT ADDRESS LEGAL AND OTHER ISSUES ABOUT YOUR HOME

The Internet has a wealth of resources to help consumers through the morass of legal and other issues of home ownership. In time, the Web will help equalize consumers with the larger companies and expensive legal system they face. So keep alert for new web sites. For general home ownership issues, consult some of the following:

- http://www.laweasy.com is a free legal web site that offers sample annotated real estate forms, real estate planning, and tax tips. Audio clips address such wide-ranging home owner- ship topics as mortgage financing (an interview with a bank lender), closing the purchase of a home (an interview with a real estate attorney), estate planning, and home office plan- ning (an interview with a CPA).
- http://list.realestate.yahoo.com is a Web address/portal that provides access to a broad array of home-related web sites and services:

  Buying a home.

  Selling a home.

  Finding an agent.

  Home sales prices.

  Neighborhood profiles.

  School profiles.

  Financing a home.

  Moving services.

  Home improvement.

  Rentals and roommates.
- http://usa.homesalez.com provides a broad array of links and services.

FINAL WORD

The goal of this book is to help you through the legal problems of home ownership, from beginning to end. If something has been missed that is of general interest, or if you have a question, contact us through the Law Made Easy Press, LLC web site, www.laweasy .com, and we'll try to add forms, planning tips, or other items to the web site to help you.

Good luck planning for your home.

MARTIN M. SHENKMAN

New York City, New York

Acknowledgments

A number of people deserve thanks for their help with this book. Michael Hamilton, my long-time editor at John Wiley & Sons, Inc., has seen me through so many books. Mike, as always, was great. Nancy Marcus Land, of Publications Development Company of Crockett, Texas—whose firm has helped in the production of so many of my books—has always remained behind the scenes so recognition of her great help (and vision of what a book should be!) and great staff is long overdue. Marsha Sheriff of KRA Insurance Agency, Inc., of Springfield, New Jersey, was of assistance. Paul Haimowitz, a student at Torah Academy of Bergen County, New Jersey, assisted with research and writing a number of sections of the book. Margaret Haas assisted in proofreading various stages of the book and helped clean up many a mess. Warren Boroson, my co-author on many real estate books, had a hand in many of the planning ideas in the book. Lee Mendelowitz of Old Tappan, New Jersey, helped identify all the web sites listed. Andrew Weissberg of Medinet Communications has helped in developing the web site www.laweasy.com which this book often refers to.

While there are many horror stories with home improvements and purchases, I've been fortunate to work with many great people. Vera Greenwald was a great broker and help. Vera and Nechama—may your signs continue to proliferate. Jane Paragano is truly an architect with flair and class. Rubin Gross did a great and practical job as an architect. Jeffrey Erdfarb of J&A Development has always shown a competence and integrity that has made home improvements easy (really!). Bill Williamson of United Landscaping makes landscaping an art. Arthur Schwartz has been of so much help so many times with patience and humor as a decorator, advisor, and so much more. Jeff Manas—the blinds are great but you still owe me a bottle of scotch!

Any mistakes or errors are my own.

M. S.

Contents

1 BUYING YOUR HOME

Buying a home is one of the most important financial decisions you will ever make. If you overextend your budget on the purchase you could face financial pressures and perhaps even lose your home. If you don't extend your price limit enough, you may not have the area, rooms, or amenities you and your loved ones need or want. Once you decide how much you can spend, you'll have to negotiate the best price possible. There are many great books and even some decent web sites to help you make these two critical decisions. After you've completed these tasks and found your home, then you're ready for the information in this chapter. Many legal issues have to be addressed. The discussion provided here is designed to help you work with your attorney, real estate broker, and other professionals to best protect your interests and save costs.

Note: For more information, see:
- Shenkman and Boroson, *How to Buy a House for No (or Little) Money Down* (3rd ed.) (John Wiley & Sons, Inc.).
- Eldred, *The 106 Common Mistakes Homebuyers Make (and How to Avoid Them)* (John Wiley & Sons, Inc.).
- Cummins, *Not One Dollar More* (2nd ed.) (John Wiley & Sons, Inc.).
- Glossbrenner, *Smart Guide to Buying a Home* (John Wiley & Sons, Inc.).

WAYS TO BUY A HOME

There are many ways to purchase a home and many types of interests you can buy in a home. The following discussion explains them.

Once you believe you know the answers for you, review your preliminary conclusions with your attorney.

Planning Tip: Don't underestimate the knowledge of an experienced real estate broker. Many have tremendous expertise from years in their profession. Good brokers have been through as many, if not more, house closings, than many attorneys. Although technical legal issues are clearly within the purview of your lawyer, bounce your questions off your broker as well.

Type of Home You Are Buying

Single-Family Residence.   The most common form of home is a single-family detached home. No particular legal issues are raised by your purchase of a home. The decision is primarily one of preference and availability given the area you've determined to search. In most cases when you purchase a single-family residence, you will purchase and own complete ownership in the property (fee simple).

Multifamily Home.   In many areas, two-, three-, or four-family units are common. If you are considering such a purchase, the fact that there are other units in the building might raise several legal issues. The title search, manner or type of ownership, insurance issues and needs, and how you should own the property, might all be affected. You need to review these issues with your attorney, using the following points to start the discussion:

- Are you buying one unit or the entire property? The title and casualty insurance, deed, and so forth will each have to be tailored to properly reflect exactly the interests you are buying.

- If you are buying only one unit, what is the legal relationship between the units? They must be governed by some type of arrangement. Are they condominiums? If not, be certain that your real estate attorney and title company investigate the ownership structure and are satisfied it is workable.

- If you are purchasing all the units, who occupies them? Who is selling? If there are tenants, do they have leases? Can the leases be assigned? Do you need the tenants' consent to buy?

Can you get the tenants out when you wish? If local rent laws give the tenants rights, you must be familiar with what these rights mean to you before buying.

- Have your accountant or financial planner, in consultation with your attorney after addressing the preceding issues, complete a budget for the cash flow on the property.

- If you plan to have a relative rent or use, say half of a two-family dwelling, still prepare a lease. What if the family member is sued, divorces, or has a fight with you?

- If you are renting to unrelated persons, consider the benefits of having a limited liability company purchase the property to limit your risks in the event of a lawsuit. If this is done, however, a host of tax issues must be addressed. Consult your accountant before the purchase.

Condominium.   Condominium is a special form of ownership that is common in many parts of the country. If you are considering the purchase of a home that is a condominium, you should understand the legal structure of a condominium, and how that can affect your purchase as well as the other legal steps in owning and maintaining your future home.

Legally a condominium is a special form of ownership. Each owner in the condominium owns a fee simple title (just like that noted for a single-family residence) to his or her unit. A unit might be an apartment in a building, a freestanding home, or an attached town house. What distinguishes the condominium arrangement from a single-family home is that when you buy a condominium you also are purchasing an ownership interest in the general amenities made available to all the other owners of condominiums in that particular complex or building (common areas). These might include a swimming pool, golf course, or clubhouse. The halls and area outside of the interior walls of your apartment (in that type of condominium) might all be considered common areas. In some instances, the common areas are owned by a homeowners' association or similar group to which every homeowner must belong. This type of arrangement might be called a planned unit development or PUD.

What is common to all condominium arrangements is that your purchase will give you outright ownership of your particular house or apartment and a shared right to use (a possessory interest in) the common areas.

A condominium is created under condominium laws (statutes) of the state where the condominium is situated. Therefore, your attorney must be familiar with these laws to help you evaluate the condominium you are buying.

In addition to the investigation (due diligence) listed later in this chapter for a general house purchase, potential buyers of a condominium unit should also consider the following specialized steps:

- Are there any issues in the state condominium law of which you, as a future condominium owner, should be aware? Are there any issues raised in the condominium plan documents filed with the government agencies required under state law that could be important for you to know about? An experienced real estate attorney (and an experienced real estate broker) can help you.

- What common areas or amenities does the condominium make available? Are these really amenities you want or need? Do the rules that govern them make them impractical for you (e.g., your grandchildren visit all the time, but children under 16 are not allowed in the pool or gym)?

- What reserves has the condominium association set aside? It's the responsibility of the condo's board to repair all common property, land around the condo units, outside walls, and the roof. If it's an old project with no reserves, you should be very concerned.

- Review (with your financial planner or accountant) prior financial statements for a history of assessments and large repairs made by the condominium association. Determine whether these were one-time improvements, or are indicative of ongoing problems. The absence of assessments and large repairs might also mean that there's a monster waiting in the wings. Be certain to determine the board's policies toward major repairs. Do they assess and set aside amounts on a monthly basis, or do they use large special assessments?

- Review any engineer reports on the building. Pay attention to any problems noted and the age of the building.

- Go to the condominium office and read the minutes of the board of directors for signs of possible problems. There might be a discussion of funding shortfalls and of alternative solutions being considered. Often there will be mention of the board's considering large assessments some time before the assessment is actually made. This can be invaluable to discover before a purchase. The boards want to protect themselves from liability by showing that they've discussed problems and considered all alternatives. You might also find comments on problem neighbors or other points of concern.

- Review the bylaws for the condominium association. When can it make an assessment for common expenses? What is included and how is it determined?

- Check to see if there are a lot of units for sale at the same time. Everyone may have just received a promotion, or it might mean there are some substantial problems with the property.

- Has the association been running at a deficit? Deficits have to be funded, and if so, you may be the potential funding source!

- What is its cash position? Some associations use fund accounting—an operating fund for daily operations and a replacement fund for repairs. The amounts of each fund might be telling.

- Look at receivables. If a lot of members have been in arrears for some time, it could indicate that there will be more serious problems to face in the future.

- What liabilities are reflected on its balance sheet?

- What is the nature and amount of assets that the association owns? Condo associations generally don't own any significant property that can be used as collateral for a loan. The owners of the individual units hold title to their respective units. This means repairs or deficits will have to be funded from the owners' pockets. What if the condo association balance sheet shows valuable assets? Be careful! If a developer turns over title to a clubhouse to the association, the clubhouse will be on the books. But what is it really worth? Would a lender accept it as collateral for a loan? The property has such a specialized use that it may not have any real market value. The association may have to secure 80 to 100 percent owner approval to sell it.

Cooperative Apartment.   A cooperative is another form of home ownership. Just as with the condominium, it presents unique legal and hence practical issues that you must understand when you are considering a purchase.

A cooperative is a form of ownership arrangement in which all the property involved in your future home—and the homes of others in the complex, building, or arrangement—are owned by a corporation, called a cooperative housing corporation. Similar to the condominium association described earlier, common areas are maintained for all residents. Unlike the condominium arrangement, you will not own fee simple title (ownership) of your apartment, town house, or other unit. Instead, you will own stock in the cooperative housing corporation that entitles you to a proprietary lease giving you the right to occupy your unit. This legal structure has important legal, tax, and financial implications. Whereas you may be able to individually finance (mortgage) a condominium unit, you cannot do so with a cooperative unit. Instead, you will have to arrange for a special cooperative loan. This entails different procedures, documents, and perhaps lenders specializing in those types of loans.

Many special income tax rules affect cooperative housing corporations. For you as an owner, the key is that if the cooperative corporation meets the necessary tax law requirements, you will be able to deduct your share of property taxes and mortgage interest paid by the cooperative corporation on your personal income tax return as if you had paid them directly to a lender and the city tax authorities. These are discussed later.

If the house you're selling is really a cooperative or condominium, you will have to deal with some additional documents and steps that aren't reflected in the contract at the end of this chapter. Your lawyer should be familiar with the procedures for a cooperative and will advise you of the extra steps you need to take. The first thing you should do, even before you hire a lawyer or find a buyer, is contact the cooperative corporation or the condominium association. Ask what procedures you must follow, what documents and other requirements they have for a prospective buyer, and what other advice they can give you. Most associations are helpful and will be able to guide you.

For a closing on a cooperative unit, your seller's stock in the cooperative corporation will have to be canceled by the corporation, and new stock issued to you as the buyer. Also, you will have a proprietary lease that entitles you to live in the particular cooperative unit you own. This will have to be assigned by the seller to you as the buyer. Often the cooperative corporation attorney will handle these matters and you as the buyer will be responsible for his fee in addition to the fee for your attorney.

Planning Tip: A prospective purchaser of a cooperative apartment should review with an attorney experienced in cooperative apartment work (not just a general real estate attorney) specific investigative steps to take before committing to a purchase. Many of the special steps will be similar to those discussed for a condominium investigation.

Time Share. When you purchase a time share, you are not purchasing an ownership interest in a home, you are really purchasing the right to use a particular apartment, facility, or selection of facilities a specified number of days, weeks, or months per year. If you are considering a time share, carefully review all of the disclosure documents to determine what you will be entitled to. Pay careful attention to how you can sell or get out of the arrangement since many are difficult to liquidate. Since this is really not a form of home ownership, it isn't discussed in detail in this book.

Special Arrangements for the Elderly. As the population continues to age, more options of special housing arrangements are being developed, and many are becoming common for senior citizens. Some of these are discussed in this section. Each entails its own special legal issues, which you should have your attorney carefully review.

Planning Tip: In most cases, the special housing arrangements for a senior citizen are best reviewed by an attorney specializing in elder law, not just a real estate attorney. In some cases, you might benefit from the expertise of both types of legal counsel: an elder law specialist and a real estate attorney. If you are dealing with an ethical attorney, he should readily acknowledge the limitations of his expertise and have relationships with attorneys in related specialties that he can call on when needed.

Retirement facilities, unlike more traditional real estate, have both a housing and a service component. The service component can include any combination of dining facilities, laundry services, transportation, personal care (assisted living or residential care), a threshold level of health care (nursing), and so forth. This presents special legal, financial, and other issues when evaluating such arrangements.

Many different structures have been used to varying degrees for retirement facilities. The following five arrangements are widely used:

1. Condominiums that combine the right to live in an apartment or town house with a significant service and facilities arrangement included as part of the common areas, all geared for seniors.

2. Rentals in which the developer owns and rents the units and can either bundle services with the rental charge or offer them on an optional basis. This offers tenants a cheaper initial outlay and more investment flexibility.

3. Refundable entrance fee arrangement in which the senior citizen, as a tenant, deposits a substantial fee up front that is, at least in part, refunded when the tenant vacates or dies. For tax purposes, this can be treated as a loan; and the complex "below market" loan rules could apply if special exceptions are not available. These can be structured in many different ways. Some will eventually return to the senior's family a portion of the deposit or even a component of the appreciation of a unit.

4. Nonrefundable entrance fee arrangement in which the senior pays a large nonrefundable fee up front in exchange for lifetime care and housing.

5. Membership arrangements that can be structured in a manner that is similar to a country club membership, except instead of (or in addition to) golf, the facility provides amenities and services designed for seniors. Depending on how the arrangement is structured, seniors may purchase a membership interest that can appreciate or depreciate in value, and that can be sold or passed on to heirs. This often will not offer any tax advantage to the seniors because they aren't generally treated as owning an interest in the underlying real estate.

Deed

For many of the forms of real estate ownership discussed earlier (single-family house, a multifamily house, condominium, and some specialized senior citizen housing), your ownership will be evidenced by a legal document called a deed, which effects the transfer of ownership from the prior owner to you. For cooperative apartments your ownership, as discussed, is instead evidenced by shares of stock and a proprietary lease. For some other forms of senior housing, a contract arrangement may be all that indicates what you own. Thus, for most forms of real estate ownership, the deed is key.

The deed is the document that transfers ownership (title) to real estate. There are several different types of deed, each of which can be used in different circumstances, and each of which conveys a somewhat different ownership interest. To understand what you are buying, you need to understand what type of deed you are getting. Always review this with the attorney assisting you on the purchase since customs and laws differ by area:

- *Committee Deed* is a deed issued by a court-appointed guardian or committee for a minor or incompetent. Be careful to avoid transferring ownership to a child or other minor heir as part of your planning because it can create problems if you later want to sell or transfer the property to another.

- *Grant Deed* or *Deed with Covenants against Grantor's Acts* is a deed that assures you no encumbrances or problems were created by the current owner (the "grantor") who is transferring the property to you while he owned the property. It does not give you assurances for prior owners.

- *Gift Deed* is a special form of deed used when you are making a gift of the property. For example, you give your three children equal interests in the family vacation home. You would use a gift deed.

- *Executor's Deed* is a special form of deed used when property is transferred by an executor following your death.

- *Bargain and Sale Deed* is a deed that conveys title to the property for a payment. Often a Bargain and Sale Deed with

Covenants against Grantor's Acts is used, which includes warranties by the owner transferring the property to you.

- *Warranty Deed* is a deed in which title is conveyed to you and which the current owner or grantor warrants forever (i.e., the covenants are said to "run with the land") that the title you are receiving is good marketable ownership (title) in the land. This is the best or most secure interest that you can receive in property.

- *Deed of Release* is a special form of deed to release an interest that a mortgage holder had on property. For example, a bank loaned you money and secured its loan with a mortgage on your property. When the loan is paid off in full, it could issue a Deed of Release, or alternatively file a document in the county clerk's office called a *Satisfaction of Mortgage*. The terminology and the forms vary by area of the country, which is why it is always advisable to use a local real estate attorney familiar with local law and custom.

- *Quit Claim Deed* is a deed in which the owner merely states that she is transferring any interest she may happen to have in the property to you. For example, an adjacent property owner may have appeared to have an easement (right of way) over part of the property you are buying. A quit claim deed merely transfers any rights the adjacent owner has to you. This type of deed is used to eliminate items that could raise issues as to your complete ownership ("clear title") to the property you are buying.

Who Should Own Your House and How (Legal Title)

Choosing the Title and Owner Is Important, but Not as Simple as You Might Think.   In previous sections, the different types of real estate interests, and deeds transferring those interests, were discussed. Next, you need to decide who should be the recipient of the deed or other form of legal ownership. The simple and obvious answer is you. The deed could be simply made out by the seller to you as "Jane Doe" (assuming that's your name). There are, however, many options for structuring ownership. These are important to understand since the owner and title can have important tax and legal implications:

- If the owner is sued, the owner's claimants and creditors can reach the property the owner owned to satisfy their claims. So if you are concerned about claims or lawsuits (which most people are) you might have the home owned by your spouse, or by you and your spouse as tenants by the entirety to make it harder for a claimant to get.

- If the house is a vacation home that will be rented a substantial part of the time to nonfamily members, having it owned by a limited liability company (LLC) could prevent a suit by a tenant from reaching your other assets. However, ownership of your primary residence by an LLC or FLP (both explained in Chapter 4) could be a tax nightmare because it may ruin your ability to claim home mortgage interest and property tax deductions, and the home won't qualify for the valuable $250,000 ($500,000 joint) home sale exclusion.

- If your estate is small and no estate tax will apply, then owning the home jointly may avoid probate. If your estate is larger or you may need more help managing your assets, a revocable living trust might be preferable.

- If you are wealthy, other estate and gift tax advantage options should be considered (e.g., bypass trust, QPRT).

The right decisions are not always as simple as most lawyers and books on purchasing a house written for laypersons make it seem. Wade through the following section, and then with the information you have learned in the preceding sections, you'll be prepared to have an informed consultation with your attorney about who should own the house you're buying and how it should be titled.

Joint Tenants. Joint tenants is a possessory interest in the same property where all cotenants own a whole or unified interest in the entire property. Each joint tenant has the right, subject to the rights only of the other joint tenants, to possess the entire property interest. The traditional common-law definition of a joint tenancy requires the presence of the four unities: unity of interest (each joint tenant must have an identical interest); unity of title (the same will, deed, or other document must confer title to all joint tenants); unity of possession (each has the right to possess the entire property interest); and unity of time (the rights of each joint tenant must vest at the same time).

The supposed benefit of joint tenancy for property is that on death the property automatically transfers by operation of law to the surviving joint owner. This is really not always the benefit many imagine. For wealthier taxpayers, it can defeat estate tax planning objectives. For many people with second or later marriages, it can defeat the desired distribution of property. Finally, it doesn't assure that the surviving tenant will respect your wishes.

Sample Language: The deed could read, "to: John Doe and Jane Smith as joint tenants and not as tenants in common."

An issue with respect to joint tenancy is the determination of the ownership interest where the title is unclear. Therefore, the preferable approach is to play it safe. If joint ownership with right of survivorship is desired, the account title should so specify. This is especially important where one of the purposes of establishing the joint ownership is to protect the property from the creditors of one of the joint owners.

A joint tenancy can be terminated (severed) in four ways:

1. Partition is the dividing up and distributing of joint property for the purpose of terminating a joint tenancy, selling part or all of the property, and so forth.

2. Mortgaging the property can terminate a joint tenancy. In some states if one joint tenant grants a mortgage on the jointly held property, this severs the joint tenancy because the mortgagee will only be permitted to foreclose on the divided one-half interest of the joint tenant who granted the mortgage.

3. Leasing the property can also destroy the joint tenancy in some states.

4. Conveying the property to a third party severs the joint tenancy by destroying the requisite four unities described earlier. For example, if the property is held by two joint tenants, "Bob and

Sam as joint tenants," Bob's transfer of his interest to Joe would result in "Joe and Sam as tenants in common."

When do you use joint tenants to own a home? When you are buying a house with someone you trust, your estates are not so large that another form of ownership is preferable from a tax perspective, and you wish to avoid probate and have the property transferred to the survivor of you and the other joint owner (you still both need wills and other planning to address what happens when you both die, e.g., in a common car crash).

Tenants by the Entirety. This is a special type of tenancy available only to husband and wife. This concept arose out of the common-law concept of treating husband and wife as a single person. The same four unities required for joint tenancy are also required here. The surviving spouse has the right to the property by operation of law on the death of the other tenancy by the entirety spouse.

Tenancy by the entirety can be distinguished from joint tenancy in that the methods to sever or terminate a joint tenancy do not apply to the tenancy by the entirety. The spouses, however, can terminate a joint tenancy by agreement or divorce. Thus, neither tenant alone can force the termination of the tenancy by the entirety or the partition of the property. For this reason, this type of ownership structure has significant value in the context of asset protection planning where only one spouse is a target for creditors or malpractice claimants.

Sample Language: If John Doe and Jane Smith were married, it might read, "to: John Doe and Jane Smith, husband and wife," which under state law may be deemed to convey title to a principal residence as tenants by the entirety. Another approach might be for the deed to read, to: "John Doe and Jane Smith as Tenants by the Entirety."

When do you use tenancy by the entirety to own your marital home? When you are buying a house with someone you trust, your estates are not so large that another form of ownership is preferable from a tax perspective, your marital/family situation is simple enough that you trust the survivor to handle the property appropriately (for second and later marriages, tenants by the entirety or any other form of joint ownership may not be the best approach), you wish to avoid probate and have the property transferred to your surviving spouse, and you want the measure of asset protection that a tenancy by the entirety provides by making it difficult for a claimant to force partition.

Tenants in Common.   A tenancy in common is where two or more persons share ownership in a property at the same time but each party has a separate undivided interest in the property (as contrasted with joint tenancy where each has an equal interest in the whole). A key consequence of this difference is a tenant in common can bequeath property anywhere he or she wishes, whereas the joint tenant property passes to the surviving tenant by operation of law.

Sample Language: The deed would read, "to: John Doe and Jane Smith as tenants in common and not as joint tenants."

When might you use a tenants-in-common arrangement? This can be used for a second or later marriage, where you want to pass the economic value of your interest on to your children from a prior marriage. But it will have to be used in conjunction with a trust to protect the surviving spouse's right to live in the house following your death. If you merely bequeath your ½ interest to your children, they may immediately pressure your surviving second (or later) spouse to leave. Tenants in common is often used if the couple's estate is larger so that they can each use ½ the value of the home to fund the tax-motivated bypass trust (explained in Chapter 7).

Community Property Laws and Your Home Purchase.   Generally all property acquired by a husband and wife during their marriage, while they are domiciled in one of the community property states, belongs to each of the marriage partners, share and share alike. They share not only in the physical property acquired but also in the income from the property (e.g., a rental vacation home). At the same time, each may have separate property. They may also hold property between them in joint tenancy and generally may adjust their community and separate property between themselves (i.e., use a transmutation agreement). Couples can state prior to marriage via a prenuptial agreement that they will not be bound by the community property laws of their state of domicile.

Generally, community property assets retain that character even after the parties have moved to a non-community-property state unless the parties are able to adjust their rights between themselves. This is an important consideration with respect to the assets held. For example, your restructuring of title to any assets presently owned individually or in joint name could affect this characteristic. Therefore, consideration of the caveats (independent and specialized counsel) should be made before proceeding. In particular, in the event of a future divorce, the steps taken by either or both of you now with respect to the title to your assets could affect your retention of assets at such time.

Real estate, including your residence, will generally retain the form of ownership assigned to it. Real estate in a community property state acquired by either spouse while married may be treated as community property without regard to the domicile or residence of the spouses. It is the law of the situs of the real estate that determines whether the income therefrom is community property.

Property acquired before marriage retains the form of ownership it had when acquired—separate, joint, or other. Property acquired during the marriage by gift or inheritance by one of the parties retains the character in which it was acquired. Property purchased with community property is community property, and property purchased with separate property is separate property. Property purchased with commingled community and separate property, so that the two cannot be separated, is community property.

Community property is included in the estate of the first to die only to the extent of the decedent's interest—generally, half of its value—and that half may be subject to probate. Transfers of community property between spouses qualify for the marital deduction.

Life Estate.   Life estates can provide a means of having more than one person own an interest in property, although those interests are not effective at the same time. In a life estate, a person is granted, instead of fee ownership, the right to use property for the duration of his life. The life estate arrangement is often used where the testator or testatrix wants to give a designated person the right to use property for life, but wishes to control the distribution of that property following the death (or some other event) of the life tenant. The life estate achieves these goals without the cost and expense of a trust. The prices to pay, however, include the inclusion of the value of the asset in the life tenant's estate where the life tenant had an interest in the property for life, potentially complex gift tax calculations, and less security and certainty than a trust provides.

A common use of a life estate is to protect a senior's right to live in a home without risking the home being taken to pay for medical and nursing home bills (see Chapter 4). Another common use of a life estate is to provide a second or later spouse the right to live in the former marital residence but to assure that children from a prior marriage ultimately inherit the home.

Caution: The common use of life estates in second and later marriages doesn't make it a great tool. If you are willing to spend the time and extra cost, a trust is often a much better approach. Discuss this with both your matrimonial and estate-planning attorneys.

Trusts.   In many cases, you will want a trust to own your house. Trusts are powerful and useful estate, tax, investment, and financial planning tool. You don't have to be rich to need or use one. Trusts for real estate can, within limits, help you achieve several important goals: management of your assets if you are disabled, management of assets for your children or family in the event of your death, avoidance of probate, avoidance of creditors, minimization or elimination of estate and other transfer taxes, protection for your loved ones, and help in controlling a valuable asset (or even a business dependent on that real estate asset).

The particular trust you should use to own a residence or vacation home will depend on your personal circumstances and how you prioritize the preceding goals. The three most common trusts for personal-use real estate are the following:

1. *Applicable Exclusion or Bypass Trust.* You are entitled under the gift and estate tax rules to give away up to $1 million on your death (this amount is to increase in future years). If you simply bequeath all of your assets to your spouse, you double up all assets in the surviving spouse's estate and could therefore trigger a tax on her death. A common approach, discussed in

Chapter 7, is to have assets bequeathed to a trust that benefits your surviving spouse without having the assets taxed in her estate. Since a home is a major asset for many people, it is commonly used to fund this type of trust.

2. *Qualified Personal Residence Trust.* If you have a large estate and want to reduce the value of your assets to minimize estate or gift taxes, or have a valuable home or vacation home that you want to assure passes to your heirs, a special house trust called a qualified personal residence trust (QPRT) can be used. This trust is described in Chapter 7.

3. *Revocable Living Trusts.* Perhaps the most commonly used trust to own a house is a revocable living trust. This trust can avoid probate on your house or vacation home and can also avoid probate in a second state (other than the state in which you live). This is called "ancillary probate" and would be required if you own real estate in another state. A revocable living trust is also an ideal technique to enable your family or friends to manage your real estate for you if you become disabled. The management of real estate in advanced age, and the eventual avoidance of probate, are major reasons that many elderly use living trusts for their home.

The living trust does not present any significant tax or legal issues because the trust is a "grantor" trust for income tax purposes. It is classified as a grantor trust because you will retain complete power over the assets, to revoke the trust, and so forth. Thus, you will have to report all the income from the trust (e.g., a rental of part of the home) on your personal tax return. This can significantly simplify the tax-reporting requirements. When a trust is taxed as a grantor trust for income tax purposes, the income, gain, and losses of the trust are reported on the grantor's (your) personal income tax return.

Note: For a sample revocable living trust form, with annotations, see the website: www.laweasy.com. For a detailed revocable living trust form, with comprehensive tax and economic commentary, see: Shenkman, *Tax Practitioner's Guide to Reviewing Legal Documents* (Practitioner's Publishing Company, Inc.).

Partnerships.   Partnerships, unlike trusts, should not be used to own your principal house because they can really only be used to hold investment or business assets, such as a vacation home that is rented, or commercial real estate (not discussed in this book). For vacation homes, if estate or gift tax planning is your objective, the QPRT discussed in Chapter 7 is often the best option. Partnerships are infrequently used with the type of residential real estate discussed in this book. If you purchase a residential rental property with a partner, then a partnership or LLC might be appropriate.

A partnership is an entity formed under state law. There are two types of partnerships: The first is a general partnership and the second a limited partnership (commonly referred to as a family limited partnership when all partners are family members). The general partnership is commonly noted by its initials "GP" and the family limited partnership by its initials "FLP."

A general partnership is a simple entity and inexpensive to form. All partners are general partners and each has the right to manage partnership property and each is fully liable for all partnership liabilities. These characteristics generally result in the use of an FLP or LLC.

A family partnership can be used to own a rental property. You could be the general or managing partner thus maintaining control.

Example: Father is a 30 percent managing partner of a family limited partnership. The partnership owns a $1,000,000 rental property. Father gifts 70 percent of the limited partnership interests to his children. On Father's death, the children already own 70 percent of the value of the partnership, so this portion of the value of the property is not included in Father's estate. The value of the FLP partnership interests are included in Father's estate in proportion to the percentage interests in the partnership he owns, not the percentages previously given to the children by gift. Although Father only owns 30 percent of the partnership interests, as general partner he retains control over the property.

An FLP has two types of partners, at least one general partner who has legal responsibility to manage the property (e.g., the parent) and who is subject to unlimited liability for a suit against the property (this is why an LLC is preferred, or why many lawyers will form a corporation or other entity to serve as general partner). The second type of partner is a limited partner who by law cannot participate in management.

Whether you use a general partnership, limited partnership, or limited liability company, you will need a lawyer to form the entity and to prepare an agreement governing the relationship between the various owners (partners for a partnership, members for an LLC).

Purchasing a House with a Nonmarried Partner. In addition to trusts, partnerships, and other arrangements for the ownership of property, sometimes a contractual arrangement is used to govern the relationship of the owners. When nonmarried partners purchase a house, a private contract arrangement is often used because the previously described approaches are simply not flexible enough, or state law is too restrictive, to provide the desired result. Also, state laws do not address the relationship between nonmarried home owners the way they do for married homeowners, so a private contractual agreement may be necessary to fill the void.

What issues should the contract between you and your partner address? What if you split up? Who should get the home, should the home be sold, how should the proceeds be divided? If one of you dies, what happens with the property? State law does not provide for equitable distribution for nonmarried partners who split, and if one nonmarried partner dies, the laws of intestacy (who receives your assets if you don't have a will) don't provide for a partner. There is also no concept similar to a spousal right of election, which enables a spouse to receive a minimum percentage of a deceased spouse's estate. If you don't address these issues contractually, you may be out of luck, or embroiled in an ugly lawsuit with your ex-partner or your deceased ex-partner's family. If a major repair is necessary, do you want to provide parameters for who should pay? There are many other issues you could consider.

Nonmarried couples face several difficulties in planning for their estates that are not problems for traditionally married couples. These additional problems stem from the bias that the tax and property laws have in favor of married couples. There is no right to transfer unlimited assets without gift or estate tax cost to a nonmarried partner as there is for a spouse. State laws that "fill-in" where wills are inadequate or nonexistent do not provide for distributions to nonmarried partners in the manner that they do for a spouse. The result is that the use of trusts, or partnership agreements (e.g., co-ownership agreements) is even more important for nonmarried couples than for married couples.

Note: For a sample real estate agreement that can be modified for nonmarried partners, see the "Tenants in Common Agreement" on the website: www.laweasy.com. See also Shenkman, *The Complete Book of Trusts* (John Wiley & Sons, Inc.) (Chapter 15).

What If the Wrong Person Signed the Offer or Contract—Assigning Your Right to Purchase. In some instances, you may sign a contract but later need to transfer (assign) the contract rights to another (this could be a contract to purchase a house, a lease, a mortgage, etc.). For example, you sign a contract under the direction of your real estate broker, but after speaking with your attorney, you might decide to have your spouse, a revocable living trust, or perhaps an LLC purchase the house. You must then assign your interests and rights in the contract to the desired purchaser.

Caution: An assignment of any contract will depend on the terms of the contract. If assignment is prohibited or permitted only with the seller's approval, you may have to adhere to those restrictions unless state law provides an out.

To assign a contract (or other right), you need a legal document to transfer that right; it must comply with any requirements of the contract being assigned; and it must comply with any requirements of state law (e.g., it may have to be notarized or witnessed). The person transferring the contract, called the *assignor,* can only transfer (assign) the legal rights which he had to the desired person (assignee). The assignment document may have to be recorded (filed with a local court or recording office).

Adverse Possession

Although adverse possession is rarely possible to plan for, it is another method of acquiring an interest in real estate. Because this legal concept occasionally arises in home purchases, it is briefly reviewed here.

There is a time limit in which a property owner must sue to recover possession of property from someone who has wrongfully used the property. If this is not done, then the wrongful user of the property will be able to obtain title to the land. This process is called *adverse possession*. The requirements for you to obtain ownership (title) to another's property by adverse possession is that it must be open and visible use of the other person's property, you must exclusively use the other's property, and your use must be continuous. In most states, a period of 10 to 20 years suffices for you to become the owner of the property.

Example: A homeowner built a new garage at the back of his house. The garage extended for 10 feet into an alley owned by the municipality in which the home was located. The city's nonuse of an alley for 30 years and failure to object to the construction of a garage 10 feet into the alley sufficed to give the homeowner the right to the property. The court stated the law to be that the protracted nonuse of property for an extended period is sufficient to create a presumption of abandonment. The acquiescence, in the placement of physical obstructions on the property, is inconsistent with any hypothesis other than abandonment.

Buying at Foreclosure

Ahhh, late-night television and an hour-long infomercial on how you can get rich buying houses at foreclosure. Well, maybe. But it is far more complex and risky than the shows imply. What is foreclosure? If a mortgage was due on a house, and the owner didn't pay, the lender has to take legal action to get the loan repaid. Although foreclosure could occur because other obligations besides payment were violated under the mortgage, this is not the usual situation. This process begins with violation of the loan (evidence of the debt) and mortgage (secures the repayment of the note by making the house collateral). The lender can then foreclose the lien on the property, take possession of the residence, and then sell it to obtain repayment of the loan amount. In some states, this is done under the rights given to the lender under the mortgage. In other states, a court or judicial process is required. If the borrower knows the property will be lost, the process is often circumvented by the homeowner/borrower transferring title to the lender by a Deed in Lieu of Foreclosure.

Any excess of the proceeds received from the foreclosure sale over the loan amount and expenses of sale is repaid to the owner. In many cases, the proceeds from the sale are less than the amount due the lender. In such cases, the lender may obtain a default judgment against the former homeowner/borrower and try to collect the balance from other assets.

Many people believe that tremendous bargains are awaiting at foreclosure sales. Although there can be, there are also substantial risks. If someone couldn't afford to pay their mortgage to the point the bank took away their home, they probably were not responsible about maintaining the home or paying other debts that could result in liens on the property. Most people don't lose their home unless their backs are against the wall. That is seldom good for the property.

Options

If you are not sure you want to buy a particular property, or if you want the property but are unsure whether you can arrange financing (your new job offer in the area might not come through, or other unusual factors exist), consider an option. You could pay the seller a set dollar figure, say $2,500, to give you 30 days within which to decide to buy. If you do buy, you will have already agreed on the terms and the property will be locked up for you (the seller can be prohibited from selling the property during the option period). If you don't buy, the seller usually keeps all of your $2,500. This can be a good approach for both parties. The seller makes some extra money and only ties up the property for a short period. Most importantly, the seller agreeing to the option may be a strong incentive for you to take the steps necessary to buy. You benefit because it is a limited-cost way of securing the right to the property while you address important issues. For you as the buyer, this will always be a better approach then signing a contract and defaulting if things don't come through.

It is critical to distinguish an option contract from a sales contract because the tax results are dramatically different. If an intended option transaction is successfully recharacterized by the IRS as a sales contract, a completed transaction will take place at what had been intended to be the nontaxable grant of an option. Since only a portion of the sales price will have been received (the intended option price), the transaction will probably be recharacterized as an installment sale. Under the general installment sales rules, the option price will be treated as a part of the payments made on the installment sales contract. Factors that are considered in determining whether a purported option contract is really a contract of sale include:

- *The price of the option.* The larger the price paid relative to the value of the property involved, the more the transaction will appear to be a sale with the purported option price being the down payment. If the option price is too large, the grantee/purchaser would assuredly complete the transaction.

- *The length of the option period.* The longer the period, the more likely for the transaction to be recharacterized as a sale since options are generally for a short duration.

- *The terms of the agreement between the parties.* If it is intended that the transaction be treated as an option, then the contract should call the transaction an option and contain terms indicative of an option and not of a contract of sale. For example, an option should not convey to you as purchaser the title or other rights normally associated with ownership of the property.

CREATIVE TIPS TO BUYING

A Little Help from Family and Friends

Family or friends can loan you money at favorable interest rates. If you have a loan from a bank as well, the family/friend loan may be unsecured or a second mortgage (the bank financing would have a priority). If a related person makes a loan and charges you an interest rate less than market rates, speak with your tax accountant as there could be tax implications.

Note: For a detailed discussion of family gift and loan planning, see: Shenkman and Boroson, *How to Buy a House for No (or Little) Money Down* (John Wiley & Sons, Inc., 2001), and Shenkman, *Complete Book of Trusts* (John Wiley & Sons, Inc., 1997). Available through www.laweasy.com.

Equity Sharing

Equity sharing is a technique in which you own some, but not all of the equity in the residence. You structure a contractual arrangement with a private (not a bank or institution) investor or lender in which you share some of the equity (ownership) or appreciation in the value of the house with the investor or lender. In exchange, you receive money you otherwise could not have received.

Note: For a detailed discussion of equity sharing, and sample forms, see: Shenkman and Boroson, *How to Buy a House for No (or Little) Money Down*. For detailed sample forms with comprehensive tax and economic commentary, see: Shenkman, *Tax Practitioners' Guide to Reviewing Legal Documents* (Practitioner's Publishing Company).

Lease Options

In a lease/option arrangement, you don't sell your house, at least not now. When the market is tight and you either can't find a buyer, or can't find a buyer at the price you want, a lease/option arrangement is a temporary step you might want to consider. You lease your house to a tenant who has also expressed some interest in buying your house. The lease agreement gives the buyer the right to buy the house at some future date. It's not a sale, but if the market is bad and you must move, it may be an approach to minimize your costs while waiting for a sale. As with any residential rental situation, there are many potential problems that you must consider before jumping into a rental.

A lease/option arrangement is best explained by considering the two components separately:

1. *Lease*. You rent your house to a tenant for a monthly rent. Generally, the tenant should also be obligated to pay the costs of all utilities, insurance, and other costs. Market conditions will largely dictate what you can and can't get the tenant to pay for.
2. *Option*. The lease gives the tenant the right to buy your house at certain times. The option could be exercisable at any time during the lease term, only at the end of the lease, or at specified times.

The lease terms provide an incentive for the tenant to purchase the house. The most common method of achieving this is to provide that some portion of each month's rental payment is to be credited against the ultimate purchase price the tenant will have to pay for the house.

Note: For a detailed discussion of the lease option method of purchasing a home, and sample forms, see: Shenkman and Boroson, *How to Buy a House for No (or Little) Money Down*. For detailed sample forms with comprehensive tax and economic commentary, see: Shenkman, *Tax Practitioners' Guide to Reviewing Legal Documents*.

Right of First Refusal

An option should be distinguished with a right of first refusal. A right of first refusal also gives you as the tenant an opportunity to purchase the house rented, but is different from an option in a very important way. If the lease gives you as the tenant a right of first refusal, the owner/landlord can't sell the house to anyone else without first giving you an opportunity to buy at the same price and on the same terms. The right of first refusal is therefore different from obtaining an option on the house. With an option—depending on how the lease is drafted—if you as the tenant haven't given the owner/landlord notice that you are exercising the option, the owner/landlord may be free to sell the house to anyone. Further, if the price of the house declines, you are unlikely to exercise an option. With a right of first refusal, you as the tenant (and option holder) must be consulted no matter what happens to the price of the house. Many potential lease/option tenant/buyers will try to negotiate both a right of first refusal and an option to buy. This dual approach can give you the best of both worlds. If the price of the house increases, you as the tenant/buyer exercise the option (if the option is at a fixed price). If the price of the house declines, you as the tenant/buyer wait until someone makes an offer at a lower price, and then you exercise the right of first refusal to buy at that price.

Note: For more information, see Shenkman and Boroson, *How to Buy a House for No (or Little) Money Down* (John Wiley).

PURCHASE CONTRACT

Once you've decided who is going to purchase the house, the type of legal interest being purchased, and how title will be taken, you can focus on the next key legal issue in acquiring a home, the contract.

The Importance of the Contract

A purchase contract or sales contract is the most important document governing your purchase of a home. It establishes your rights to the property, what you will pay, and the conditions necessary for the transfer of the property to you (closing) taking place. The terms of the contract affect all the legal issues and the steps to be taken.

How to Review the Purchase Contract

The "For Your Notebook" section at the end of this chapter includes a detailed sample home purchase contract with notes and cautions throughout. Use it as a guide in working with your attorney, identifying issues that are important to you, and understanding the draft contract the seller's broker or attorney prepares.

CHECKING OUT YOUR PROSPECTIVE HOUSE (DUE DILIGENCE)

When you buy a car, you have to first "kick the tires." Same for a house, but the tires are complicated. The following discussion will guide you, when read in conjunction with your actual contract and the tips in the sample contract following this chapter. The most important guides, however, are common sense, your gut feeling, and a skeptical attitude. Question everything that seems important or problematic. Work with all your professionals, your broker, attorney, home inspector, and so forth. Many books will provide you with details as to how to conduct a physical inspection, interpret cracks in the walls, test electrical outlets, and so forth. What most of those books fail to do, however, is address many of the legal due diligence or investigative steps that need to be taken. The following discussion, while providing an overview of the entire investigation process, focuses on legal issues.

Title

Title is the ownership of the property. You want to make sure that you have clean and clear ownership. If there are any issues or problems (exceptions), you want to be sure your attorney has explained them to you and that you can live with them.

- Order a new title policy and have your attorney clear problems (exceptions) with the title company.
- If an easement or other right to access the property is necessary or desirable, address the issue before buying. Don't rely on a court to later correct the problem. One homeowner learned that courts will not help out just to make access easier if it isn't really essential.

Example: An easement by necessity across grantor's land was denied because there was an alternate means of reaching the extension of grantee's property. An easement will not be implied or granted where there is another reasonable means of access.

- Items that might come up on a title search could include an easement granted to a public utility to have lines across the property. If this is a concern, there is probably little you can do except not buy the house. Most such easements aren't anything to be concerned about, but review them with your attorney so you understand what they mean.

- If there are mortgages or mechanic liens (claims by a repairperson or contractor who did work on the house in the past), these will have to be cleared before you take ownership (title) to the house. Your lawyer will address this with the seller's attorney and they will be handled before or at the closing (see later in this chapter).

- The title report should reflect the results of tax, lien, and judgment searches, survey reading, certificate of occupancy, and other items. It should also address any issues on fire and building department violations, street widening or changes, street report, and other issues that your attorney can identify for you.

- Speak with your attorney and real estate broker about suggestions for a title company. In some areas, the prices are basically governed by law so that the only distinguishing feature is service. This is nothing to minimize when you are under pressure to close by a specified date. In other cases, you may be able to decline portions of the title company service or obtain them at lower prices. Your professional advisers can help you.

Tax Search

Your lawyer will obtain and review copies of the real estate tax bills. These will indicate whether there are past due or delinquent taxes, special assessments due, and so forth. If there are and you have to pay them, you may not be entitled to a tax deduction (see Chapter 3).

Judgment and Lien Search

Any mechanic or other lien will have to be cleared before you take ownership (title) to the house. Your lawyer will address this with the seller's attorney and they will be handled before or at the closing (see "Closing the Purchase," later in this chapter). These may be paid at closing or perhaps the seller will contact the person listed in the lien and have them remove it because the bill was paid or some type of error made in filing it on the property (filing it in the county clerk's office where deeds and other records affecting title to property are filed).

Often judgments or liens that are identified against the seller of the property (not against the house itself) must be dealt with before you close. In many cases, these are liens against another person with a similar name. If that is the situation, then an affidavit should be prepared by your attorney, to the satisfaction of the title company (since they will have to remove the exception from the report), stating that the lien or judgment is against another person with a similar name.

Physical Inspection

The bottom line on a physical inspection is clear. Hire a competent engineer or home inspector, have the property inspected, and obtain a written report. Accompany the home inspector on the inspection. Make your own notes, use common sense, and ask questions. If there is an area the seller says can't be inspected (e.g., the seller won't remove a trapdoor that is nailed shut), either don't buy the property or negotiate an arrangement to have it opened (you could agree to pay for the cost of repairing the trapdoor if you don't buy the house). Use common sense, ask questions, and be skeptical (to a reasonable degree). If there is a matter that the inspector cannot address for lack of experience, bring in a specialist.

Finally, the physical inspection goes hand in hand with the other due diligence steps you must take. You should be sure to review and coordinate the due diligence you, your attorney, the broker, home inspector, surveyor, and others complete.

Don't be careless in your physical inspection of the property. A court may not have much sympathy for your plight if it was self-inflicted.

Example: A buyer contracted for a house subject to engineering and termite inspections. Termites were discovered after closing and the buyer sued the seller. The court held the doctrine of caveat emptor (buyer beware) applied and that the buyers should have been aware of the extent of the termite damage.

You should also not rely solely on the professional responsibility of the real estate broker to disclose everything. Although brokers must adhere to strict professional and regulatory standards, and many brokerage agencies have their own rules as well, none of these are a guarantee that the broker must disclose everything to you as a prospective buyer. Do your homework.

Example: A couple purchased waterfront property with the intent of building their retirement home. After the purchase, they discovered that soil conditions and the natural terrain prevented the use of a conventional septic system, thus rendering the property uninhabitable. The purchasers sued the sellers and broker. The district court dismissed the complaint, concluding that the seller and broker had no legal duty to investigate or disclose the conditions and that the "as is" clause in the contract required dismissal of claims. On appeal, the court held that the as is clause, which read: "all improvements on this property . . . are accepted by the purchaser 'as is,' " applied to improvements and not to the natural features of the property which were in issue. The court found that there was a question of fact as to whether the sellers, who had been notified by the state of the septic problem, had intentionally deceived the purchasers. The broker, however, was not shown to have had any knowledge of the problems and thus could not be held accountable. The court would not impose a fiduciary duty on the broker to investigate and report defects to buyers since this would conflict with the duty that the broker owed the seller.

Survey

A survey is a formal legal sketch of the property you are buying. It is formal in that it reflects the exact legal description of the property from identifiable landmarks such as metal stakes placed in the ground and street corners. In more technical terminology, it traces the metes and bounds description of the property. The survey will reflect the outside boundary line of your property, the footprint of your house, and other improvements (garage, patio, shed, etc.), and any other items affecting the property, such as a fence or utility easement. This is important to identify potential issues:

- *Setback requirements.* These are often imposed by the municipality. If the house is too close to a neighbor's property or the street, there could be a problem. If you know you want to improve the house, is there room to add on without violating setback (or other) requirements?

- *Easements.* In addition to the title report already discussed, the survey can highlight visually road, utility, or other easements that affect your property.

- *Encroachments.* Fences belonging to a neighbor may cross your boundary line and have to be addressed. It is often easier to let the seller who may have a relationship with a neighbor deal with this than for you to do it as the "new kid on the block." If a neighbor's fence has visibly cordoned off a meaningful part of the property, an issue of adverse possession, discussed earlier, could arise. In such a case, the survey might identify this and your attorney might request the neighbor to move the fence and give a quitclaim deed to the property in issue to assure that there are no claims.

- *If you are getting a mortgage, the survey will have to meet the requirements of your lender.*

- *A surveyor can provide different levels of service.* You might be able to save some cost if you carefully select only the services you need. For example, the surveyor can place metal stakes at the corners of the property. This may not be required by the lender, and perhaps you can save money by avoiding it. If you plan to erect a fence, however, the fence company will need the stakes to properly place the fence, and it will be less expensive to do this at the time of the survey. As with so many decisions you make concerning your home, there are no standard answers. You have to select what works best for you.

- *Read the survey metes-and-bounds description* to the sketch of the property and be certain that it flows properly from the beginning point, around the property, and back to the beginning point.

- *Ask your attorney, lender, and surveyor* if you can save money by getting an old survey the seller has updated.

- *Get at least one extra original survey* (it will have a raised seal on it) and keep it in your safe deposit box for future use (e.g., construction of an addition, sale of the house, refinancing).

Environmental Issues Generally

The contract should include provisions permitting you to cancel the contract without obligation if other environmental issues are identified. These might include an oil tank that may have to be removed or abated (cleaned and filled with sand), asbestos pipe covers that might have to be removed or encapsulated (e.g., plastered to avoid particles dissipating into the air), and so forth. If your general home inspector identifies any possible environmental issue, or if your lawyer or real estate broker believes the house may have these issues, or that these issues are common in the area, bring in a specialist in that particular environmental problem. Don't rely on just the home inspector.

Oil Tank

Oil tank woes. If your house-to-be has an unused oil tank *don't* accept anything less than proper abatement of the tank, in full accordance with all applicable laws, by a licensed company, prior to closing. Further, make sure your lawyer insists that the seller is fully liable for *all* removal and cleanup costs and that this survives the closing and transfer of the deed. Unless this language is specifically added, the seller's responsibility ends at the closing and transfer of title (ownership) to you. Cleanup costs can be horrendous. You're probably intending to buy a house and not an environmental disaster, so don't compromise. If the seller won't agree, buy another house. Don't assume that if the tank is removed the problem is over. A leak from the tank could spread beyond the immediate area of the tank. If you're unfortunate enough to be near an underground stream, that spread could be tremendous, and the cleanup costs exorbitant. Even if extreme disasters are unusual in residential situations, is it worth the risk?

Radon

Radon, a colorless, odorless, tasteless, but radioactive and potentially dangerous gas, is a common concern in many real estate transactions. Ten percent of the structures in this country may have radon levels above the current recommended guidelines. Worse yet, misinformation abounds. Most importantly, radon problems can affect far more properties then many buyers imagine.

Contrary to what some believe, problems are not limited to certain areas of Pennsylvania, New Jersey, and New York, particularly areas within what is known as the Reading Prong. There can be higher risks outside these areas. For example, Canada, Florida, and Arizona have some areas of substantial exposure. In some parts of the country, people assume that there is no problem so they don't test. These areas may, in fact, have substantial problem areas, but insufficient data is available to know. In Florida, you could build a house over a phosphate area. You'd have severe problems that you couldn't get away from. Elevation is an important factor. People in Denver, about a mile above sea level, have twice the gamma radiation that people experience living at sea level (say, in New Jersey). You can't do anything about this. But gamma radiation is only responsible for 40 to 80 millirems of the average 150 millirem dose that Americans receive each year. Radon is a basic element in nature. People in every state should have some concern although those who live in states with naturally occurring uranium deposits must have the greatest concern.

If it's a problem, it usually can be fixed. And, the cost to fix is often modest compared with the costs of addressing other types of environmental concerns. But if you're negotiating the purchase of a house, you want to be sure you know in advance what your responsibility will be. If you can, you may want to reduce the purchase price, make the purchase contingent on the seller addressing the problem, or take other action.

The goal of every radon test is to obtain a year-round average of the radon levels in a subject property. The time constraints of a real estate closing, and purchaser's cost considerations, often conflict with this objective. People lose site of the goal because they're trying to finish off a real estate transaction quickly.

The radon reading must be properly conducted. This entails many factors. Any violation of the tests, or variations in conditions that aren't factored into the analysis, can dramatically affect the results. The measurement should be made in the lowest occupiable, not livable, level of the building. The best level is where the floor is in direct contact with the ground. Tests must generally be conducted in closed conditions. All doors, windows, and other openings should be closed 12 hours prior to beginning the test. Although opening a door or window a few hours during the test may not significantly affect the results, the longer the violation, the greater the likelihood of inaccurate readings. The objective of the closed conditions is to reach an equilibrium where as much radon is coming into the building as is decaying away. You can't get a false high from this, since the amount of radon in the soil is not changing. So once the equilibrium level is reached, the readings won't increase. You want to measure under actual conditions of use. To obtain an accurate indication of the radon levels, long-term testing is generally essential.

Extreme changes in environmental conditions can change a reading 50 to 100 percent. For example, if a heavy storm front is approaching the area, it will usually be preceded by a low pressure front. This front can reduce the air pressure in the subject building and suck in radon from the ground below. If you measure at this point, your reading can be abnormally high. If you measure shortly after this point, you might find an abnormally low reading because the radon immediately below the building has been temporarily depleted. A short time after this, the readings should be back to their normal level. Thus over a short time period readings could vary substantially. This is why experts prefer long-term testing. The problem is that it is impossible to control conditions in a home for such a period if the home is occupied, and few house-closing timetables permit longer testing.

Violation of test conditions is also a substantial risk where short term or passive tests are conducted. The practicality of the closed house requirement being met is questionable. How can you keep a house closed in the summer when you have kids? Where the house is occupied by the seller, it is easy to violate test conditions, whether intentionally or by mistake. A seller can open a window or door, turn on a fan, and so forth.

Other factors can also affect the results where the charcoal canister test is used. Cleaning sprays (almost anything made to remove grease) can use up the active sites on the charcoal that would otherwise absorb radon. Moisture can substantially interfere with the accuracy of results. So a wet basement after a rain can have a significant impact. Results could even be skewed by kids having water fights in the same room as the test canister. The labs that analyze the canisters can tell if there was moisture, but many simply give a reading and don't factor this into the analysis. They may not be able to identify whether cleaning sprays interfered. If a correction is not made to reflect moisture, the reading will be inaccurate.

Ask your lawyer to what extent these issues can be addressed in the contract.

Sample Language: Seller recognizes that closed conditions are necessary for a proper radon test and will reasonably endeavor to keep doors and windows closed and avoid use of cleaning products and other aerosol sprays in the basement area during the test period.

Review the issues involved, and the practicality of addressing them with your attorney, broker, and real estate inspector.

Certificate of Occupancy

Some, but not all, municipalities, require that a residence have a certificate of occupancy (CO for short). This, depending on the municipality and its building codes, can be a positive for you as a buyer because it means that the municipal inspector will investigate certain matters to assure they are at the level required by the local building code and other laws. In other cases obtaining a CO may mean that a seller will have to incur costly and unnecessary home repairs or modifications that you may not want. In such cases, confer with your attorney. There may simply be no choice because the changes are required, or there may be a way to avoid some of the costs. Why do you care what it costs the seller? Because the more the seller has to pay for obtaining a CO, the less he will be willing to concede on other issues important to you.

CLOSING THE PURCHASE

The closing is the meeting at which the seller receives the sales price for the house, and title (ownership) passes to the buyer. The closing is the culmination of the entire transaction. Other documents and checks will likely pass hands. Exactly what happens, and when will vary depending on state law and local custom. Therefore, the following discussion provides only general guidelines. You'll have to rely on your lawyer, escrow agent, and broker for specifics. One important point is relevant to all closings. If everyone does their homework in advance, the closing should be a relatively simple and easy process. You always want to avoid last-minute negotiations and fights where emotions could ruin an otherwise "done deal."

How to Prepare for Your Closing

The more you plan and prepare for the closing of your house purchase, the simpler and cheaper the process is likely to be. The attorneys and brokers (yours and the sellers) should complete in advance whatever they can. Although at this point, there will be a host of professionals working on the closing for you and the seller, don't assume that everyone has addressed the matters within their responsibility unless you make sure of it. If your attorney has a secretary or paralegal helping him, that may be the best person for you to review matters with. You should contact each professional helping you and ask if there is anything you can do in advance to make the closing smoother. Develop a checklist as you go. And when you attend the closing, bring every piece of paper that you have received as well as all of your notes. In case something comes up, you'll be prepared to handle it.

Planning Tip: What if you can't be at the closing? If your house closing is scheduled and you will be out of town, say on vacation or attending to a personal emergency, you can use a special power of attorney to authorize someone to handle the closing for you. See the sample power of attorney form in the "For Your Notebook" section of Chapter 4. That sample form can be restricted so that the person you name to act on your behalf, your agent, can only complete the house closing, and not take any other action. Be certain to have both attorneys, bank, and title company review and approve the power of attorney in advance of your going. Even if you can sign all documents in advance of the closing, it's still best to have an authorized person (i.e., agent under an approved power of attorney) attend just in case something else arises.

Make certain you have secured mortgage financing and have advised your lender in advance of the closing. You should do your part by making sure that your lawyer has received all the calculations and requested check amount well in advance. Find out if the seller might prefer several checks in different amounts instead of one check for the whole amount so that he or she can sign over the checks for other uses, such as buying a replacement house.

Make sure your lawyer has reviewed every document and letter received from the seller's lawyer and notified the seller's lawyer of any questions or problems well in advance of the closing.

Be certain you have completed all necessary inspections, or have waived the right to do so (perhaps as a result of the lapse of the time allotted in the contract).

The following checklist will help, but be sure to tailor it to your area and specific transaction:

☐	Deed to you	☐	Termite report
☐	Mortgage application, commitment, etc. (lender will bring final mortgage)	☐	Home inspection report
☐	Note (lender will bring)	☐	Radon report
☐	Affidavit of title (mortgagors)	☐	Hazard insurance policy
☐	Affidavit of title (sellers)	☐	Flood certification
☐	Affidavit of consideration	☐	Flood insurance policy
☐	Notice(s) of settlement (in some areas)	☐	Payoff statement for all of seller's loans (seller to bring)
☐	Survey (several raised seal originals)	☐	Contract for sale
☐	Survey affidavit	☐	Riders to contract
☐	RESPA—HUD-1 Form (prepared by seller's attorney)	☐	Checks for each specific fee, with copies of bills or estimated bills: realty transfer fee, recording fee, brokers, seller's balance due, lawyers, title company, etc. (your lawyer may handle)

(continued)

☐   Title binder   ☐   Check for additional items
                                        such as personal property
                                        (with a Bill of Sale prepared by
                                        seller's attorney), etc.

☐   Approved attorney letter   ☐   Other items:
    (for lender)   _____

☐   Title policy   ☐   Other items:
    (____ Loan or ____ Owner)   _____

☐   Recent tax bill

Who Should Attend the Closing

Although custom, local law, and convenience of the parties all affect who will be present at the closing, the following are possible
candidates:

- *Buyer's Lawyer* Your lawyer will have to be present for the
  same reasons the seller's lawyer attends the closing. In some
  states, the buyer's lawyer represents the mortgagee/lender
  and possibly the title company (which insures the buyer's title
  to your house). In these instances, the buyer's lawyer may have
  to be approved by the lender and/or title company to perform
  the necessary functions. Although the house closing may be a
  rather simple transaction that one lawyer could handle effec-
  tively, this is rarely advisable. The buyer and the seller each
  have different interests that often are best represented by independent lawyers.

- *Seller's Lawyer* The seller's lawyer should be present at the
  closing to represent that party's interests. Documents that
  may not have been available before the closing might have to
  be reviewed. Often minor last-minute decisions must be made.

- *Seller's Mortgagee* If the seller has a mortgage outstanding,
  the seller's bank may require that its representative (perhaps
  its lawyer) attend the closing to obtain the check from you for
  the outstanding mortgage balance due. In some instances, it

may be possible to avoid having the bank's representative present (thus saving any fee the bank might charge) and simply
have your lawyer represent the bank (the buyer wants to be
certain the mortgage is paid off so it doesn't remain a lien on
the house) and forward documents and payments to the
seller's bank at a later date. The result is that the buyer won't
obtain written confirmation that the seller's mortgage has
been satisfied at the closing.

- *Escrow Agent* This is usually an independent party, perhaps
  a representative of the title insurance company or of the
  bank. Whether you'll use an escrow agent depends on the
  custom in your part of the country. The escrow agent han-
  dles all of the money and paperwork associated with the closing. The escrow agent will generally use the sales contract as
  a guide to assure that all the terms of the contract are ad-
  hered to, the monies are appropriately applied (to pay outstanding real estate taxes, utility bills, etc.). Sometimes a list
  of steps (perhaps called the escrow instructions), is prepared
  to summarize the escrow agent's responsibilities, as well as
  the money and documents the buyer and seller must each
  furnish to the escrow agent. The escrow agent may arrange
  for the recording of documents, payment of repair or insurance costs, proration of insurance or taxes, and other matters
  necessary to effect the closing.

- *Real Estate Broker* At the closing, the real estate broker picks
  up the commission check and provides a statement indicating
  the commission has been paid in full. The broker also assists
  in resolving any questions or disputes between the buyer and
  seller concerning the condition of the property, personal property involved, or other matters.

- *Buyer's Mortgage Lender* The lender advances the buyer the
  funds for closing (if the buyer is closing simultaneously on the
  mortgage and house).

- *Title Insurance Company* A representative may be present to
  provide the buyer with the title insurance binder, to clear up
  any title exceptions that are resolved at the closing, and to collect the payment due to the title company.

Documents to Address at the Closing

Again, the nature of the transaction, local custom, and state law all affect which documents will be involved. However, the following items are usually seen:

- *The deed to the house prepared by the seller's attorney and given by the seller to the buyer.* The deed must be the specific type of deed required in the sales contract. The legal description of the house in the deed should match the information contained in the title insurance binder (a commitment to give insurance, a preliminary policy) the buyer receives.
- *Title insurance reports and searches* as contained in the buyer's title insurance binder (a record of all title matters identified in the public records).
- *Payoff statement from the seller's lenders* (first mortgage, second mortgage, home equity lender, etc.).
- *Survey.*
- *House keys, garage door opener, and so forth turned over to the buyer.*
- *Settlement sheet or closing summary listing all payments and documents involved.* Sometimes a RESPA (Real Estate Settlement and Procedures Act) form required by the U.S. Department of Housing and Urban Development is used. This contains all the insurance, property tax, real estate transfer fees, fuel, and other adjustments and reconciles all payments and amounts due to the seller and paid from the buyer.
- *Affidavit of Title given by the seller to the buyer in some states.* The seller represents to the buyer that the seller has owned the property, is the sole owner, has never used any other names other than those listed, has paid for all fixtures on the property, and is not subject to any lawsuits. There may be a judgment against another person with the same name as the seller. The buyer will want you to provide a statement, under oath, that the judgment is not against you, but is against another person with the same name as you.
- *Transfer taxes.* In states and counties where there are real estate transfer taxes, there will typically be forms and affidavits

to complete for filing. For example, if the sale of the house is exempt from the tax, an affidavit to that effect may have to be filed.

- *An old survey.* If an old survey is relied on, the title insurance company, lender, or buyer may require the seller to sign an affidavit stating that there have not been any material changes since the date of the prior survey.

- *A signed receipt by the broker* acknowledging receipt of the commission check and that the amount received discharges the seller from all liabilities to the broker.

- *Insurance.* If the seller is turning over the insurance policy for the house to the buyer, the policy should be given over (be sure the insurance company approves). This is rarely done.

- *Bill of sale* that the seller gives the buyer as evidence that the buyer has taken title to the personal property sold in the transaction. Be certain that your attorney reviews the bill of sale to assure that it complies with any local legal requirements. These might include a witness, notary, and statement of consideration such as some dollar figure (even if nominal) since the money paid under the separate purchase contract may not suffice. Check with your accountant as sales tax might have to be paid on the amount of property transferred with the bill of sale.

Note: For a sample bill of sale, see: Shenkman, *The Beneficiary Workbook* (John Wiley & Sons, Inc.) and the website www.laweasy.com.

- *Mortgage and note for the buyer's loan used to buy the house.* The note may be referred to as a bond in some areas. A bond or note is a legal document (instrument) that provides evidence that a debt exists. A note must at minimum state the requirement to pay an amount of money, at a certain time, to the specified party and any conditions relating to the payment. A note is illustrated in the "For Your Notebook" section of Chapter 2.

- *Inspection reports* (house, radon, termite, other).

Financial Transactions at the Typical Closing

Every transaction has its own nuances; however, the following payments are often involved:

- *Deposit monies initially paid by the buyer.* Depending on the area's custom, these funds may have been held by your attorney in his or her attorney escrow account. In other areas, the real estate broker, the title insurance company, or an independent escrow agent will hold the funds. In many instances a single statement, the RESPA form, is used to calculate many of the expenses previously listed, so fewer checks may be needed to cover the net due as a result of all the amounts listed.

  Make certain that all checks total the required amount, that every check is properly made out as payable to the correct party, that bank or certified checks are provided where required and that every check has been properly endorsed. At some closings, the escrow agent completes all of the checks involved and only a single check must be paid to the escrow agent.

- *Payment of the commission due the broker.* The seller generally pays for the commission unless alternative arrangements have been made.

- *Payments of any outstanding liens on the property.*

- *Checks to or from the buyer or seller* to reconcile the proration of taxes, insurance, rental income, and so forth.

- *Payment of the lawyer's and escrow agent's fees.*

- *Payments for property and other taxes as allocated.*

- *Insurance (fire and hazard) payment by the buyer.* This is very important if the seller is holding a purchase money mortgage on the property because the seller wants to be sure that the buyer has adequate insurance coverage on the house.

- *Title insurance premium.* Paid by the buyer to the Title insurance company selected by the buyer.

- *Payoff of the seller's outstanding mortgage on the property.* In many cases, the cost of using an overnight mail carrier to get the check to the bank the next day will be cheaper than the interest cost incurred during the three or four days it would take regular mail to reach the bank. Make sure the check is sent out in the appropriate manner to keep costs as low as possible.

- *Balance of payments due to the buyer's mortgage lender.* This can include points for origination and discount fees.
- *Fee to the mortgage lender's review attorney* for the preparation and review of the documents.
- *Payments of charges for document recording (e.g., deed).*
- *Mortgage recording fee or tax.*
- *Realty transfer tax depending on local rules.*

Things to Do after the Closing

Despite all the matters you've addressed before, and then at the closing, there is more to address after closing:

- Make a list of all items that still need to be done. Use this section as a starting point, but ask your lawyer, broker, and other professionals at the closing what else you should follow up on.
- Eventually your lawyer will send you a final title report showing that all matters cleared at the closing (e.g., a mortgage lien of the seller) were in fact eliminated as exceptions on the title report. The final title report should also reflect you as an owner. Find out when you can expect the final report. Note the date on your calendar and if you don't receive it within a few weeks of that date call your lawyer or the title company. When you get the final title report, read it. It will be much shorter than the preliminary reports. Be sure no exceptions are listed that you believe should have been eliminated. Be certain the amounts are correct and that the proper owner is listed.
- Notify the utility companies of the purchase and have service continued in your name. Have newspaper, telephone, and other services billed under your name.
- File a change of address form with the post office and the IRS. You can also obtain a helpful change of address kit from the post office to notify friends, family, vendors, and so forth.

Planning Tip: Moving? Tell the IRS. When you move, file Form 8822, "Change of Address," with the IRS. Not only will this assure that your blank tax forms arrive, but most importantly, a pesky penalty notice won't go unanswered. Failing to reply to an IRS notice could result in penalties and interest charges that you can't deduct! Worse yet, a long failure to reply could trigger the IRS pursuing collection of the amount it believes due. This could include a lien on your bank account and worse.

- Be certain to set up a file with copies of all final documents pertaining to the purchase.

Planning Tip: Make an extra copy of the HUD Form 1 RESPA and place it with your current year's tax papers. At almost every closing, there is an allocation of the property taxes on the sale. Since this won't come up on your regular bank escrow reports, or canceled property tax checks, you could easily overlook this valuable tax deduction come April 15. If an adjustment was made at closing for property taxes that you reimbursed the seller (since the seller paid for taxes, in advance, for the quarter in which the closing occurred) you're entitled to a deduction for this amount.

- Place the original deed, an original survey, and other key documents in your safe deposit box, after making copies for the file.
- Notify your accountant of the change and be sure to assemble a file of moving information and expenses in case you will qualify for a tax deduction.
- Photograph everything in the new home during and after the move (see Chapter 4).

WEB SITES TO HELP YOU BUY YOUR HOME

There are many web sites for buying and selling homes. Because web sites change often, you should always engage in a search of current sites through online search engines like google.com. Here are a few sites that might be of interest:

- *http://www.forsalebyowner.com* This web site includes the following features: buy a home, sell a home, service directory, mortgages, neighborhood research, moving and relocation, insurance, appraisals, and more.

- *http://www.homegain.com* This web site endeavors to help homeowners navigate the home selling-and-buying process. Homegain focuses on three primary areas: finding out what your current or future home is worth; preparing your home for sale; and finding the right real estate agent. The site includes home searches (for buying), a mortgage center, moving help and advice, home improvement resources (tools, projects, contractors), and more.

SUMMARY

This chapter (and the following "For Your Notebook" section) walks you through many of the legal and related issues of purchasing a house. Your house is an investment, and possibly your largest investment. You owe it to yourself to pay attention to and understand the legal and other issues to assure that everything is handled in the way that is best for you.

FOR YOUR NOTEBOOK

SAMPLE REAL ESTATE PURCHASE
CONTRACT FORM FOR SELLER AND BUYER
TO DISCUSS WITH YOUR ATTORNEY

Note: Rather than reprint a sales contract for sellers in the "For Your Notebook" section of Chapter 6, one contract form is used here to identify planning issues for both buyer and seller.

Note: For a detailed house purchase contract form, with comprehensive tax and economic commentary see: Shenkman, *Tax Practitioner's Guide to Reviewing Legal Documents*. For additional information and ancillary closing document forms, with annotations, see the website: www.laweasy.com.

a. Names of the Parties

Note: Be sure the right person is listed as the buyer. If you are buying the house, or your revocable living trust, or even you and your spouse as tenants in common, the contract can reflect this.

CONTRACT of sale dated June 3, 2002, between John and Jane Seller, residing at 456 Sell Street, Sellville, Anystate (the "Seller"), and Bob and Brenda Buyer, residing at 123 Main Street, Buyville, Anystate (the "Purchaser").

Note: Be certain that the seller/buyer signed his or her full legal name at the end of the document. In addition, any changes penned in on a printed form should be initialed by both you and the buyer to show that both of you have agreed to the changes. If the buyer is married, get the buyer's spouse to sign as well. This makes the spouse liable as well if the buyers default. This is particularly important in a buyers' market since a buyer who defaults will have plenty of other houses to choose from. If you've spent the time and legal fees to get a contract signed, and have held your house off the market, you want to make certain that the buyers will be held to their end of the agreement. If the contract is not properly signed, this may be more difficult.

Occasionally, someone other than the buyer may show up to sign papers at the closing. Your primary concern is to be certain that the responsible party is obligated on the contract.

For example, the buyers live out-of-state and have someone attend the closing on their behalf. Be certain to obtain an agreement through which the actual buyers authorize the person attending the closing on their behalf to do so. The document may be a power-of-attorney. It must be signed by the actual buyers and should specifically give the person attending the closing the right to sign documents on their behalf to buy real estate. Have your attorney review it to be certain that it meets any special state law requirements. If the buyer is a partnership, corporation, or other entity, this raises special problems. You will need to be certain that the partnership or corporation has the right to buy the property. You will also have to ascertain who has the authority to bind the entity (e.g., the president, a general partner). Be certain to have a lawyer carefully review this issue and obtain all the additional documents necessary to assure that the buyer has the authority and competency to consummate the purchase (e.g., minutes of the corporation's board of directors approving the purchase and the name of the officer authorized to sign the contract, copy of a shareholders' agreement, a certificate of incorporation).

---

b. Sale

The Seller agrees to sell, and the Purchaser agrees to buy the property, including all buildings and improvements thereon, erected, situated, lying, and being in the City of Sellville, County of Oakland, State of Anystate, more particularly described as follows:

Note: The detailed legal description is often attached as a schedule. If so, the contract should say something like "See Schedule A, attached." If it does, then be sure it is attached. Also, compare the formal legal description in the contract with the description in the survey and title insurance policy. Advise your lawyer of any differences.

ALL that tract or parcel of land and premises, situate, lying and being in the City of Sellville, in the County of Oakland, and State of Anystate. BEING known and designated as Lot No. 3 in Block No. 13 on a certain map entitled "Map of Janes Town, Sellville, Anystate, O.L.P. Rogers, Surveyor, dated June 10, 1932" and filed in the Register's Office as Case 34338-NN-5.

BEGINNING at a stake in the Northeasterly side of Main Street, at a point therein distant 60.2 feet Southeasterly from the intersection

formed by the said Northeasterly side of Main Street and the Southeasterly side of Glenwood Road; thence running (1) North 45 degrees 22
minutes East, a distance of 90 feet to a stake for a corner; thence running
(2) South 43 degrees 12 minutes East a distance of 58.32 feet to a point
for another corner; thence running (3) South 85 degrees 32 minutes
West a distance of 14 feet to a point in the aforesaid line of Main Street;
thence running (4) North 54 degrees 18 minutes West a distance of 83
feet to the point or place of BEGINNING. BEING also known as 123
Main Street, Buyville, Anystate.

BEING known as Lot 4 in Block 32, Account No. 13-44G on the official tax map of the City of Sellville, Oakland County, Anystate (the
"House").

Note: The description should be complete and accurate. The complete
legal description, not a mere address or lot and block number should be
included. Generally, it will come from a copy of the deed you obtained
when you purchased the house. However, the description on the old deed
shouldn't be accepted blindly. It should be carefully compared with the
description contained in the survey done of the property and any differences investigated.

Note: If there are any problems with the title to the property, or with
the information reflected in the survey, discuss them with your lawyer
before you complete negotiations with any potential buyer. If the problems can be resolved ahead of time, it may facilitate the sale of the property. If the problems can't be changed (e.g., a neighbor has an easement
to use your driveway to reach his house) it's probably best to be up front
with prospective buyers. Its almost always easier to deal with problems
that are known up front, than with those discovered after the transaction has progressed. In the latter case, the buyer may suspect your hon-
esty, which could affect the entire transaction.

---

c. Street Rights

Note: As part of your title search, a street report should be obtained
which identifies that the street has full access, etc.

This sale includes all the rights, title, and interest, if any, of the Seller in
and to any land lying in the bed of any street, in front of or adjoining the
House, to the center line of such street.

d. Condemnation

Note: Although condemnation rarely occurs, its consequences are so significant that it has to be addressed. If a municipality or other government agency forces the sale of the property by the owner to the agency, what happens? It is critical to provide for exactly what is to happen depending on what stage the purchase/sale is at. If the contract has not been signed, there is no issue since the property is still owned by the sellers. If the contract is signed, then the contract terms, or perhaps state law, may determine the outcome. If the contract is vague, a drawn-out legal battle could ensue as the parties negotiate whether the sale should be concluded, who is entitled to the condemnation proceeds, and what the sales price should be. This provision should be read in conjunction with the later section discussing the obligations of the seller when seller can't deliver to the buyer the property the buyer was intending to buy.

This sale also includes any right of the Seller to any unpaid award by reason of any taking by condemnation any damages to the House. The Seller shall deliver, at no additional cost to the Purchaser, at the closing, or after the closing, on demand, any document which the Purchaser may require to collect any such award.

e. Personal Property

Note: More fights and heated emotions flare up over personal property than any other issue in a house closing. Often the amounts are far less than the battle is worth. Keep your perspective. Don't risk losing a sale/purchase over what personal property is and is not included. It's rarely wise to cancel a sale over a personal property dispute. Even if the bookcase the buyer wants is worth $500, that's probably a pittance in comparison to the sales price of the house.

Note: This section specifies precisely which items of personal property are included and which are excluded from the sale. Personal property is generally movable property, such as furniture. Personal property that is not permanently attached to the house or land is not included in the sale unless the contract says it is. This is distinguished from real property—the house and the land—which are automatically included in the sale. Property known as fixtures is personal property that is attached to the house or land. Fixtures are generally included automatically in the sale. The law is not always clear as to what property is personal property or fixtures, and even if the law is clear, your buyer may not be. Therefore, the best approach is to list everything in detail.

Although this is probably the simplest provision in a sales contract, in many sales it can cause the most problems. Too often, the buyer and seller disagree as to what items should and should not be included in the sale.

The best advice is as follows: (1) If there are any important personal items that you don't want to include in the sale, move them out of the house before you begin showing it to prospective buyers. What buyers don't see, they can't argue about. (2) If you can't move out the items you really want to take with you, then tell prospective buyers up front that those items have sentimental value to you and you will take them. (3) Be certain to carefully list every item of personal property that is to be included and excluded in the contract before it goes to the buyer. It's much easier to get a buyer to accept that certain items are excluded if it is in the first contract the buyer sees. It is much harder to get a buyer to agree to let you add something to the excluded list after the buyer has seen the contract. Don't rely on the broker or your lawyer to know what to include and exclude; they can't read your mind. The best approach is to walk through your house before you first meet with a broker or lawyer and prepare lists of what you want to exclude from the sale, and what you're willing to include. At your first meeting, give the list to whoever will be preparing the contract. Again, if it's really a buyers' market, whatever you do, don't lose the sale over some small item of personal property.

(1) Included in this sale are all fixtures and articles of personal property attached to or used in connection with the House, unless specifically excluded. The Seller represents that the fixtures and personal property are paid for and owned by the Seller free and clear of any security interests or liens or they shall be satisfied at the time of the closing from the proceeds of the sale in order to convey an unencumbered property. Fixtures and personal property included in this sale are the following: heating, air conditioning, plumbing, electrical and lighting fixtures (except the breakfast room ceiling fixture), bathroom and kitchen fixtures and cabinets, storm windows and doors, screens, shades, mail box, wall-to-wall carpets, sump pump, shrubbery, fences, range, refrigerator, freezer, washing machine, clothes dryer, dishwasher, and drapery in the dining room, including the hardware and rods.

Note: Once seller and buyer have agreed on the personal property included, they can still fight over the condition. Be sure the contract indicates exactly how it is being sold. The following paragraph is what most sellers will want.

(2) All personal property listed above is being sold in AS IS condition. Seller makes no representations as to the functioning, quality, or condition of such property.

(3) Not included in this sale are the following: furniture, drapes (other than the dining room), curtains, microwave oven, fireplace equipment, breakfast room ceiling fixture, and lawn ornaments.

f. Purchase Price

Note: Make sure the purchase price properly reflects what you've agreed to with the buyer. If the price was to be, for example, $350,000, but the buyer has agreed to pay you an additional $1,250 for lawn furniture, list the price as $351,250, or perhaps, even itemize in this provision that the price is $350,000 for the house and $1,250 for the lawn furniture, for a total of $351,250. This will make it easier for everyone involved to understand the final number. A separate bill of sale can be used for the lawn furniture or other personal property, and it can be excluded from the contract price under the real estate purchase contract. If this is done, be certain all of this is clearly stated in all agreements.

The purchase price for the House is Three Hundred Fifty Thousand Dollars ($350,000).

g. Payment of Purchase Price

Note: You must specify not only the amounts of payments, but the other details as well. When will the payments be made and in what form? How much of the price can a buyer cover with a personal check? How much will be in the form of a certified or bank check? Can funds be wired from buyer's bank to the attorney's trust account so good funds are available? Understand the nuances of a bank check in advance since it is not an absolute guarantee of payment.

The aggregate purchase price of Three Hundred Fifty-One Thousand Two Hundred Fifty Dollars ("$351,250") (the "Purchase Price") shall be paid as follows. By check on the signing of this Contract, to be held in escrow by Seller's attorney $_____. By a Purchase Money Mortgage and Note from Purchaser to Seller $_____. By certified, bank, escrow, or lawyer's trust account check at closing from buyer's mortgage $_____. The balance due and payable at closing $_____.

Note: If significant money is held in escrow, request an interest-bearing account with the interest paid to you.

Sellers should generally try to obtain as large a down payment as possible. In many parts of the country, a large down payment is customary. However, if an accommodation to the buyer will help close the deal and enable the buyer to get the necessary funds together, there is no problem accepting less, so long as the seller understands the risks. It is very important to specify the type of payment that will be acceptable. If the contract doesn't state that a bank or certified check is acceptable, the buyer may try to pay with a regular check. If the seller is planning to close on a new house he or she is buying shortly after the closing on the house being sold/bought under this contract, it's critically important to the seller to have readily available funds from the buyer. The best approach for any seller, however, is to have funds wire transferred so that they are immediately available.

Example: Where you are to be receiving a substantial amount of payments at closing and are going to close shortly on a new home you're buying, you might want to have the buyer provide several checks in amounts that correspond to payments you as the seller (and buyer of the second house) need for the closing of the house you're buying.

Assume you will be receiving $250,000 at the closing of the house you're selling in the morning, and will be going to the closing for the house you will be buying that afternoon. You might want to ask your buyer, prior to closing (since you probably won't have exact numbers when the contract is signed) for three checks totaling $250,000 rather than one check. Assume that the seller of the house you will be buying in the afternoon owes his bank approximately $100,000 on a first mortgage, and a private lender $75,000 on a second mortgage. Assume that the purchase price of the house you'll be buying is $325,000. It might smooth your purchase if you ask the person buying your house in the morning for three checks: (1) $100,000, which you will sign over at the afternoon closing to the bank that holds the first mortgage on the house you'll be buying; (2) $75,000, which you will sign over to the private individual holding the second mortgage; and (3) $75,000, which you'll sign over to the seller of the house you'll be buying as part of the remaining $325,000 purchase price. Make sure to coordinate all of this with your attorney and the buyer of the house you're selling, and the seller of the house you're buying. You want to make certain that the checks will be acceptable to the bank of the seller whose house you are buying.

Note: Specifying the exact payments is not sufficient. It is critical to include detailed provisions elsewhere in the contract and the closing statement or the RESPA (HUD-1 form) of sale specifying all of the details of a mortgage, or mortgage assumption, and so on.

---

h. Method of Payment (Alternate Provision)

All money payable under this contract shall be paid, unless otherwise specified, as follows:

Note: Make sure to get photocopies of all checks used at the closing and to save them in your house file. You should also make an extra copy of the contract and give it to your accountant to make sure everything is properly reported for tax purposes.

---

(1) Cash, but not over $1,000.

(2) Certified check of the Purchaser, or an official check of any bank, savings bank, trust company or savings and loan association having a banking office in the State, payable to the order of the Seller.

(3) Money other than the purchase price, payable to the Seller at closing, may be by check of the Purchaser up to the amount of $1,000, or

(4) As the Seller or Seller's attorney may otherwise agree in writing.

i. Escrow; Interest

All monies held in escrow shall be held in interest-bearing accounts and the Purchaser shall be entitled to all interest earned.

Note: Escrow is an arrangement through which a third party holds monies and contracts pending completion of the closing of the sale of the house. The person who does this is someone other than the buyer or seller. It is often the seller's attorney, but the person may vary depending on the custom in your part of the country. It is important to specify whether the monies will be held in an interest-bearing account and who should get the interest, the buyer or seller. Occasionally, the buyer and seller split the interest. Always check with your lawyer as to what is customary in the location where your house is located. And just because it's customary doesn't mean you cannot negotiate something better. The contract should also state who should get the money and other documents held in escrow, if the house purchase/sale doesn't happen, and what the obligations and responsibilities are of the escrow agent. Many escrow agreements provide that the escrow agent should get paid for the job.

Planning Tip: If the deal will have an escrow arrangement, get the escrow agreement attached to the contract of sale as an exhibit, or begin negotiating it as soon as possible. Don't ignore the escrow agreement as mere legal boilerplate. If the deal goes bad, the escrow agreement could be as important as the contract in protecting your rights.

Note: This sample contract does not reflect seller financing. If seller financing is to be used, it will have to be reflected in the contract. If you will be helping the buyer finance part of the purchase (taking back "paper" from the buyer) be certain that the amount of purchase money mortgage is properly reflected in the contract. In addition, the key terms of the loan you will make to the buyer should also be noted in the contract so that these items will be agreed to before the closing. The key terms, in addition to the amount of the loan, include maturity date (when the loan comes due), amortization period (period over which payments are calculated which can exceed the maturity date), interest rate, and any personal guarantees (e.g., a parent of a young buyer). See: Shenkman, *How to Buy a House with No (or Little) Money Down* for sample seller financing documents.

Note: When the buyer will assume an existing mortgage, the terms of the contract have to be adjusted if feasible. Caution: Before assuming that a buyer can benefit from a seller's mortgage, check with a lawyer and get the lender's approval. This is not often possible. This has not been reflected in this sample contract. Where it's possible for the buyer to assume your mortgage, this can be a substantial plus to making a sale. If you as seller have a low rate fixed mortgage that is assumable, this will make it easier for the buyer to afford a larger down payment or purchase price than would be the case if the buyer had to pay market interest rates on all borrowed monies. If you're the buyer, it can provide a significant incentive.

Note: In a strong real estate market, it might become common for sellers not to give buyers a mortgage contingency clause. This means that if you are a buyer, you will have to arrange financing in advance and take the risk of losing your deposit if you later cannot get the loans you need. For sellers, this means one less risk of a deal not going through. However, even in such a market, a seller who is willing to be a bit flexible might be able to negotiate a better deal to sell.

Note: In almost all home sales, the buyer will have to get a mortgage to complete the sale. To avoid being in default under the sale contract, buyers will endeavor to negotiate the inclusion of a mortgage contingency clause. This provides simply that if the buyer, after reasonable efforts, can't get the required mortgage, the sale doesn't go through. The issue for sellers is, What must the buyer do before the mortgage contingency clause can be used to get out of the contract? In this regard, all contract clauses are not created equal. Many contracts almost give the buyer carte blanche to get out. Others may just require application for a mortgage that is denied. If you're the buyer, that's great. If you're the seller, you should try to negotiate a more reasonable clause that requires the buyer to take minimum specified actions. If the buyer is not willing to commit to take reasonable steps to get a mortgage, you have to ask whether it is really worth tying your house up to wait.

Have the buyer to commit to make a timely, complete application to at least two or three lenders and comply with all reasonable requests of each lender (why should the buyer get out of buying your house because his mortgage application was rejected for not providing required papers). The buyer should be required to accept a mortgage at prevailing or market interest rates and terms.

---

j. Mortgage Contingency Clause

This contract of sale is contingent upon the buyers obtaining a written mortgage commitment by November 15, 2001, from a reputable bank, savings and loan association, credit union, or mortgage company, in an amount not less than One Hundred Eighty-Five Thousand Dollars ($185,000.00). The terms of the mortgage shall not be less favorable than an interest rate of Eight and One Half percent (8.5%), with an amortization period of not less than Fifteen (15) years, and points not in excess of Three (3) percent of the principal balance borrowed. The loan must be a conventional, Conventional-MGIC, or adjustable rate loan and mortgage. The buyers shall make an immediate application to a lending institution, and shall endeavor in good faith to obtain a mortgage loan on terms at least as favorable as those set forth herein. Buyers shall pay the application, appraisal, and credit report and other fees relating to such mortgage application. The buyers shall promptly supply all information and forms requested by the lending institution. If the buyers, after reasonable and diligent efforts are unable to obtain a mortgage commitment, this sale contract shall be void and all funds and documents shall be returned to the respective parties, and neither the buyers nor the sellers shall have any rights against each other.

k. Flood Area

Note: Flood zones are an important issue to address up front in any sale or purchase of a house. If you're selling and unsure, determine before putting your house on the market whether the house is located in a flood area. Be up front and disclose it. Buyers should inquire from local attorneys and brokers about insurance programs before committing. If you haven't as a buyer had ample time to investigate, don't sign a contract unless there is an express clause giving you time to research the flood zone issue and make a decision.

If the House is located in a state or federal flood hazard area, Purchaser may cancel this Contract on written notice to Seller within Ten (10) days from the date of this Contract, in which case the provisions of the section of this Contract governing termination shall apply.

l. Mortgage Estoppel Certificate

Seller agrees to deliver to the Purchaser at the Closing a certificate dated not more than Thirty-One (31) days before closing signed by First City Savings Bank, in a form appropriate for recording, and certifying the amount of the unpaid principal and interest, date of maturity. The Seller shall pay the fees for recording this certificate.

m. Violations

Note: Local laws vary substantially, so you really need the input of a local real estate expert to understand the implications of the following clause. Don't assume, as either a buyer or seller, that it's appropriate to use this clause without obtaining expert local advice. A provision similar to the following one could result in the seller paying for substantial repairs, or even improvements, and taking other steps necessary to bring the house up to the standards of the local building code. Some municipalities require that a certificate of occupancy or some other type of inspection certificate be obtained. As a precondition to issuing the certificate, an inspection might be performed and specified repairs required.

Although some expense might be involved, there may be no choice if you as a seller must absolutely sell your house. If not, you should discuss with your lawyer putting a limit on the amount you might have to spend.

All notices of violations, any regulations, codes, laws, ordinances, orders, or other requirements by any governmental agency affecting the House at the date of this contract, shall be complied with by the Seller, at Seller's expense, subject to the limitations contained in this Contract, and the House shall be conveyed free of any violations. This provision shall survive closing.

n. Assessments

Note: Talk to local realtors, lawyers, and others, to find out if the municipality has any planned assessments. If assessments have already been made by the local town or county, they become a lien on the property that the seller will be responsible for, unless the contract states otherwise. Since this is fairly standard, it may be difficult in a buyers' market to change the standard form. In a seller's market, different treatment could be negotiated.

If, at the time of closing, the House is subject to any assessment which is, or may become, payable in annual installments for improvements which have been made, and the first installment is then a lien, or has been paid, then for the purposes of this contract all the unpaid installments shall be deemed to be due, and shall be paid, by the Seller at closing.

o. Adjustments at Closing—Calculation

Note: Set up a checklist for every closing item. Review with your broker and attorney any items that might have to be adjusted at the closing. Work out the necessary arrangements so the figures can be determined and agreed on prior to the closing to keep the closing smooth and efficient. You need to do this in advance since arrangements often have to be made with utilities and other companies.

(1) The following items are to be apportioned as of midnight of the day before closing: (i) interest on the Mortgage; (ii) taxes; (iii) water charges; (iv) sewer rents, if any, on the basis of the fiscal year for which assessed; and (v) heating oil, if any.

(2) If the Closing shall occur before a new tax rate is fixed, the apportionment of taxes shall be based upon the old tax rate for the prior period applied to the latest assessed valuation.

Note: Estimates obtained in advance will help smooth the closing and avoid disputes. Get the readings within a week of the closing and write all of the utility companies and notify them of the date of the closing to cut off future liability.

(3) If there is a water, electric, or other utility meter on the premises, the Seller shall furnish a reading to a date not more than Ten (10) days prior to the Closing, and the charges, if any, shall be apportioned on the basis of the last reading.

p. Adjustments at Closing

The Seller may credit the Purchaser, as an adjustment to the purchase price, with the amount of any unpaid taxes, assessments, water charges, and sewer rents, together with any interest and penalties, to a date not less than Ten (10) days after the Closing, provided that the official bills, computed to that date, are provided to the Purchaser at Closing.

Note: Although not common, other adjustments also can arise at a house closing. Inquire as to whether adjustments will have to be made for insurance premiums. If a tenant is renting the house, adjustments may need to be made for rent and security deposits (and legal steps taken to remove the tenant if necessary). Be sure to comply with any applicable lease terms and advise the tenant to pay rent to the new owner.

q. Default by Seller

Note: Title is the ownership interest in the real estate that you are sell-ing to the buyer. The title or ownership interest that you will have to transfer is described in the section called "Quality of Title." If the title defect (e.g., an easement or lien) can be corrected without a substantial cost, it may pay for the seller to correct the title defect instead of cancel-ing the sale. The tougher the market, the more sellers should consider re-solving the title issue and not canceling the contract. It may be wise to clarify your right to cure the title defect by stating in the contract that the seller has the option of curing the title defect, if possible.

If the Seller is unable to convey title in accordance with the terms of this Contract, the sole liability of the Seller will be to refund to the Pur-chaser the amounts paid on account of this Contract, plus all reasonable charges made for examination of title and any additional searches made under this Contract, including the survey, termite, and structural in-spection charges, such expenses in the aggregate being not more than Five Hundred Dollars ($500.00). Upon such refund and payment, this Contract shall be considered canceled, and neither the Seller nor the Purchaser shall have any further rights against the other by reason of this Contract.

r. Closing

Note: The closing is the final meeting where escrow is broken and all monies and documents evidencing the title to the property are trans-ferred. There is one key word that applies to both buyer and seller—*pre-pare*. Every closing is different. Although many are simple and smooth, some are not. You don't want to be at the ones that aren't. Talk to all of your professionals (lawyer, realtor, accountant, inspector, insurance con-sultant, and perhaps others) and make a list of everything you are re-sponsible for and be sure it's done.

The closing of this transaction shall include the payment of the purchase price to the Seller and the delivery to the Purchaser the deed described below (the Closing). The Closing will take place at the office of the Buyer's attorney's, or the mortgagee's office at 100 Legal Street, Big Town, Anystate, on or about 11:00 A.M., January 15, 2003.

s. Deed

Note: The deed is the legal document that transfers the title to (the ownership of) the land to the buyer. There are many types of deeds, each of which has been described in this chapter. A bargain and sale deed with covenants against grantor's acts transfers all of the seller's right, title, and interest in the property to the buyer. If you are the seller, you also promise the buyer that you haven't done anything while you owned the property that could jeopardize the buyer's obtaining good title. You do not, however, make any promises about what prior owners have done to the property. A warranty deed goes beyond the rights granted in the bargain and sale deed.

Deeds have different names in different parts of the country so if there is any question as to what is appropriate, consult with your lawyer.

At the Closing, the Seller shall deliver to the Purchaser a bargain and sale with covenants against grantor's acts deed in the proper statutory form for recording to transfer full ownership, fee simple title, to the Premises, free of all encumbrances except as stated in this Contract (the Deed).

t. Quality of Title

Note: Title is a technical legal concept that generally neither buyer and seller will have to address. However, you need to understand the nuances in case an issue arises with respect to the house involved in the sale. In some situations, you may have to make a decision as seller to incur some additional cost to fix (cure) a problem with title. Buyers may have to make a decision—which should only be done with legal guidance—to accept a house with an imperfect title. A court will generally require a buyer to accept marketable title. This assures the buyer the right to sell the property if he so chooses, the right to use the property, and the right to hold the property peacefully. Marketable title basically assures the buyer that he shouldn't have to be subject to litigation to take and use the property. Many factors could affect marketability such as liens, mortgages, judgments, past-due real estate taxes, physical encroachments (e.g., a neighbor's driveway extends two feet over your property line), an improperly handled probate proceeding, an invalid divorce proceeding.

---

(1) The Seller shall give and the Purchaser shall accept such title as a reputable title company which regularly conducts business in this State will be willing to approve and insure at standard rates with

their standard form of title insurance policy. This title insurance policy must transfer ownership of the property to the Purchaser free of any rights and claims except the following: (i) restrictive covenants of record which do not and will not impair the normal use of the property; (ii) utility and similar easements which do not impair the normal use of the property or inhibit the Purchaser from constructing any reasonable improvements or additions to the House; (iii) laws and government regulations that affect the use and maintenance of the House, provided that they are not violated by the existing House and improvements or by their current use; (iv) consents by the Seller or any former owner of the House for the erection of any structure or structures on, under, or above any street or streets on which the House may abut but which are not within the boundary lines of the House.

(2) Seller shall deliver to Purchaser an affidavit of title at Closing. If a title examination discloses judgments, bankruptcies, or other returns against other persons having names the same as or similar to that of the Seller, the Seller shall state in the affidavit showing that they are not against the Seller.

Note: For example, if your name is Jane Doe, there might be another Jane Doe who has a judgment against her for failing to pay a debt. You don't have to pay the other person's debt, but you will have to give a sworn statement (affidavit) to the buyer stating that you're a different Jane Doe, and that the judgment isn't against you.

(3) If required pursuant to local law, Seller shall deliver to Purchaser, at Seller's sole expense, a certificate of occupancy. Seller shall make any repairs necessary to obtain the certificate of occupancy at Seller's sole expense up to a maximum of Two Thousand Dollars ($2,000). If repairs in excess of such amount are required and Purchaser is unwilling to assume the cost, then either party hereto may cancel this Contract, and the provisions of this Contract shall apply.

u. Risk of Loss

Note: Many contracts are written using a percentage of the purchase price, with 10 percent being common. As the seller, you want a fairly high threshold to make it more difficult for the buyer to back out of the contract. As a buyer, you may wish to negotiate a dollar figure that you are willing to live with.

The risk of loss or damage to the premises by fire or other casualty until the delivery of the deed is assumed by the Seller. If there is a fire or other casualty to the House prior to the Closing and the cost of repairing the damage exceeds Ten Thousand Dollars ($10,000), Purchaser may cancel this Contract and the provisions of the section "Default by Seller" shall apply.

v. Transfer and Recording Taxes

The Seller shall deliver a check at the Closing payable to the order of the appropriate State, City, or County officer in the amount of any applicable transfer tax, recording tax, or both, payable by reason of the delivery or recording of the Deed together with any required tax return. The Purchaser's attorney, at Purchaser's expense, shall complete any tax return and cause the check and the tax return to be delivered to the appropriate office promptly after Closing.

w. Broker

Note: Every contract should specify the real estate agents that seller and buyer have dealt with on the transaction. Each of the seller and buyer should hold the other harmless in the event of a suit by another broker. Try to get bills from the brokers in advance of the closing.

The Purchaser and Seller state that neither has dealt with any broker in connection with this sale other than Joe's Real Estate Company, Inc., and the Seller agrees to pay the broker the commission earned pursuant to a separate agreement at the rate of Five Percent (5%). Each party agrees to hold the other party hereto harmless in the event of any misrepresentation as to the use of brokers.

x. Condition of the House

Note: The buyer should have had an inspector review the house and should rely on the report of the inspector, not on the seller's representations as to the house's condition. Nevertheless, they should be negotiated. You don't want to find the inspector missed something that the seller knew existed.

Sellers should be careful of representing that appliances and systems are in "good" working order. *Working order* probably means that if you turn them on they work. But what does *good working order* mean? If you have a 25-year-old freezer that works, it's in working order. But could it ever be in good working order? Sellers should try to limit the representations so that they don't "survive closing." If the buyer finds a problem after closing, you might not be held liable. However, if as a seller you are aware of a defect, the law in your state may obligate you to disclose it. Consider whether the disclosures should be made in the contract. The advantage then is that you are on record as having made any required disclosures, and the buyer can't claim that he wasn't aware of those problems when the contract was signed.

The Purchaser agrees to purchase the Premises, buildings, and personal property as is, which shall mean in their present condition subject to reasonable use, wear, tear, and natural deterioration between the date of this Contract and Closing, except as specifically provided otherwise in the section "Inspections." The Premises and personal property shall be delivered in broom-clean condition, and all personal property not included in this sale shall be removed. All systems and appliances shall be in working order. The roof shall be free of leaks and the basement free of seepage. Purchaser shall have the right to inspect the House prior to the Closing to verify the condition of the House.

y. Inspections

Note: Home inspections for structural problems are almost universal. Inspections for radon and termites, in some parts of the country are a necessity. Your concerns as a seller are that the buyer not delay the closing for any lengthy period, since your house will be off the market during that time. If the buyer doesn't notify you, then he will have waived his rights to object based on an inspection.

The Purchaser has Ten (10) days from the signing of this contract to obtain a termite inspection of the Premises, and a structural inspection by a qualified home inspection service or engineer, at the Purchaser's sole cost and expense if Purchaser so chooses. If the inspection reports indicate the presence of termite infestation or any structural problem, the Seller shall eliminate the infestation or correct the structural problem at Seller's expense, if the cost does not exceed One Thousand Dollars ($1,000). If the costs exceed such amount, and Purchaser is unwilling to bear the additional cost, this Contract will be canceled and the provisions of the section "Default by Seller" shall apply. Notice of the Seller's intent to cancel this Contract must be given to the Purchaser's attorney within Ten (10) days after Seller's receipt of the termite or structural inspection report. If notice is not given to the Purchaser's attorney within this Ten (10) day period, it shall be the Seller's responsibility to eliminate the reported problem at the Seller's sole cost and expense. If the attorney for the Seller has not received the termite or structural inspection reports within Ten (10) days from the signing of this contract, this paragraph shall be unenforceable and of no effect.

z. Entire Agreement

All prior understandings and agreements between the Purchaser and the Seller are superseded by this Contract which contains their entire agreement. This Contract is entered into after full investigation by both parties and no reliance is made on any matter not set forth in this Contract.

aa. Modification

This Contract may not be changed or terminated except in writing signed by both parties. However, each of the parties authorizes their respective attorneys to agree in writing to any change in dates and time periods provided for in this Contract.

ab. Binding Effect

This Contract shall apply to and bind the heirs, executors, administrators, successors, distributees, and assigns of the respective parties.

IN WITNESS WHEREOF, this contract has been executed by the parties:

SELLERS:

_____   _____
John Seller   Jane Seller

BUYERS:

_____   _____
Bob Buyer   Brenda Buyer

[Witness of Notary forms omitted.]

SAMPLE ASSIGNMENT OF HOUSE PURCHASE CONTRACT TO REVOCABLE LIVING TRUST TO DISCUSS WITH YOUR ATTORNEY

Note: You may have signed a broker-prepared contract before consulting your attorney, or a contract reviewed by your attorney before consulting with your other planners. If so, you may then want to assign the contract to another person or entity to close on the purchase of the new house. To do this, you have to assign the contract to that other person. In this illustrative contract you are assumed to want to assign the purchase of your new house to your revocable living trust to avoid probate and provide for the management of the property in the event of your disability.

THIS AGREEMENT made as of the [Month, Day, Year] between [Trust Name], residing at [Trustee Address] (Assignee); and [Your Name], an individual who resides at [Your Address] (Assignor).

Note: Have your attorney review all underlying contracts and verify that no impediments to transfer to the contract exist and that all local legal requirements are complied with.

   If this form is being adapted to assign a lease or mortgage, the terms of lease or mortgage must be reviewed, as well as local transfer tax and reporting requirements and any third party contractual requirements (e.g., those of a lender).

WHEREAS, the Assignor wishes to assign all his right title and interest in that certain House Purchase Contract between [Your Name] as buyer and [Seller Name] as seller, dated January 3, 2003, attached in full and described in Schedule A hereto (hereinafter called the Contract); and Assignee wishes to accept the assignment of the Contract.

   NOW, THEREFORE, THIS AGREEMENT WITNESSETH that the parties hereto covenant and agree as follows:

Note: Although the following language indicates that this assignment is subject to the rights of others (in this example, the seller under the House Closing Contract), your attorney should obtain their consent in advance (if necessary) and be certain all legal requirements are met.

---

a. In consideration of One Dollar ($1.00) and other good and valu-
able consideration, the receipt and adequacy of which is hereby acknowledged, Assignor hereby assigns, transfers and sets over unto
Assignee the said Contract and all rights, titles, and interests of
Assignor therein and thereto, together with all rights, benefits,
privileges, and advantages of Assignor to be derived therefrom,
subject to the rights of certain third parties to approve, or consent
to such assignments, as provided in the Contracts.

Planning Tip: Have the assignment include an exact reference, and
even repeat the exact language, of the provision in the contract that permits assignment. This will help assure that you comply with the exact requirements to make the assignment valid. Many contracts include Notice
provisions. They should be expressly complied with as defined in the contract. Since the seller's approval was required in the hypothetical original contract, a signature line for seller is provided below.

---

b. This Assignment is made in accordance with the terms and provisions of Section X-3 of the Contract which states: "This Contract
may be assigned before Closing, on Notice to Seller, and Seller's
consent, which may not be unreasonably withheld."

c. The Assignor covenants and agrees with the Assignee that Assignor
shall at the request of the Assignee, do and perform all such acts
and things, and execute and deliver all such consents, documents,
and other writings as may be required to give full force and effect
to the assignment herein contemplated.

d. Assignee accepts the within assignment to it of the said Contracts
and agrees with Assignor to assume, carry out, observe, perform,
and fulfill said Contracts in accordance with their terms.

e. This Agreement shall, subject to the terms and conditions of the
actual Contract, enure to the benefit of and be binding upon the
parties hereto and their successors and assigns.

f. This Assignment of Contract has been executed to complete the
transfer of the single family residence located at 123 Main Street,
Anytown, USA, by [Your Name], assignor's revocable living trust
[Trust Name], [Trustee Name], in accordance with the terms of
the Contract.

IN WITNESS WHEREOF, the parties hereto have executed and delivered this Agreement as of the day and year first written.

ASSIGNEE:

[Trust Name], Assignee

By: _____
    [Trustee Name], Trustee

ASSIGNOR:

_____

[Your Name], Assignor

In the Presence of:

_____

Witness

ACCEPTED AND AGREED TO BY SELLER:

_____

[Seller Name]

(Notary forms omitted.)
       Schedule A: Contact Attached [omitted here]

SAMPLE AFFIDAVIT OF TITLE ON PURCHASE OF HOME FORM TO DISCUSS WITH YOUR ATTORNEY

Note: When a house is purchased or sold, both the buyer and seller may give a statement under oath (an affidavit) as to their correct legal name, status of the property being sold, marital status, and other information necessary to obtaining proper title. This form illustrates this.

---

a. Affidavit of Title

State of [State Name]
County of [County Name]   SS.:
    [Your Name] and [Spouse Name] say(s) under oath:

b. Representations

If only one person signs this affidavit the words "we," "us," and "our" shall mean "I," "me," and "my." The statements in this affidavit are true to the best of our knowledge, information, and belief.

c. Name, Age, and Residence

Note: If the seller is not a United States citizen, certain tax reporting or withholding requirements may apply.

We have never changed our names or used any other names. We are citizens of the [Country of Citizenship] and at least 18 years old. After today, we will live at [Property Address].

d. Ownership and Possession

We are the only owners of property located at [Property Address] called "this property."

    We now mortgage this property to [Mortgage Company].

    The date of the mortgage is the same as this affidavit. This mortgage is given to acquire a loan of [$Loan Amount]. We are in sole possession of this property. There are no tenants or other occupants of this property. We have owned this property since [Month, Day, Year]. We have always obtained all necessary permits and certificates of occupancy. All charges for municipal improvements such as sewers, sidewalks, curbs, or similar improvements benefiting this property have been paid in full. No building, addition, extension, or alteration on this property has been made or worked on within the past [Number of Months]. We are not aware that anyone has filed or intends to file a mechanic's lien or building contract relating to this property. No one has notified us that money is due and owing for construction, alteration, or repair work on this property.

e. Liens or Encumbrances

We have not allowed any interest (legal rights) to be created which affect our ownership or use of this property. No other persons have legal rights in this property, except the rights of utility companies to use this property for the purpose of serving this property. There are no pending lawsuits or judgments against us or other legal obligations which may be enforced against this property. No bankruptcy or insolvency actions have been started by or against us. We have never been declared bankrupt. No one has any collateral interest in any personal property or fixtures on this property. All liens (legal claims, such as judgments) listed on the attached judgment or lien search are not against us, but against others with similar names.

f. Marital History

Note: If the seller was divorced, the title company or your attorney may need to verify that the other spouse has no claims on the house you are attempting to buy. If only one spouse was on the deed, you may need a deed or other document from the other spouse waiving certain marital rights to obtain clear title (dower or courtesy).

Select the appropriate status:

[   ] We are not married.

[   ] We are married to each other. We were married on [Marriage Date]. The maiden name of [Spouse Name] was [Maiden Name].

[   ] This property has never been occupied as the principal matrimonial residence of any of us. (If it has, or if it was acquired before a date specified in your state's laws, each spouse must sign the mortgage and affidavit.)

[   ] Our complete marital history is listed.

[   ] Our complete marital history is listed. This includes all marriages not listed above, and any pending matrimonial actions. We include how each marriage ended. We have attached copies of any death certificates

and judgments for divorce or annulment including any stipulations in these judgments for divorce or annulment including any stipulations in these judgments which relate to this property.

g. Exceptions and Additions

The following is a complete list of exceptions and additions to the above statements. This includes all liens or mortgages which are not being paid off as a result of this mortgage.

[Exceptions]

h. Reliance

We make this affidavit in order to obtain the mortgage loan. We are aware that our lender will rely on our being truthful in the statements made in this affidavit.

Signed and sworn to before me on   _____
[Month, Day, Year]   [Affiant]

_____   _____
[Attorney]   [Affiant Spouse]

Attorney at Law of [State Name]

DOCUMENTS FOR PURCHASE OF COOPERATIVE APARTMENT SHARES AND LEASE: SAMPLE ASSIGNMENT AND ASSUMPTION OF PROPRIETARY LEASE

Note: If you are purchasing a cooperative apartment, you will need special documents to complete the transaction. See discussion in this chapter. The assignment and assumption of proprietary lease and stock certificate is a closing document for the transfer of the shareholder's rights to an apartment in the cooperatively owned building and the assumption by the assignee of the lessee's obligations under the proprietary lease and stock certificate.

---

a. Know All Men by These Presents that [Assignor Name], in consideration of the sum of [Dollar Amount] [$] dollars, paid by [Assignee], and for other good and valuable consideration, does hereby assign unto the Assignee a certain Proprietary Lease dated [Month, Day, Year] by and between [Lessor Name] and [Lessee Name], covering apartment [Apartment Number] in the building known as [Building Name].

b. To Have and To Hold the same unto the Assignee and Assignee's personal representatives and assigns, on and after [Assignment Date] for the balance of the term of the Proprietary Lease, and any renewals or extensions thereof and subject to the pledges, circumstances, and restrictions therein contained.

c. In order to encourage the Lessor to consent to this Assignment and Assignee to accept this Assignment, the Assignor represents to Lessor and Assignee that:

   i. Assignor has full right, title, and authority to allocate the shares in the Lessor and the Proprietary Lease appurtenant thereto.

   ii. Assignor has fully effected all the terms, pledges, and prerequisites of the Proprietary Lease on Assignor's part to be performed to the effective date hereof.

   iii. Assignor has not done or permitted anything to be done which might impose any disadvantage on the Lessor or Assignee.

   iv. There are no claims, security interests, or liens against the Proprietary Lease, or the shares in the Lessor corporation apportioned to the apartment to which the Proprietary Lease is appurtenant, or to any fixtures and/or personal property installed by Assignor in the apartment.

d. In order to encourage the Lessor to agree to this Assignment of the proprietary Lease and the shares of the Lessor to which the Proprietary Lease is appurtenant, and in consideration of such Assignment and the consent of the Lessor thereto, the Assignee hereby assumes and agrees to perform and comply with all the terms, pledges, and prerequisites of the Proprietary Lease to be performed or conformed with by Lessee on and after [Month, Day, Year], the effective date of this Assignment, as if the undersigned had originally executed the Proprietary Lease as Lessee, and further agrees that at the request of the Lessor, the undersigned will relinquish the assigned Proprietary Lease to the Lessor and enter into a new Proprietary Lease of said apartment for the remainder of the term thereof, in the same form and on the same terms, pledges, and prerequisites as the assigned Proprietary Lease.

e. It is Hereby Certified by the Lessor that it has consented to this Assignment of the Proprietary Lease and the shares allocated to the apartment of the Assignee. Such consent has been given in writing by a majority of the now authorized number of directors of the corporation or by duly adopted resolution by its Board of Directors at a meeting duly held.

f. It is Further Certified that all rent, maintenance or other charges due under the Proprietary Lease have been paid up to and including [Month, Day, Year].

g. The pledges and representations herein shall survive the delivery hereof, but any action based thereon must be instituted within one year from the effective date of this assignment.

In Witness Whereof the assignor, Assignee, and Lessor have executed this Assignment on [Month, Day, Year].

_____

[Assignor Name]

_____

[Assignee Name]

by Cooperative Corporation:

_____

[Officer Name]

SAMPLE HOME SALE ORGANIZER AND RECONCILIATION

The following illustrative home sale postclosing checklist and organizer can be used as a model to organize all records and documents pertaining to the closing, assure that nothing has been missed, and reconcile and prove out all payments. You will have to adapt it to your particular transaction. If you invest the time shortly after the closing to organize all records, it will prove infinitely easier than trying to locate documents at a later date. In most cases, your attorney will not complete this form of documentation for you (or if he did, the cost would be more than you might be willing to incur).

a. The Closing

BOB and BETTY BUYER purchased the house located at 137 SETON HALL STREET, BIG CITY, USA, from Arthur and Susan SELLER. The closing took place at the law offices of Adam Attorney Some Street, Some City, New Jersey on August 29, 2002.

b. People in Attendance at the Closing

(1) Adam Attorney, Esq., attorney for buyers.

(2) BOB and BETTY BUYER, buyers.

(3) Adam Attorney, counsel to Central Jersey Mortgage, lender to buyers.

(4) Rita Realtor, real estate broker, Hot Broker Agency.

(5) Harry Hustler, real estate broker, Joe's Realtors Co.

(6) Larry Lawyer, counsel to Sellers.

c. Documents Presented at Closing

(1) Deed.

(2) Tax Collector Notice.

(3) Tax Information Notice.

(4) Itemization of Amount Financed.

(5) Central Mortgage Lenders Corp. Amount Financed Statement dated APR—8/29/02.

(6) Big Mortgage Corp. Amount Financed Statement dated APR—8/14/02.

(7) Assignment of Mortgage to Almost Independent Bank.

(8) Note for $182,000 to Jersey Mortgage—one signed copy.

(9) Settlement Agent's Certificate.

(10) Certificate in lieu of an affidavit.

(11) 1099-S—to be completed by Larry Lawyer.

(12) Mortgage.

(13) Certificate of Occupancy.

(14) Certificate of Transfer.

(15) Tax Information Worksheet.

(16) Mortgage Loan Commitment (prior to closing).

(17) Affidavit of Title—Buyers—1 copy.

(18) Affidavit of Title—Sellers—3 copies.

(19) Survey.

(20) RESPA HUD-1.

(21) Survey Affidavit.

(22) Notice of New Escrow Account—Tax Bill Authorization—ABC Attachment A.

(23) Tax Certification of Your Mortgage Escrow Agreement.

(24) Copy of all Checks issued at and Relating to Closing.

(25) Big Title Insurance Company—binder.

(26) Notices of Settlement—2.

(27) Fundamental Bank Payoff Statement.

(28) First National Bank Payoff Statement.

(29) Insurance Binder number 30-68-8906—State Insurance Co.

(30) Mortgage Disclosure Statement.

(31) Mortgage Loan Closing Statement.

(32) Letter from Harry acknowledging full payment of commission.

(33) Letter from Joe's Realtors Co. acknowledging full payment of commission.

d. Monies Available at Closing

$5,660.89 Check on Savings Association to LL Trust Account. Check No. BR-0617094 dated 8/23/02.

34,278.70   Check on First Bigg Texas to LL Trust Acct. Check No. 704656 dated 8/23/02.

100.00   Harry Hustler Number 3448 dated 8/29/02.

3,803.00   Check from Joes Sandwich to LL Attorney Trust Account. Check No. 528280 dated 8/23/02.

7,761.00   Check from Big Joes Auto to LL, Attorney Trust Account. Check No. 22419 dated 8/23/02.

(1,396.80)   Refund to BOB and BETTY BUYER; LL Trust Account check No. 1052.

8,765.79   Check from Larry Lawyer Attorney Trust Account.

175,314.61   Check (net of deductions) from Central State Mortgage Corporation. Check No. dated 8/29/02.

$234,287.19   Total proceeds at closing.

101.00   Additional check for Blinds from Larry Lawyer.

$234,388.19   Total funds available.

e. Reconciliation of Net Mortgage Check

$182,000.00   Total mortgage from Central State Mortgage.

40.00   Assignments.

75.00   Bank service fee.

300.00   Lender's attorney's fee.

25.00   Certified check fee.

147.87   Interest for balance of August.

77.66   Hazard insurance escrow for two months.

559.86   Property taxes for two months to escrow.

5,460.00   Loan origination fee (points).

$ 6,685.39   Total deductions.

$175,314.61   Net check.

f. Payments Made at/after Closing

$ 6,650.00   Harry's Realtor—commission.

7,000.00   Joe's Realty—commission.

900.00   Adam Attorney, Esq., Esq.—legal fee, Buyers.

1,400.00   Larry Lawyer, Esq.—legal fee, Sellers.

977.75   Land Title Agency, Inc.—title search & ins.

85.00   County Clerk/Adam Attorney, Esq.—recording mortgage from Central Jersey.

912.50   County Clerk Adam Attorney, tax.

80.00	County Clerk/Adam Attorney, Esq., E⟨ Seller's two mortgages.
30.00	County Clerk/Adam Attorney, Esq., notices of settlement.
350.00	Gerry Surveyors & Associates—survey.
17.50	All America—flood hazard certification.
279.93	Adam Attorney, Esq., Esq.—Attorney Trust Account— for telephone, facsimile, Federal Express charges, etc.
97,977.14	Fundamental Mortgage.
117,146.66	Citizens Last National Bank.
$233,806.48	Total disbursements.
581.71	Final disbursement to BUYER.
$234,388.19	Total disbursements.

g. Reconciliation of Curtain Amount

Sources of Additional Payments to BUYER:

(a)	Reduction in mortgage payoff Northern Bank	$ 90.64
(b)	Reduction in mortgage payoff First Natl Lenders, Inc.	115.00
(c)	Reduction in [Attorney Name] legal fee	100.00
(d)	Reduction in [Attorney 2 Name] legal fee	100.00
(e)	Reduction from Broker—Harry Hustler	100.00
(f)	Additional payment from seller	101.00
(g)	Additional disbursement from Larry trust account of excess funds	55.00
	Total	$661.64

Amount Remitted to Buyer with This Closing Statement

Total remitted per above	$581.71
Additional out-of-pocket expenses over amounts estimated at closing (details provided in bills attached)	79.93
Total amount which should have been disbursed	$661.64

h. Follow-up after Closing

(1) Detailed accounting to the Employer (with bill for additional costs to reimburse BUYER, or refund of excess). Letter sent August 19, 2002, to the Employer with a copy to the BUYER.

(2) Documents to Record:

    (a) Seller's mortgage—Still not received—see below.

    (b) Seller's mortgage—Still not received—see below.

    (c) Deed—Done via messenger day following closing.

    (d) Buyer's mortgage—Done via messenger day following closing.

    (e) Payoff two Seller's mortgages via Federal Express. As of October 23, 2002, the canceled mortgages have not been received. Certified letters were sent to the lenders on October 22, 2002, requesting the canceled copies of the mortgages.

(3) Title Company: Final title policy will be requested after above mortgages have been received and filed for cancellation.

(4) Form 1099-S filing—to be completed by Adam Attorney.

2 FINANCING YOUR HOME

Home financing takes many shapes and forms. You can use a mortgage for the purchase of your house; you can refinance to obtain funds for personal use or to improve your house; or you can take out a home equity line on your house. In all these situations, the key economic decisions will be finding the best price. This will mean the lowest interest rate, the least likelihood of increases in the rate in future years, the least points, and the smallest closing costs. These critical issues have been addressed in a host of real estate books and are not discussed further in this chapter.

If you are dealing with a large commercial lender, which is the most common situation, you will not have much choice in reviewing the mortgage and related documents. It's basically a take-it-or-leave-it proposition.

Planning Tip: This doesn't mean that you don't review the documents with your attorney. You must understand what your obligations are under the mortgage and must review the documents to make sure they are correct. Even the largest of institutions can sometimes make a mistake that is costly to you.

In other situations, you may be able to have some input on the terms of the loan. Most loans are sold by banks and other lenders into what is called the secondary market. The loans are grouped (packaged) and structured so that investors can buy interests in securities reflecting ownership interests in the mortgages (securitized). When this is to occur, the lender has little flexibility in how the mortgage will be structured. If eventually thousands of mortgages will be grouped for securitization, they must conform to specified requirements or the eventual securitization won't be feasible. If, however, the lender will retain your mortgage loan in its own portfolio, it may be in a position to negotiate any special terms its loan committee permits. Inquire as to what the lender will be doing with the loan. This knowledge may help you identify a lender where you can negotiate terms or obtain a loan even though you face special circumstances.

Many legal terms are used in the context of home financing and mortgages. Understanding the terminology, particularly as it relates to financing your home, will help you understand the legal issues involved. Much of this chapter is focused on explaining home finance terms, and how they relate to you.

THE MORTGAGE COMMITMENT

When you shop for a loan to buy a house, several weeks or longer may pass between the discussions with the bank or other lender and the closing on your purchase of the house. You may want to lock in an interest rate so that you know you will have the financing you need, at a cost you expect. To do so, you have to ask prospective lenders what arrangements they are willing to make and then get it in writing in the form of a contract called a *commitment letter*. For a fee, the bank or other lender may be willing to guarantee you a loan of a specified amount, at a particular rate, if you meet their required conditions.

The commitment is a vital part of your structuring a home purchase. Be sure to carefully read each clause of the commitment and understand what it means to you. Have your real estate attorney review the commitment before you sign it. Discuss it with your real estate broker since he may need to know the dates involved.

When reviewing a commitment letter consider the following:

- What is the lender charging you in exchange for guaranteeing a particular loan? Is it worth the cost?
- How long has the lender agreed to lock in the loan cost (rate, points, etc.)? Does the lender's time frame in the commitment appear reasonable in light of how the negotiations for your home purchase are progressing? Can you extend the commitment?

Will the bank agree to a longer term for the rate lock-in (say 60 days instead of only 30 days)?

- What conditions has the lender required of you to proceed with the loan? Can you meet them?
- Has the lender included any unusual or special provisions that cause concern?

Planning Tip: Once the commitment is negotiated, be certain that before you sign the final mortgage documents at the closing your attorney has compared the final terms and provisions with the commitment to assure that the bank is not charging more than it is entitled to and that the final terms conform with the commitment.

SECURED OR UNSECURED LOANS FOR YOUR HOUSE

Unsecured Loan

An unsecured loan is a loan made to you without your providing any particular collateral. The only thing backing up the repayment of an unsecured loan is your good faith and moral obligation to pay. If you default on the loan, the lender can sue you for repayment, but has no priority right to any particular asset of yours to assure repayment. The most common type of unsecured loan for a house is a loan from a family member to help you cover the down payment, moving expenses, or the costs of new furniture.

Caution: When family or friends help you with your down payment by loaning you funds, your bank may require them to sign a letter stating that the monies were a gift so that it would really be your funds, not family loan dollars, used for the down payment.

Secured Loan

Most real estate loans are secured. This means that in addition to your promising to repay the lender, you give the lender the right to satisfy the debt out of some specific asset. For your house, it is the house itself that is pledged as security for the loan. The document that accomplishes this is called a *deed of trust* or a *mortgage,* depending on which part of the country you reside in. In a deed of trust arrangement, you as homeowner convey the house in trust to a third party to hold pending your repayment of the loan. The mortgage provides your pledge of your ownership in the house to the bank in the event of a default. If you purchase furniture for your house and finance the purchase at the store, they will retain a lien on the furniture to secure the loan. If you don't make payments on a timely basis, the store can repossess the furniture to secure the repayment of the loan.

LEGAL DOCUMENTS THAT YOU WILL SEE

Mortgage

The mortgage is the document whereby the buyer/borrower of a house agrees to make it serve as collateral for the loan. If the buyer doesn't repay the amount due, the seller can foreclose on the house and sell it to repay the amount still owing. In most cases, the seller will only loan the buyer part of the purchase price. The buyer will make some down payment and the balance of the purchase price will typically be provided by a commercial lender (bank, savings and loan, etc.). In this typical scenario, the seller's loan (purchase money mortgage) will be a second mortgage, coming behind the bank's first mortgage. Although a second mortgage by an unrelated lender to the buyer is sometimes also called a purchase money mortgage, the emphasis in the following forms and comments is on the situation where the seller is the provider of the second mortgage financing.

Different Types of Mortgages

There are many kinds of mortgages. The key distinction for you as a prospective borrower is which type of loan will provide you with the best financial deal and best fit your personal circumstances. From a legal perspective, you must be certain that you understand how the different types of mortgages affect you and that they are properly reflected in the legal documents you will have to sign.

First and Second Mortgages. Since most home loans are secured by mortgages, the question could arise, What happens if there is more than one mortgage? A bit of legal background will help you understand the distinction and how it can affect the different types of mortgage you might have. Most real estate legal documents are part of a recording system that is based on a rule that what is filed with the county clerk (or other designated official place to "record" documents) has priority over a document filed later. Under this general rule, a mortgage that is recorded first would have priority on collection against your house over a mortgage recorded at a later date. The first recorded mortgage could be called a first or senior mortgage. The next recorded mortgage could be called a second or junior mortgage.

Example: Your house is worth $200,000. You have a first mortgage for $150,000 and a second mortgage for $45,000. You default in paying your mortgage and the house is foreclosed on. At the time of the foreclosure, the house is sold for $175,000. The first mortgage holder is paid in full. The second mortgage holder receives what is left, $25,000 on a $45,000 loan.

The distinction between a first and later mortgage is very important. This is why banks take several steps to assure that the bank's mortgage is a first mortgage on your house. The preceding example also illustrates why you often will pay a higher rate for a second mortgage.

Fixed Rate Mortgage. A fixed rate loan retains a specified interest rate throughout the life of the loan. Changes in the market interest rates won't affect your loan. In addition to the interest rate, you must address the number of points required and the term of the loan, 15 to 35 years are common. These terms should be reflected in the commitment and final mortgage. These legal documents should specify the rate agreed to and that it cannot be increased. Be certain that other than the ability of the lender to charge a higher rate if you default (which is a common protective device of lenders), there is no right to change the rate.

Adjustable Rate Mortgage (ARM).   Unlike fixed rate mortgages, adjustable rate mortgages are influenced by changes in overall market interest rates. Therefore, when the overall market interest
rate goes down, your payment for the following month will decrease
as well. Conversely, if overall market rates go up, your payment will
increase. This type of mortgage is ideal for those who only require
short-term mortgages, and are therefore unconcerned with possible
rising interest rates. Also, those who have secure finances and can afford possible rises in interest rates may use this type of mortgage.
Adjustable rate mortgages tend to have lower initial rates of interest than fixed rate mortgages, which adds to their appeal. Addi-
tionally, two caps are often placed on the level to which the rate of
interest may rise. One cap is based on a percentage of the previous
rate per month. In other words, a mortgage's interest rate may only
rise a certain amount each month. The other cap is an overall cap on
the mortgage, which only allows the mortgage to rise to a certain
rate over the course of the entire mortgage. The commitment and
mortgage for an adjustable rate mortgage should clearly state the
rate you will be charged, how and when any increase will be determined, that you will be notified in advance of any increase, and that
there is a maximum increase that can occur in any year (or other
period) and over the life of the mortgage.

Choosing between a Fixed and Adjustable Mortgage.   How do
you choose between a fixed rate and adjustable rate mortgage?
Fixed rate mortgages generally have a higher rate because the bank
is taking the risk that if interest rates go up, it will be stuck getting
a lower rate from you. Variable rate mortgages have, at least at first,
a lower interest rate than fixed rate mortgages since you, and not
the bank, are taking the risk of interest rates increasing. Don't get
fooled by special introductory deals on an adjustable rate mortgage. The annual percentage rate (APR) may be misleading. Be sure
to read the fine print. The Truth in Lending laws guarantee that
you should get the information you need. Even being able to deduct
mortgage interest for tax purposes won't do you much good if you
can't afford the monthly payment after the bank has raised the rate.
Understand when the rate can be raised, how the amount of the
increase is determined, the maximum amount the rate can be raised
(and more importantly what this does to your monthly payment),
and all other terms.

Buy-Down Mortgage. An unusual type of mortgage is some-times called a buy-down mortgage. The seller, to encourage the buyer to make the deal, may deposit a sum of money with the buyer's bank to be used to pay down or lower the interest rate the buyer will have to pay. The tax consequences of such a trans-action are tricky and will depend on what the loan and house sale documents say. One possible outcome is that the seller's payment will be considered a reduction of the purchase price. The buyer may be able to deduct the payments made to the lender as interest ex-pense as the payments are made.

Planning Tip: As with all legal transactions, be certain that the con-tract document clearly specifies how the buy-down will occur, what ex-actly will be paid, and how it will be treated. Be certain that the buy-down is disclosed to the lender and that you consult an accountant as to the tax treatment before signing. Even if the result is the tax equiva-lent of a reduced purchase price, the legal consequences, especially if there is a default, may not be. Check with a lawyer.

Graduated Payment Mortgage (GPM). This is a mortgage with payments that will start off low and increase in a few years.

Note: The legal documents must clearly indicate how the mortgage pay-ments will be determined and when and buy how much they will rise. In-terest on the underpayments must be paid, but you need to know when and at what rate. The legal documents should clarify this. Be certain that you are working with an attorney who understands this type of transac-tion because many real estate attorneys may be inexperienced with non-conventional transactions.

A GPM may seem just perfect, at first glance, for a young couple or person who just started work and will probably be making more in later years. Pay less now when you cannot afford it, and more later when you can. This type of loan has a major financial risk that you should carefully consider before thinking about the tax conse-quences. The monthly payments you will have to make in a few years could be substantially more than the payments you make initially. Will you really be able to make them? Will those guaranteed op-tions you have be worth the paper they're printed on in five years?

Do you have contingency plans in case you can't make the payments? Once you have resolved these issues, take a look at the tax results. This type of loan will likely have you paying less in the early years than the interest due. The interest you aren't paying gets added to the principal balance of the loan so that after the first few years you will actually owe the lender more money than you originally borrowed. This is known as negative amortization. You cannot deduct any interest amounts until you actually pay them.

Reverse Mortgage. With a reverse mortgage, a lender/investor pays the homeowner a check each month, and at the end of the mortgage term, the lender will own the house. Reverse mortgages can also help senior citizens access the equity in their houses to supplement their retirement income without taking out a home equity loan. When you obtain a mortgage from a bank, you will have to make monthly payments for a period of time until you repay the mortgage. After you have paid off the mortgage, you will own the house outright. A reverse (annuity) mortgage is a similar concept, but in reverse. Under this scenario, a lender (or an investor) agrees to make monthly payments to you (or perhaps a large payment at inception). At the end of the payment term (which could be after a certain number of years or death) the lender or the investor will own a portion or all of your house. Your house may then be sold and the lender or investor will be repaid the funds loaned with interest, and possibly with some of the appreciation in your house as well, depending on how the transaction was structured. Meanwhile, you have had the opportunity to continue living in your own house as desired, and have presumably been able to supplement your retirement income.

Note: As with all nonconventional real estate transactions, be certain you retain an attorney who understands these transactions. They are still relatively new and remain unusual in most parts of the country. Don't assume any documents are standard or boilerplate. Read and carefully understand exactly what you will be paid, whether changes in interest rates will affect the payments, when the lender/buyer will have the right to force you to buy your home, what happens if the home is condemned during the time you are receiving payments, and other issues your attorney raises.

Caution: Reverse mortgages are almost only used by senior citizens. Elder law planning to protect your assets from nursing home and related medical care providers is common among the elderly. Before entering into a reverse mortgage, or any other transaction concerning your residence, consult with an elder law attorney to determine the impact in your estate, on your eligibility for various governmental programs, and so on.

Shared-Equity Mortgage. In a shared-equity mortgage (SAM), a lender agrees to give you a lower interest rate and you agree to share some portion (percentage) of the profit when the property is sold, or when the mortgage terminates (which may be prior to when you sell). If the mortgage terminates before you sell, the amount of profit you have to pay the lender will probably be determined by having the home appraised. The profit amount paid to the lender is really contingent interest. This profit amount is deductible as interest when you actually pay it to the lender. Although it's tough to find a lender willing to loan on a shared-equity mortgage, these mortgages make sense if you cannot find another way to get into a home, or you know a friend or family member who likes the investment possibilities. Be sure to use an attorney familiar with these loan instruments. They are not your run-of-the-mill documents. Equity sharing can be structured as a mortgage with an equity kicker, as a partnership arrangement, or as a straight mortgage.

Note: See Shenkman and Boroson, *How to Buy a House with No (or Little) Money Down* for a detailed discussion and sample documents for SAMs.

Deed of Trust

Generally, mortgage documents are used in the eastern part of the country and deeds of trust in some western states. The purpose of the documents is similar.

Note

The note is a legal document whereby the buyer acknowledges owing you money, agrees to the terms of the loan (interest rate, maturity date, etc.), and most importantly, agrees to personally repay the amount due. Thus, if the buyer defaults and the price of the house has declined so that it cannot be sold for enough money to repay the loan (either due to declining prices or damage done by the buyer), the lender can sue the buyer personally for any amount still due. In some cases, the note and mortgage will be combined into a single document called a "Note and Mortgage." Your lawyer can advise you what approach will be used.

Caution: You should only sign one note. The note is the document that creates your legal liability. When you repay the entire loan due, the note should be canceled and the bank should give you a document to have filed in the same government office where the mortgage was filed canceling the mortgage (i.e., the lien) on your house. This can be a document called a "satisfaction" of mortgage or "discharge" of mortgage. The customs and terminology vary by area.

Gift Letter

It is common, especially for first-time homebuyers, for a parent, other relative, or even friend to give some money to use for the down payment. The banks want to make sure that you really own the money you're using for the down payment. If it's your money, you are more likely to be responsible to take care of the house. If the friend was really loaning you the money, there is really less equity in the house. If you recently received a check for a gift for the down payment, the lender will typically require a signed letter in which you and the person making the gift state that the money they transferred to you was really a gift to you and is now your money. Each lender has its own standard form of letter. Be sure you understand the terms and what you are signing. If the money involved was really a loan and not a gift, talk to your attorney.

Guarantee

If the buyer/borrower doesn't repay the loan, and if the house isn't of sufficient value when sold to repay what is due, and the buyer personally doesn't have enough assets, or can't be found (i.e., he skipped town), what can the lender do? Not much, unless another person has signed an agreement to pay the balance. This is called a guarantee. A guarantee is a legal document in which a person other than the homeowner (referred to as a "third party" since he is not one of the parties to the loan transaction) promises (guarantees) to repay the loan if the borrower defaults. A common situation is for a parent to guarantee a loan for a child buying a first house.

Guarantees are not standard documents. Whether you are the lender and have a parent or other person guaranteeing your loan, or you are the person giving the guarantee (called the *guarantor*), you must understand the terms of the guarantee, how much you could be liable for, and when the lender can call the guarantee (must the borrower default first, must the lender first sue the borrower and not collect, or can the lender proceed immediately against the guarantor if there is a late payment?).

The note boxes in the sample form in the "For Your Notebook" section at the end of this chapter highlight the issues you should consider when a guarantee is used.

TAX CONSEQUENCES OF YOUR MORTGAGE

The tax laws severely limit the ability to deduct personal (consumer) interest expense. However, qualified residence interest is still deductible. This will generally permit the deduction of interest expense on acquisition indebtedness on a qualified residence or home equity indebtedness on a qualified residence. You must be familiar with a few buzz words to understand the rules. Your principal residence and qualifying second or vacation home are called qualifying residences. The mortgage debt used to acquire your qualifying residences is called acquisition indebtedness.

Caution: When negotiating a loan, be certain that you and your attorney are cognizant of the tax rules for deducting interest expense. A misunderstanding of these rules could result in the loan being mishandled from a tax perspective, thus jeopardizing your tax deduction.

Qualified Homes on Which Mortgage Interest Can Be Deducted

To deduct mortgage interest, the home must be a "qualified home" for purposes of the home mortgage interest rules. A qualified home includes a house, condominium, cooperative (see later in this chapter), mobile home, boat, or similar property that provides basic living accommodations, including sleeping space, toilet facility, and cooking facilities. It doesn't include any portion of the home used for nonresidential purposes (home office or rental). Both your principal residence and one second home, which you designate, can qualify. For a second home to qualify, you or your family must use it for personal purposes for the greater of either 14 days or 10 percent of the number of days it is rented at a fair rental value (see Chapter 5 for a discussion of vacation homes).

Acquisition and Home Equity Debt

Acquisition indebtedness is interest incurred in acquiring, constructing, or substantially improving a qualified residence, and which is secured by the residence. Further, the principal balance cannot exceed $1 million. Home improvements are items that add to the value of your home, prolong its useful life, or adapt it to new uses. The value of the time you spend fixing or renovating your home can't be included. Repairs that maintain your home in good condition, such as repainting, are not home improvements. Items that may be included might be insulation, a new water heater, new roof, or a swimming pool.

Note: Ask your tax accountant how the IRS will classify different items and how they will define "substantial."

In addition to the preceding acquisition indebtedness, you are allowed to take out an additional amount of debt up to $100,000 and deduct the interest on it. This debt must be secured by a lien on your residence. This debt is called home equity indebtedness. This home equity debt can be used for any purpose. Thus, home equity indebtedness is debt, other than acquisition indebtedness, that is secured by the taxpayer's residence. It cannot exceed $100,000 (or the fair market value of your home less acquisition indebtedness).

Example: Henry Homeowner purchased a home for $100,000, taking out an $80,000 first mortgage. Two years later, when the house was worth $225,000, Henry built an additional bedroom at a cost of $15,000. Henry financed this with a home equity loan. The maximum amount of financing on which interest can be deducted as acquisition indebtedness is $95,000. If Henry borrowed $120,000 on his home equity line, the interest on the additional $105,000 loan [$120,000 borrowed—$15,000 used for improvements] would be deductible as home equity indebtedness mortgage interest up to the maximum $100,000 amount. The interest on the remaining $5,000 loan will be treated as personal (consumer) interest. This personal interest expense will not be deductible.

The maximum qualifying mortgage debt you can deduct interest on is $1,100,000. This is the sum of the maximum amount of acquisition indebtedness and home equity indebtedness.

Both the $1 million and $100,000 limitations are reduced to half in the case of married persons filing separately. Married persons filing separate tax returns are considered one person for purposes of determining the principal residence on which mortgage interest can be deducted. One spouse is allowed to deduct interest on the principal residence and the other spouse can deduct interest on a qualifying second residence or vacation home if the couple has one.

Note: The rules are a bit more lenient if you took out a home mortgage or equity loan before October 13, 1987. If you took out your mortgages prior to August 17, 1986, you are generally not subject to any of the rules discussed in this chapter. Talk to your tax adviser.

Securing Debt by Your Residence to Deduct Interest

To deduct mortgage interest, the loan must be secured by your residence to qualify for the home mortgage interest deduction rules. To qualify, the debt must be secured by a legal document or instrument (mortgage or loan agreement) that makes your ownership interest in the qualified residence (your principal residence or

qualified second home) specific security (collateral) for the repayment of the loan. The lender's security interest in your residence
must be recorded (filed with the appropriate government agency)
in accordance with applicable state law.

Caution: A family member or friend who loans you money may not believe it is necessary to go through with the formality of filing the mortgage with the county clerk (or other government body, depending on
location). However, their trusting you and not filing could jeopardize
your income tax deduction.

The lender's security interest may be sufficient for the loan to be
a qualified residence mortgage even if local laws make the security
interest ineffective or only partially enforceable.

If you own an apartment in a cooperative building, you can qualify a mortgage you took out to buy the cooperative apartment so
that you can deduct the interest. Owners of cooperative apartments
(or town houses) are really tenant-shareholders. A corporation,
known as a cooperative cooperation, actually owns the building and
other real estate. The owner is a shareholder in the cooperative corporation. Each shareholder gets the right from the cooperative corporation to use a specific apartment (a proprietary lease). Even
though you own stock, you can treat it as a principal residence for
the home mortgage interest rules.

Caution: Some cooperative corporations' rules (in the bylaws or cooperative agreement) prohibit owners (tenant-shareholders) from mortgaging their apartments. Some state laws create technical problems with
obtaining a mortgage on cooperative apartment stock.

Refinancing Can't Circumvent the Mortgage
Interest Rules

If a home mortgage is refinanced, only an amount up to the remaining principal balance on the loan refinanced can qualify for
tax deduction.

Example: Henry Homeowner purchased his home for $150,000. The home is now worth $320,000. His current mortgage balance is $120,000. He refinances this mortgage with a new mortgage for $155,000. Henry isn't so lucky with his tax deductions. Only interest on $120,000 of the new mortgage will qualify for interest deductions, unless the additional $35,000 [$155,000 new loan − $120,000 original loan balance] is used to improve his home, or counts as part of his $100,000 home equity loan amount.

How the Date a Debt Was Incurred Affects the Deduction of Interest Expense

Determining when a mortgage was incurred to purchase a home is not always so clear. What if you use bridge financing and four months later get a permanent mortgage on the property and pay off the bridge loan? Will the interest be deductible? If the bridge loan is not secured by the new home, the interest on it may not be deductible. The mortgage obtained later provides additional problems. Interest on a mortgage will be deductible if the proceeds of the debt can be traced to the acquisition or construction of the home. Mortgage interest will also qualify if the payments to acquire the home were made reasonably before or after you incur the debt. Dates are thus important to remember when you and the lender set the closing on a mortgage. Taxpayers may, however, elect to treat the mortgage as incurred on the date a written loan application was made if the proceeds are disbursed within a reasonable time (30 days) after the application is approved. The rules are complicated, and you should always check with your accountant before completing the transaction to be sure everything is handled properly.

These rules raise potential traps that the attorney responsible for the house and mortgage closing can assist you in avoiding. Occasionally, a buyer will use a bridge loan secured by a former residence or other property, or cash, to consummate the closing. If the home isn't financed within the requisite time, the interest on the mortgage eventually placed on the home won't be deductible.

In addition to the preceding requirements, for a mortgage to qualify, the lender must have a security interest in the home that is perfected under local law. As a result, "friendly" loans from a relative or friend may also turn out not to be so friendly. Make certain the loan is evidenced by a mortgage on your home that is recorded.

Planning Tip: The best thing to do is to set up a separate bank account. Deposit all of your loan proceeds in that account. Pay for all of your home improvements from that account. Check with your bank concerning fees or other charges. Hopefully, banks will begin setting up special accounts for home improvement loans that will minimize your bank charges and help you keep track of your payments.

Mortgages That Violate the Rules

Home mortgage interest that can't be deducted because of these rules is treated as personal (consumer) interest expense and no deduction is permitted for consumer interest expense.

Deductibility of Points

Points are a cost most lenders charge for making a loan and are usually based on a percentage of the loan made. Points are really interest expense paid up front when the loan is made. Since this interest expense relates to the entire term of the loan, the proper tax treatment would be to deduct (amortize) the points equally over the loan term.

Example: Mary Mortgager borrows $100,000 and pays 3 points, or $3,000. The mortgage is for 30 years. Under the general rules, Mary should deduct $100 per year in additional interest [$3,000 points divided by 30 years].

A special rule lets homeowners deduct points in the year they are paid. To qualify for this favorable treatment, the loan must (1) be used to buy or improve your principal residence; (2) be secured by your principal residence; (3) the number of points can't exceed the number of points generally charged in the area where the loan is made; and (4) paying points is an established business practice in the area where the loan is made. If deductible points are paid on a debt incurred to purchase or improve a principal residence, such points are considered qualified residence interest and will be deductible under the mortgage interest rules.

Loan processing and other service fees are not interest and can't be deducted.

General Tax Rules Affecting the Value of Your Mortgage Interest Deduction

So you've run the gauntlet of the preceding rules and have survived (and not fallen asleep). You're still not home free. The tax laws are not designed to be simple. You still need to consider factors that will affect the value of your home mortgage interest deduction:

- *Marginal Tax Rates* The higher your tax bracket, the higher the value of your deduction. The government frequently tinkers with tax rates. Most recently in the 2001 Tax Act, marginal income tax rates were slightly reduced, thus reducing the value of your tax deduction.

- *Itemized Deductions* You have to itemize deductions to benefit. This means your deductions have to exceed the standard deduction amount and you cannot be subject to the phaseout of itemized deductions in the year you seek a home mortgage interest deduction. In 2000, the standard deduction for a married couple filing a joint income tax return was $7,350. High-income taxpayers have been subject to a complex array of phased-out itemized deduction tax benefits. The result is that over certain amounts, these tax benefits were phased out and effectively eliminated. Not only did this have an adverse tax effect on certain income taxpayers, it also made planning complex. The 2001 Tax Act proposes to reduce these overall limitations and thus eventually eliminate what has really been an increased tax rate applicable to these high-income taxpayers. The limitation on itemized deductions will be reduced by one-third in the years 2006 and 2007, by two-thirds in 2008 and 2009 and completely eliminated in 2010. You must determine how this will affect you.

- *Alternative Minimum Tax (AMT)*   The AMT is an alternative tax system that seeks to apply a minimum rate of tax to a broader base of income by taxing income that may not be taxed under the regular tax system, and limiting or prohibiting deductions that may be permitted under the regular tax system. Although home mortgage interest is deductible for AMT purposes, if you are subject to the AMT, the next tax benefit from any deduction (including home mortgage interest) may differ from what you expect.

SUMMARY

Home mortgages are essential to most people acquiring a home. But they don't come in only one shape and size. There are lots of options, many legal issues that vary depending on the type of mortgage and where you reside, and many tax issues. The result is that one of the most common financial transactions is complex and fraught with legal, tax, and other issues. Be certain you understand precisely what you are doing, why you are doing it, and how it will affect you. Consult with an experienced mortgage broker, realtor, and attorney. Even if you check the Internet, don't forget your local banker. Be certain that you use an experienced local real estate attorney. If you are buying a house, don't overlook the knowledge an experienced real estate broker can provide. Ask lots of questions and read the documents. Even though you have professionals, it's a huge transaction. Be responsible and careful.

FOR YOUR NOTEBOOK

SAMPLE NOTE FOR HOUSE LOAN TO REVIEW WITH YOUR MORTGAGE BROKER AND ATTORNEY

Note: In a negative amortization mortgage, the amount may increase. In a shared appreciation mortgage, an additional amount will be due in addition to the amount stated in the note.

$[Mortgage Amount]

Note: The state where the loan is created may be important to the applicable usury and other laws. Usury laws limit the rate of interest that can be charged, which can be important at times when interest rates are high or a default occurs.

[Borrower Address]
[Month, Day, Year]

a. Statement of Loan

FOR VALUE RECEIVED, the Undersigned promises to pay to the order of [Lender Name], or the holder hereof ("the Payee") at [Lender Address], or at such other place as the Payee may designate in writing to the Undersigned, the principal sum of Thousand Dollars ($[Loan Amount].00) in lawful money of the United States of America.

b. Maturity; Payment

Note: In a shared appreciation or reverse mortgage, a detailed maturity provision will have to be included.

This Note shall be repaid in full upon the maturity hereof, on [Maturity Date], unless required to be repaid at an earlier date in accordance with the provisions following. Repayment shall include all then unpaid principal and any accrued but unpaid interest on this Note.

c. Security; Collateral

Note: In this sample Note, the lender is accepting your interests in the house, secured by a mortgage on the house, as collateral for the loan. If your credit isn't sufficient, the lender may ask for additional collateral or a guarantee (e.g., by a parent or spouse). If the home is not made the collateral for the loan, no home mortgage interest deduction may be permitted.

The Payee does hereby accept as security for the Loan herein contemplated, the pledge to Payee for the security for the payment of the obligations under this Note, the entire right, title, and interest in the single family residence located at 123 Main Street, Anytown, USA, owned by [Your Name] (the "Premises"), in accordance with a Mortgage Agreement of even date, and no other security.

d. Application of Payments

Payments made hereunder shall first be applied against payments of interest and then toward the reduction of principal.

e. Interest

Note: For every loan, carefully review and understand how the interest will be calculated. Be certain that the Note (and Mortgage) conform with the commitment and what you understood the arrangement was. When will interest be compounded? In an adjustable rate mortgage (ARM), the rate will be increased. When will this occur and subject to what limitations? How will increases be determined? All this must be specified.

Interest shall accrue on this Note at the rate of [Rate] Percent ([Rate]%) per annum. Interest shall be due and payable monthly, on the first day of each month.

f. Prepayment

Note: If you are the seller, do you want to permit prepayment? If the interest rate is high, or you incurred costs in obtaining the mortgage and note, you may want a penalty for prepayment. As a borrower/buyer, you ideally want the right to prepay anytime without penalty so that you can refinance if rates come down.

The Undersigned shall, at any time, have the right to prepay, without penalty or premium, all or any portion of the loan evidenced by this Note.

g. Grace Period

Note: Grace period is a break you as the borrower get if the payment is not made on time. It is preferable to get as liberal a grace period provision as you can. Lenders, on the other hand, want limited grace periods so that if the borrower is not paying, they can put the loan in default, accelerate payment, and be paid back.

The Payee shall not exercise any right or remedy provided for in this Note because of any default of the Undersigned to pay the sums due hereunder, until after the expiration of a Fifteen (15) days' grace period from the Undersigned's receipt of any demand for payment. No more than Three (3) grace periods shall be given during the term of this Note.

h. Action to Enforce

(1) If the Payee shall institute any action to enforce collection of this Note, there shall become due and payable from the Undersigned, in addition to the unpaid principal and interest, all costs and expenses of such action (including reasonable attorneys' fees) and the Payee shall be entitled to judgment for all such additional amounts.

(2) The Undersigned irrevocably consents to the sole and exclusive jurisdiction of the Courts of the State of [State Name] and of any Federal court located in [State Name] in connection with any action or proceeding arising out of, or related to, this Note.

(3) The Undersigned waives presentment, demand for payment, notice of dishonor and all other notices or demands in connection with the delivery, acceptance, performance, default, or indorsement of this Note.

(4) In any such proceeding, the Undersigned waives personal service of any summons, complaint, or other process and agrees that service thereof shall be deemed made when mailed by registered or certified mail, return receipt requested to the undersigned. Within Twenty (20) days after such service, the undersigned shall appear or answer the summons, complaint or other process. If the undersigned shall fail to appear or answer within that Twenty (20) day period, the Undersigned shall be deemed in default and judgment

may be entered by the Payee against the Undersigned for the amount demanded in the summons, complaint, or other process.

i. Additional Covenants

Planning Tip: A Note may include a host of additional commitments by you as borrower, called "loan covenants." Loan covenants can be very detailed and explicit. If you are the borrower, don't assume that they are standard legal language you can ignore (boilerplate). They are critical to read and understand. If you violate any the loan can be called. If you are the lender be certain that the covenants are crafted carefully to protect your interests.

Undersigned further expressly covenants and agrees as follows:

(1) Undersigned shall pay all taxes, water charges, assessments, insurance premiums, or similar charges affecting the Premises.

(2) Undersigned becomes a member of the Condominium Association in which the Premises is located and pay all dues and comply with all rules and regulations thereof.

(3) . . . [other covenants].

j. No Waiver

No delay or failure on the part of the Payee on this Note to exercise any power or right given hereunder shall operate as a waiver thereof, and no right or remedy of the Payee shall be deemed abridged or modified by any course of conduct.

k. State Law

This Note shall be governed by and construed in accordance with the State of [State Name] applicable to agreements made and to be performed in [State Name].

1. No Oral Change

This Note cannot be changed orally.

UNDERSIGNED:

BORROWER:

_____   Dated: [Month, Day, Year]

[Borrower Name]

Address for Communication:
[Borrower Address]

State of [State Execution]

                                : ss.:

County of [County]

    On [Month, Day, Year], before me personally came [Borrower Name], to me known and known to me to be the individual described in and who executed the foregoing instrument, and he duly acknowledged to me that he executed the same.

_____

Notary Public

SAMPLE MORTGAGE FORM TO DISCUSS
WITH YOUR ATTORNEY

Note: Most home mortgages are provided by banks or other commercial lenders and will be on their forms, which you will have little choice but to sign. This sample form can still help you understand what the mortgage terms mean to you. If something is really offensive, you can ask for it to be changed. The lender might just agree, although probably not. You have nothing to lose by asking, and in either event, you will at least understand what you have committed to. In a private loan transaction, where a friend, family member, private investor, equity sharing lender, or other noncommercial lender is involved, you may have substantial latitude in negotiating mortgage terms. However, even if you are unsuccessful, this sample will help you understand questions to ask so you understand what the documents mean.

Note: If there is primary or first bank financing, and a private second (or later loan), the mortgage (and note) will have to reflect this. In such cases, the second lender will have to generally agree that his or her loan (and mortgage security) is after, or second to, the first mortgage (i.e., is subordinate to the commercial lender's mortgage). This is common when a seller "takes back" a mortgage from a buyer for part of the purchase price with the balance being supplied by the buyer's down payment and the first mortgage loan from a bank. Taking back a mortgage from the buyer will permit the seller to report any gain for income tax purposes on the installment method, as payments are received.

This Mortgage, made on December 1, 2002, by Paul Purchaser and Pat Purchaser of 456 Redwood, Apt. 12E, Ridgewood, Anystate (the Mortgagor), and Sam and Sue Seller of 123 Main Street, Centerville, Anystate (the Mortgagee).

a. Mortgage, Collateral

Note: The dollar amount of the mortgage must match the dollar amount set forth in the note. The collateral (the house involved) must also be clearly stated.

That Mortgagor, jointly and severally, for and in consideration of the sum of [Loan Dollars] Dollars ($000) applied toward the purchase price of the house described below as the property subject to this Second Mortgage, mortgages to Mortgagee all buildings and improvements thereon, erected, situated, lying, and being in the City of Centerville, County of Oakland, State of Anystate (the Property or House).

Note: The Mortgage (and note) must be signed by all the buyers, usually being the husband and wife, and the mortgage must state that both are jointly and severally bound. This gives the lender the right to sue both, or either borrower individually for the entire balance due.

Note: The detailed description is often relegated to an attached exhibit. It should include the street address, lot and block numbers, and a detailed step-by-step legal description, called *metes and bounds*.

The Property is more particularly described as follows:

ALL that tract or parcel of land and premises, situate, lying and being in the City of Centerville, in the County of Oakland, and State of Anystate. BEING known and designated as Lot No. 3 in Block No. 13 on a certain map entitled "Map of Free Land, Centerville, Anystate, O.L.P. Fitzgerald, Surveyor, dated June 10, 1932" and filed in the Register's Office as Case Number 38-CH-4.

BEGINNING at a stake in the Northeasterly side of Maintowne Street, at a point therein distant 50 feet Southeasterly from the intersection formed by the said Northeasterly side of Main Street and the Southeasterly side of Glenwood Road; thence running (1) North 36 degrees 01 minutes East, a distance of 100 feet to a stake for a corner; thence running (2) South 54 degrees 18 minutes East a distance of 48.02 feet to a point for another corner; thence running (3) South 35 degrees 42 minutes West a distance of 100 feet to a point in the aforesaid line of Main Street; thence running (4) North 54 degrees 18 minutes West a distance of 48.57 feet to the point or place of BEGINNING. BEING also known as 123 Main Street, Centerville, Anystate.

BEING known as Lot 3 in Block 13, Account No. 10-504B on the official tax map of the City of Centerville, Oakland County, Anystate (the House).

Note: The legal description of the property should be identical to the description contained in the sales contract. The description will generally be taken from the deed you receive when you purchase the property. However, the survey should also be consulted.

Note: It is important that the document make clear that the property that serves as collateral include not only the land, but all other property permanently attached to the land—structures such as sheds and fixtures (personal property, i.e., movable items that have been permanently attached to the land). If the buyer defaults the lender doesn't want an issue to arise as to which property is included in the claim.

Together with all the appurtenances attached thereto, all easement, rights of way, buildings, structures, improvements, and fixtures thereto.

b. Security Interest in Personal Property

Note: Is personal property to be pledged as security? Is this reasonable? If you as the borrower own a valuable coin, stamp, art, or other collection, is this acceptable?

The Mortgagor grants to the Mortgagee a security interest in all personal property located on or at the house. The Mortgagor also authorizes the Mortgagee to file, with or without the Mortgagor's signature one or more financing statements as allowed by law to perfect Mortgagee's interest in this Mortgage.

c. Note, Term, Principal, Interest

This Mortgage is intended to secure the payment of a certain Secured Promissory Note made on the same date as this Mortgage (the "Note"), the terms of which are hereby incorporated by reference into this Mortgage, in which Mortgagor promises to pay to Mortgagee or order for value received, on or before February 1, 2007, the sum of [Loan Amount] Thousand Dollars ($000), to be paid in equal monthly installments of [Installment Amount] Dollars ($000) on January 1, 2001 and on the 1st day of each month following until the whole shall have been paid, inclusive of interest thereon at the rate of ten percent (10%) per year, the interest on each installment being payable when it becomes due, and, if not then paid, to bear interest at the same rate as the principal. Payments shall be applied to interest, then principal.

Note: The payments under this mortgage are on a fully amortizing, self-liquidating, basis. This means that over the 10-year life of the second mortgage that you, as the lender, are giving the buyer, all of the interest and principal will be repaid in equal monthly payments. This is the safest method since you have your money outstanding for less time so it is at risk for a shorter period. Many purchase money second mortgages are structured as shorter term, say 5-year, balloon mortgages and calculated with a long, perhaps 25-year amortization period. This would result in smaller payments being made in each month. Then at the end of the 5-year term of the loan, the buyer would still owe you a substantial portion of the original loan. Still other purchase money second mortgages are interest-only payments so that the buyer will still owe you the entire principal at the end of the loan. The options are myriad.

It is important to provide that if the buyer doesn't make payments on time that interest will accrue (be charged) on the unpaid interest. This is the only way to protect your economic return on the loan. Further, the documents should provide that all payments are first applied to reduce outstanding interest owed to you. Only after all outstanding interest is paid should the principal amount due be reduced by the buyer's payments.

It is critically important that you have your lawyer verify that the interest rate charged does not violate the usury laws of your state. Usury laws set maximum amounts of interest that can be charged for certain types of transactions. If the interest rate charged is greater, you may not be entitled to the extra interest. In some states, you could risk losing the right to collect any interest at all. Some usury laws may exclude purchase money mortgages because it would be easy for you to simply increase the purchase price in exchange for having to lower the interest rate charged. If the usury laws restrict your interest rate, discuss with your lawyer whether you can negotiate a somewhat higher sale (and mortgage) amount to compensate you.

The principal and interest are payable in lawful money of the United States of America.

d. Default

Note: What happens when the buyer doesn't pay on time? Lenders need reasonable protection. However, buyers/borrowers don't want to lose the house because the mail is a few days late one month. The default clause should give the borrower reasonable flexibility while protecting a lender.

A common protection lenders always require is called an *acceleration clause,* which makes the entire loan due and payable immediately if the buyer defaults. If this were not done, then the lender would have to sue separately for each installment payment when it individually was late.

In case of a default in the payment of the principal, or any installment thereof, or any interest, as provided in the Note, the entire principal and interest shall be due at the option of Mortgagee, their successors, or assigns, and suit may be immediately brought and a decree issued to sell the House, with all of the appurtenances, or any part thereof, in the manner prescribed by law. Out of the money arising from such sale, the Mortgagee is to retain the principal and interest, although the time for payment of such principal sum may not have expired, together with the costs and charges of making such sale and of suit for foreclosure, including reasonable attorney fees, and also the amounts, both principal and interest, of all such payments of liens or other encumbrances as may have been made by Mortgagee by reason of the permission hereinafter given, and the remainder, if any, shall be paid, on demand, to Mortgagor, his successors, or assigns.

e. Covenants, Representations, and Warranties of the Mortgagor

Mortgagor, for themselves and their successors and assigns, do hereby covenant, represent, warrant and agree:

f. Principal and Interest

Note: If you are the buyer/borrower, try to negotiate what is called a right of offset. If you as the buyer feel that the lender/seller has violated some provision of the sales (i.e., purchase) contract, you will want the right to automatically reduce what you must pay under the mortgage (or deed of trust) and note. For example, if the seller represented in the purchase contract that the basement didn't leak and you need a boat, a right of offset means that if you spend $5,000 to fix the problems, a $5,000 reduction would immediately be made to the amount due you under the mortgage, etc.

Sellers/lenders will oppose such a provision since it puts the buyer in control of the situation. If the buyer is still paying what is due under the mortgage, the seller/lender will have more clout in negotiating a settlement of the basement or similar issue. If the buyer can simply stop paying on the mortgage by virtue of having a right of offset, the seller/lender is out the money until the issues are resolved. This shifts the balance of power in the negotiating process to the buyer.

To pay all the principal and interest and other sums of money payable by virtue of such Note and this Mortgage, or either, promptly on the days respectively they are due. Mortgagor shall not have any right to offset any claim for any matter arising out of a Sale Contract of even date, against any other payments due Mortgagee under this Mortgage.

g. Taxes, Etc.

Note: The phrase "or the highest rate permitted by law" would lower the 12 percent rate if the state's usury limit was lower. It is generally best to charge a greater interest rate where you as seller have to advance monies for expenses the buyer/borrower hasn't paid. This should serve as an incentive for the buyer to pay what is required, and it should reward you as seller for the extra efforts the buyer is forcing you to make.

To pay all the taxes, assessments, levies, liabilities, obligations, and encumbrances of every nature on the House. If these are not promptly paid, Mortgagee, may at any time pay them without waiving or affecting the option to foreclose or any right hereunder, and every payment so made shall bear interest from the date thereof at the rate of twelve percent (12%) per year, or the highest rate permitted by law, and shall be repaid with such interest by Mortgagor.

h. Costs and Fees

To pay all the costs, charges, and expenses, including attorney fees, reasonably incurred or paid at any time by Mortgagee because of the failure of Mortgagor to perform and to comply with each stipulation, agreement, condition, and covenant of the Promissory Note and this Mortgage, or either, and every such payment shall bear interest from the date thereof at the rate of twelve percent (12%) per year, or the highest rate permitted by law.

i. Insurance

Note: If you are the buyer/homeowner/borrower, you want to have the house properly insured. The lender has similar concerns. If there is not adequate insurance and there is a casualty the lender's ability to collect the amount due on the loan of you walk is limited. Therefore, every lender must make sure the house is adequately insured against fire or other loss, and that the lender is a named insured in the policy so that the lender can collect (see Chapter 4).

To keep the House insured against loss by fire and other casualties, included in the standard form of house insurance policy with extended coverage insurance. At an amount of not less than [Minimum Insurance] Thousand Dollars ($000) with a company rate not less than A by Bests Insurance and which is licensed to do business in the state in which the House is located. The policy or policies shall contain the standard clause used in the state in the name of the Mortgagee. In the event any sum of money becomes payable under such policy or policies, Mortgagee, shall have the right to receive and apply the proceeds on account of the debt secured by this Mortgage, or to permit Mortgagor, his successors, or assigns, to receive and use it, or any part thereof, for other purposes, without waiving or impairing any lien or right under or by virtue of this Mortgage. In the event Mortgagor, his successors, or assigns do not so keep the building or buildings insured and furnish such policy or policies, as agreed, Mortgagee, his successors, or assigns may pay for such insurance or any part thereof, without waiving or affecting the option to foreclose or any right hereunder, and each and every such payment shall bear interest from the date thereof at the rate of twelve percent (12%) per year and shall be repaid with such interest by Mortgagor, his successors, or assigns, to Mortgagee, his successors, or assigns. Mortgagee shall insure the house for any other reasonable risk requested by the Mortgagee within thirty (30) days after Mortgagee receives notice from Mortgagor demanding such additional coverage.

j. Repair and Maintain Property

Note: All lenders want the borrower to maintain the property. If buyer fails to do so, the lender should be able to call the loan to protect the collateral. Buyers need to protect themselves from unreasonable clauses that would give the lender the ability to call the loan for a meaningless infringement.

Not to commit, permit, or suffer any waste, impairment, or deterioration of the premises or any part thereof.

k. Perform Agreements

To perform and comply with, every stipulation, agreement, condition, and covenant in the Note and in this Mortgage.

l. Receiver

In the event that at the beginning of or at any time pending any suit on this Mortgage, to foreclose it, to reform it, or to enforce payment of any claims hereunder, Mortgagee, his successors, or assigns, may apply to the court having jurisdiction of that suit for the appointment of a receiver that court may and should appoint a receiver of the House. That receiver should have all the functions and powers that a court may entrust to a receiver. That appointment may and should be made by the court as an admitted equity and a matter of absolute right of Mortgagee, his successors, or assigns, without reference to the adequacy or inadequacy of the value of the premises or to the solvency or insolvency of Mortgagor, his successors, or assigns, or of the defendants in that suit.

m. Estoppel Certificate

Note: Lenders should always have an estoppel certificate or similar clause in every mortgage since there may be times when you will need written confirmation from the borrower of the amount of the loan. You might need this if you are trying to sell the mortgage to an investor, or perhaps for a personal financial statement. It's best to have this requirement in the Mortgage so that the buyer will have to take the time to comply.

Within five (5) days of receiving a written request by Mortgagee, give the Mortgagee a signed statement stating the amount due under this Mortgage and the Promissory Note.

n. Inspections

Note: Lenders reasonably need the right to periodically inspect the house to make sure that no major damage has been done that could jeopardize their collateral, the home. Borrowers, however, don't want the lender over for dinner every Wednesday. The trade-off can be a clause giving the latter reasonable opportunity to inspect after reasonable advance notice, or in the event of an emergency.

Permit Mortgagee, or any person reasonably authorized by Mortgagee, to enter and inspect the House at reasonable times.

o. Title to House

That Mortgagor is the lawful owner of the House, that it is free of all encumbrances and liens except as specifically set forth in this Mortgage, and that Mortgagor has good right and lawful authority to sell or mortgage the House and will defend the same against the lawful claims of any person.

p. Assignment

Note: Lenders want to assure that if the buyer dies, his estate remains liable for all the provisions in the mortgage. However, the lender probably doesn't want to let the buyer transfer or sell the house unless the loan is first repaid. Some lenders may be willing to evaluate the buyer and decide if the mortgage loan can continue. However, from the lender's perspective it's usually better to call the loan and negotiate a new deal with the buyer.

This Mortgage applies to, and inures to the benefit of, and binds the Mortgagee, the Mortgagor, their respective heirs, legatees, administrators, devises, executors, assigns and successors. Notwithstanding anything in this Mortgage to the contrary, this Mortgage shall become due and payable upon the sale, transfer, or assignment of the house by the Mortgagor.

q. Notice

Any notice required to be given under this Mortgage, shall be a written notice, given by personal delivery, Federal Express, Express Mail, or certified mail return receipt requested, postage and mailing costs prepaid, to the address of the parties listed above, unless notice of a different address is given as specified in this section. Notice by personal delivery shall be effective upon receipt, Notice by Federal Express or Express Mail shall be effective on the next business day following the day the Notice was sent, and Notice by certified mail shall be effective on the Fourth (4th) day following the day it was sent.

r. Waiver or Modification

No modification or waiver of any right by the Mortgagee under this Mortgage shall be effective unless contained in writing signed by the Mortgagee. Any waiver by the Mortgagee of any right or power under this Mortgage, shall not be deemed to constitute a waiver as to any future right or power. If the Mortgagee accepts any payment by the Mortgagor after the due date for the payment, or if the Mortgagee performs any act which is the obligation of the Mortgagor (including but not limited to the payment of insurance premiums, property taxes, or the cost of repairs, on the house), the Mortgagee will not, but such actions do, waive the right to declare the Mortgagor in default under this Mortgage.

s. Governing Law

Note: Every legal document should specify which state law governs. If you are the borrower and the lender is a large institution, the state law of the state in which the lender is based may apply. In such cases, there is little you can do to change such a clause. What this clause means is that in the event of a suit, the laws of the state named (unless there is insufficient connection to that state) must be used.

This Mortgage shall be construed in accordance with the laws of Anystate.

t. Miscellaneous Provisions

The use of masculine, feminine, or neuter, singular or plural, shall, wherever the context so requires, include the masculine or feminine or neuter, the singular or the plural. Captions and section headings are inserted for convenience only and shall not be used to limit or interpret any provision of this Mortgage.

IN WITNESS WHEREOF, Mortgagor has executed this Mortgage the day and year first hereinbefore written.

_____

[Borrower Name], Mortgagor

Note: For real estate finance forms, with comprehensive tax and economic commentary see: Shenkman, *Tax Practitioner's Guide to Reviewing Legal Documents*. For additional information and ancillary finance forms, with annotations, see the website: www.laweasy.com.

SAMPLE GUARANTEE OF MORTGAGE
LOAN DOCUMENT TO DISCUSS
WITH YOUR ATTORNEY AND LENDER

Note: A guarantee is used when the lender wants more assurance that the loan will be repaid. This can occur where a young couple is buying their first home and don't have much of a credit history.

THIS GUARANTEE is made the 1st day of December by Gary Grandparent and Gertrude Grandparent, residing at 425 Rich Avenue, Hightown, Anystate, (the Guarantor) and Sam and Sue Seller of 123 Main Street, Centerville, Anystate (the Lender).

RECITALS

Note: The amount guaranteed usually matches the amount of the loan, but doesn't have to. The lender may accept a guarantee for less. If the guarantee is given in the context of a negative amortizing loan, a larger amount, or formula, will have to be used.

WHEREAS, Paul Purchaser and Pat Purchaser of 456 Redwood, Apt. 12E, Ridgewood, Anystate (the Mortgagor) has borrowed from the Lender a loan in the principal amount of [Guarantee Amount] Thousand Dollars ($000) (the Loan), to be evidenced by Mortgagor's Promissory Note of the same date (the Note) payable to Lender's order in such amount, with interest at the rate of eleven percent (11%) per year, and a Mortgage of the same date (the Mortgage) securing certain real property located at 123 Main Street, Centerville, Anystate (Lot 3 in Block 13, Account No. 10-504B on the official tax map of the City of Centerville, Oakland County, Anystate) (the House).

WHEREAS, the Lender requires the unconditional personal guarantee of the Guarantor on the Note, and the Mortgage securing the Note, on the terms and conditions contained in this Guaranty, as consideration and inducement for extending the Loan to the Mortgagor.

NOW THEREFORE, the Guarantor hereby agrees as follows:

a. Unconditional Guaranty

(1) Guarantor unconditionally guarantees to the Lender the payment of all principal and interest due under the Note and Mortgage on

the due dates contained in the Note and Mortgage (with consideration to any grace periods permitted). Guarantor acknowledges that the due dates for these payments may be accelerated according to the terms of the Note and Mortgage and agrees to such accelerated due dates.

Note: The following language assures the lender that the guarantor can be sued before the actual borrower since the guarantor is guaranteeing the actual payment. This may not be agreeable by the guarantor in which case the terms will have to be negotiated. If the buyer/borrower is nearly broke, the lender doesn't want to have to sue him and demonstrate that the money is not collectible from him before suing the person guaranteeing the loan. If the person guaranteeing the loan is merely a guarantor of collection, this is what the lender's rights will be.

---

(2) Guarantor guarantees the actual payment and not the mere collection of the amounts due under the Note and the Mortgage. The liability of the Guarantor under this Guaranty is primary, direct, and immediate and not conditional or contingent upon the Lender pursuing any remedies he may have against Mortgagor, or Mortgagor's successors and assigns, with respect to the Note, Mortgage, or law. Without limiting the generality of the foregoing, Lender shall not be required to make any demand on the Mortgagor, or otherwise pursue or exhaust its remedies against the Mortgagor, before, simultaneously with, or after enforcing its rights and remedies under this Guaranty against the Guarantor.

(3) The genuineness, validity, or enforceability of the Note and Mortgage, or any other circumstance that might constitute a legal or equitable discharge of a guarantor, shall not affect the unconditional nature of this Guaranty.

b. Costs

Note: Guarantors must carefully read the guarantee document. The following paragraph, which is typical, provides that the guarantor can be held liable for legal fees of the lender as well. This means that the guarantor can be required to pay more than the actual amount of the loan.

Guarantor unconditionally guarantees to the Lender the payment of all costs, charges, and other expenses due under the Note and Mortgage, including but not limited to insurance, property taxes, and the costs of repairs. If this Guaranty is enforced by suit or otherwise, or if Lender exercises any remedies provided in the Note or Mortgage, Guarantor will reimburse the Lender for the expenses so incurred, including, but not limited to, reasonable attorney's fees. These amount shall be payable by the Guarantor within ten (10) days of receiving Notice that such amounts are due from the Lender.

c. Rights Waived by Guarantor

The Guarantor hereby waives:

(1) Presentment and demand for payment;

(2) Protest of nonpayment;

(3) Notice of acceptance of this Guaranty;

(4) Notice of any default under this Guaranty, the Note, or the Mortgage;

(5) Demand for performance or enforcement of any terms of this Guaranty, the Note or the mortgage; All other notices and demands required by law which the Guarantor may lawfully waive; and

(6) Trial by jury.

d. Guarantor Loans to Mortgagor

Note: If the guarantor loans money to the borrower to help out and then the lender still sues on the guarantee, the guarantor may be out both the amount on the loan to pay the lender under the guarantee and the amounts loaned to the borrower.

If the Guarantor loans any money to the Mortgagor, or if the Mortgagor becomes indebted to the Guarantor, these debts shall be subordinated to all amounts due and owing to the Lender, and nothing in this Guaranty shall be construed to give Guarantor any right of subrogation in the Note until all amounts owing the Lender have been paid in full.

e. Certain Rights of Lender

Note: If any change is made to the note or the mortgage, it changes the deal the person giving the guaranty made. This could terminate the guarantee agreement and eliminate the protection the guaranty was supposed to provide. To prevent this from happening, the guaranty agreement should provide you as lender with reasonable flexibility to take certain actions your lawyer considers necessary, without jeopardizing the guaranty.

The Guarantor agrees that the Lender may, in the Lender's discretion, without notice to the Guarantor, and without in any way affecting the Guarantor's obligations and liabilities:

(1) Agree to the exchange, release, or dispose of all or any portion of the House referred to in the Mortgage;

(2) Modify or amend any provisions of the Note or the Mortgage;

(3) Grant extensions or renewals of the Note or the Mortgage;

(4) Effect any release, compromise, or settlement of the Note or Mortgage;

(5) Make advances for the purpose of performing any term or covenant contained in the Note or the Mortgage concerning the Mortgagor;

(6) Assign or otherwise transfer the Note, the Mortgage, or this Guaranty or any interest in any of these agreements;

(7) Waive compliance with, or any default under, the Note or the Mortgage; and

(8) Conduct matters with the Mortgagor, as if this Guaranty were not in effect.

f. Lender's Rights

All rights and remedies afforded to Lender by reason of this Guaranty, whether under the terms hereof or by law, are separate and cumulative and the exercise of one shall not in any way limit or prejudice the exercise of any other such rights or remedies, No delay or omission by Lender in exercising any right or remedy shall constitute a waiver of that right. No waiver of any rights and remedies under this Guaranty, and no modification or amendment hereof, shall be deemed made by Lender unless in writing and duly signed by Lender. Any written waiver shall apply only to the particular instance specified in that waiver and shall not impair the further exercise of any right or remedy of the Lender. No single or partial exercise of any right or remedy hereunder shall preclude other or further exercise thereof or any other right or remedy.

g. Construction

This Mortgage shall be construed in accordance with the laws of Anystate. The use of masculine, feminine, or neuter, singular or plural, shall, wherever the context so requires, include the masculine or feminine or neuter, the singular or the plural. The captions shall not limit or affect the interpretation of this Guaranty.

h. Successors and Assigns

This Guaranty shall inure to the benefit of, and be enforceable by, Lender and its successors and assigns as owners and holders of the Note and Mortgage, and shall be binding upon, and enforceable against, Guarantor and his heirs, executors, administrators, successors, and assigns.

i. Notice

Note: The guarantor should try to insist on getting notice of any default notice or similar problem that the lender notifies the borrower of so that the guarantor can deal with any problems before the loan is in final default.

Any notice required to be given under this Guaranty, shall be a written notice, given by personal delivery, Federal Express, Express Mail, or certified mail return receipt requested, postage and mailing costs prepaid, to the address of the parties listed above, unless notice of a different address is given as specified in this section. Notice by personal delivery shall be effective upon receipt, Notice by Federal Express or Express Mail shall be effective on the next business day following the day the Notice was sent, and Notice by certified mail shall be effective on the fourth (4th) day following the day it was sent.

j. Termination

This Guaranty shall not terminate until the Mortgagor makes the final payment in reduction of the principal indebtedness under the Note in the amount of some Thousand Dollars ($XX,000.00), which payment is due and payable on February 1, 2007, and the payment of all other expenses then owing under the Note and Mortgage.

IN WITNESS WHEREOF, Guarantor has duly executed this Guaranty as of the day and year first above written.

_____

Gary Grandparent

_____

Gertrude Grandparent

SAMPLE MORTGAGE OPINION LETTER
(TO DISCUSS WITH YOUR LAWYER WHEN AN ENTITY, SUCH AS A PARTNERSHIP, ACQUIRES PROPERTY AND OBTAINS A MORTGAGE)

Note: If you and a group of friends buy a vacation home as partners, the lender may request that you have a lawyer give the lender a legal statement (opinion) as to certain important legal issues that the lender will have to rely on to make the loan. This sample will give you an idea of some of the issues you may have to address.

[Month, Day, Year]

[Lender Name]
[Lender Address]

Gentlemen:

Note: Review with your lawyer the type of entity to use before signing any contract. Options include tenants in common, general partnership, limited partnership, and limited liability company.

---

a. We have acted as counsel to [Realty Partnership] associates, Ltd. ([Realty Partnership]) and [GP Name], as general partner of [Realty Partnership] and individually, in connection with the execution and delivery of:

  (1) The restated note (the Note) dated October _____, 2003, in the initial principal amount of $525,000, executed by [Realty Partnership] and [GP Name], in favor of [Lender Name].

  (2) The indemnity and undertaking (the Indemnity) dated as of October _____, 2003, executed by [Realty Partnership] and [GP Name] in favor of the Lender.

  (3) The guarantee agreement (the Guarantee) dated as of October _____, 2003, executed by [GP Name] in favor of the Lender.

  (4) The pledge agreement (the Pledge) dated as of October _____, 2003, executed by [GP Name] in favor of the Lender.

(5) Uniform Commercial Code Financing Statements executed by [Realty Partnership] and [GP Name], as debtor, in favor of the Lender, as secured party (the Financing Statements).

(6) The Note, the Mortgage, the indemnity, the Guarantee, the Pledge, the financing Statements, and all other documents, instruments, and agreements executed and delivered by [Realty Partnership] and/or [GP Name] in connection with the transactions contemplated by the foregoing, including, without limitation, all demand notes and demand mortgages executed and delivered by [Realty Partnership] and [GP Name], being collectively called the "Loan Documents" and (b) the transactions contemplated by the Loan Documents.

b. We have examined the originals or certified, conformed, or photographic copies of such documents, records, agreements, and certificates as we have deemed necessary as a basis for the opinions hereinafter expressed.

c. Based upon the foregoing and having due regard for such legal considerations as we deem relevant, we are of the opinion that:

(1) [Realty Partnership] is a limited partnership duly organized, validly existing and in good standing under the laws of the State of [State Name].

(2) [Realty Partnership] has all power and authority, and has all governmental licenses, authorizations, consents, approvals and permits, necessary to own its property and carry on its business.

(3) [Realty Partnership] is duly qualified to transact business in the State of [State Name].

(4) [Realty Partnership] is duly qualified to transact business in all other jurisdictions in which the nature of the business conducted by it or its property makes such qualification necessary.

(5) [GP Name] has all power and authority, and has all governmental licenses, authorizations, consents, approvals and permits, necessary to own his property and carry on his business.

(6) There are no proceedings or actions in any court or by or before any governmental authority or agency now pending or threatened against or affecting [Realty Partnership] or [GP

Name] or any of its or his property (including, without limitation, any relating to condemnation or eminent domain).

(7) There are no arbitration proceedings or actions now pending or threatened against or affecting [Realty Partnership] or [GP Name] or any of its or his property.

(8) The execution, delivery, and performance of the Loan Documents, the consummation of the transactions contemplated thereby and the compliance with the terms thereof do not conflict with, result in a breach of or require any consent under:

(a) The partnership agreement of [Realty Partnership], the certificate of limited partnership of [Realty Partnership], or any other organizational documents of or relating to [Realty Partnership].

(b) Applicable law, ordinance, statute, regulation, rule, or requirement of any court or any Federal, State, or municipal government or any authority or agency thereof.

(c) Any order, writ, injunction, or decree of any court or governmental authority or agency.

(d) Any indenture, agreement, or instrument to which [Realty Partnership] or [GP Name] is a party or by which [Realty Partnership] or its property or [GP Name] or his property may be bound or subject.

(e) The execution, delivery, and performance of the Loan Documents shall not result in the creation or imposition of any lien or encumbrance upon any of the properties of [Realty Partnership] or [GP Name] pursuant of any indenture, agreement, or instrument of the character referred to herein (except for the liens and encumbrances arising out of the Loan Documents).

(9) Each of [Realty Partnership] and [GP Name] has all necessary power and authority to execute, deliver, and perform its respective obligations under the Loan documents. Such execution, delivery, and performance by [Realty Partnership] have been duly authorized by all necessary partnership action and proceedings and the consent of the limited partners of [Realty Partnership] thereto has been duly obtained.

(10) None of the Loan documents, the loan evidenced thereby or the interest and other charges payable in respect thereof is usurious, violates, or otherwise contravenes any applicable law concerning the payment or receipt of interest, discount, or other advantage or is otherwise legal under applicable law.

(11) The Loan documents constitute the legal, valid and binding obligations of [Realty Partnership] and [GP Name], as the case many be, enforceable in accordance with their respective terms.

(12) No authorizations, consents, approvals, licenses, permits, filings, or registrations with any governmental authority or agency are necessary for the execution, delivery, or performance by [Realty Partnership] or [GP Name] or the Loan documents or for the validity or enforceability thereof.

Very truly yours,
[Lawyer Name]

3 OWNING YOUR HOME

Your home is likely to be the largest, or one of the largest, assets you own. Earlier chapters outlined steps to take to purchase and finance your home with the best legal, tax, and other results. Although those chapters may have seemed long and complex, the work doesn't stop once you've purchased your home. You still need to take steps to protect and maintain your home. There are important tax issues that can affect the ownership and operation of your home. There are also a host of legal issues that can arise. While some are more common then others, the goal of this chapter is to provide you with an analysis of many of the steps you must take.

RECORD KEEPING: MAINTAINING THE INFORMATION YOU NEED

One of the most important steps to safeguard your home and to address a variety of legal and tax issues that can arise is to keep *detailed records*. Photograph everything and keep the photographs in a safe deposit box outside of your home. Photograph the outside and the grounds from each direction necessary to obtain a complete view. Photograph each room with furniture drawers and closet doors open to expose contents. You could also video the house while recording a description of the contents. You can set up a home inventory account using Quicken or other software.

A detailed home inventory can be useful in many situations, including:

- To determine how assets should be distributed and how to file an estate tax return in case of death.

- To prove damages to support a tax deduction claimed on your income tax return, for a casualty loss.

- Casualty loss to prove damages to the insurance company.

- To prove compliance with a town ordinance.

- To prove use of an easement.

Note: For more information on record keeping and a computer diskette with sample forms, see Martin M. Shenkman, *The Beneficiary Workbook* (John Wiley & Sons, Inc.).

MOVING INTO YOUR HOME

Moving into a new home is one of the most difficult and traumatic events for many people. You must address the legal issues of the contracts with the movers, complex tax rules, not to mention boxes and boxes of belongings. While you're on your own with the boxes, the following discussion will help with the other points.

Hire the Right Mover

While it's important to review the contract from any moving company before you sign it, it's important to do your homework before picking a mover. Pick a good mover and contract issues will be less likely to arise. If a problem arises, a reputable mover will more likely resolve the matter fairly without resorting to legal actions. If possible, inquire among acquaintances as to what company they have used in the recent past. Experienced local realtors are probably one of the best referral sources.

Try the Internet for information as well. One web site, http://www.monstermoving.com, can provide resources and goods needed to successfully manage all stages of the relocation process. This site offers access to a comprehensive array of moving-related services as well as relocation tools designed to reduce the time, cost, and stress associated with moving. It includes:

- Finding a place.
- Mortgage and finance center.
- Moving and planning.
- Living and shopping.

Contracts and Other Legalities

Once you've done your homework and selected a reasonable mover, you still have to protect yourself. Including the contract, here are some practical suggestions:

- Label boxes and maintain a list separate from the items being moved.
- Photograph the process using a camera with a date and time stamp.
- Review the contract and be sure it addresses everything you were told when you received a bid. If the contract differs from what you were told, be very cautious. Was it a mere mistake or an effort to trick you?
- Be sure that the movers have all appropriate licensing and insurance coverage and that the contract states that they do. Ask them to provide you with a certificate of insurance.
- Review the moving contract generally and be sure it is reasonable. What does it say about damaged items? Is the date one you can live with? Is it guaranteed? Within how many days (or longer) of the specified time. Does it contain clauses that unreasonably limit the amount you can claim if the mover is late, loses things, or damages something?

Moving Expense Tax Deductions—Let Uncle Sam Help

Moving is one of life's more unpleasant experiences, but at least you end up in your new home, and Uncle Sam may give you a tax break. The value of tax deductions for moving expenses has been an important benefit to employees and self-employed people relocating. The requirements for the various deductions, the categories of costs which can, or cannot, be deducted are complex.

The bottom-line tax result will vary for different taxpayers depending on their circumstances.

Planning Tip: The best way to estimate your deductions and perhaps plan to maximize them is to fill out IRS Form 3903 and review the instructions to the form. This is the form you will have to attach to your tax return to claim moving expense deductions.

The moving expense deduction is claimed to arrive at adjusted gross income (AGI). If you do not itemize deductions, this assures you a deduction.

Direct Costs Are Deductible without Limit.   The following deductions are permitted for moving expenses if you meet the requirements indicated:

1. Moving household goods (furniture, clothing, dishes, and so forth) from your former home to your new home. This can include costs to pack, crate, insure, move, and store (up to 30 days) your household possessions. Other preparation costs, such as disconnecting appliances in preparation of the move, can be deducted.
2. Traveling from your old home to your new home (including hotels, but not meals) for yourself and your family is deductible.

Common Moving Costs That Are Not Deductible.   Expenses in the indirect category (house hunting, temporary living, and expenses of selling, buying and leasing a residence) are not deductible. A number of other common moving expenses are not deductible: losses on terminating club memberships, mortgage penalties, forfeited tuition, expenses to refit carpets and drapes, moving costs of a nurse or maid, among others.

Planning Tip: Often the key between a deductible cost and a nondeductible cost is good records. Keep all receipts and a log of what costs are incurred, when, and for what purpose. Review this chapter and IRS Tax Form 3903 before completing your log so that you will use the correct language to help support deductions.

Requirements for Deductions.   The following requirements have to be met to qualify to deduct the moving expenses you paid to move to a city where your new job is:

1. *Distance test:* The distance (measured by the most commonly traveled route, not as the crow flies) between the location of your new job and your old home has to be at least 50 miles more than the distance from the location of your old job and your old home under prior law. If you are moving to get a better commute than you would have had if you stayed in the same house and commuted to your new job, it is not deductible. If the distance between your new place of work and your new residence is greater then the distance between your old residence and your new place of work, the IRS may disallow the deduction under the work connection test described next.

2. *Work time test:* During the 12-month period immediately after the move, you must work full time for at least 39 weeks. The 39 weeks of work do not have to be consecutive. You do not need to have the job lined-up before you move. However, if you do not actually work, no deduction is allowed. If you become self-employed before meeting this test, you must meet the self-employed test described next. If you are self-employed, you must work full time for a minimum of 78 weeks in the 24-month period immediately after the move. A self-employed person is considered to have begun work when substantial arrangements to begin work have been made. If either you or your spouse meet the appropriate test and you file a joint return, you qualify to deduct moving expenses. You can add together the time spent working on different jobs to meet these requirements.

3. *Work connection test:* The move must be connected with your starting work at the new location at a new principal place of work. The move must be reasonably proximate in both time and place to the commencement of your new job. A new principal place of work is defined for an employee as the plant, office, shop, store, or other property where services are performed. For a self-employed person, it is defined as the center of his or her business activities. The principal place of work

of someone employed by a number of employers on a short-term basis through an employment agency is the employment agency. The moving expenses must be incurred within one year from the date you first start your new job, unless you can demonstrate extenuating circumstances.

4. *Reasonableness test:* Only reasonable expenses may be deducted. For example, travel expenses would be reasonable if they are incurred along the shortest and most direct route from your old home to your new home. Costs to travel a longer but more scenic route or to permit a stopover are not allowed.

INSURANCE FOR YOUR HOME

While you own your home, you must keep it properly insured. While you should have purchased insurance before the closing when you bought your home, you will have to monitor and update your insurance coverage periodically. (See Chapter 4.)

TITLE INSURANCE

The use of title insurance for your home was discussed in Chapter 2. Generally, there is no change made to title insurance while you own the home. However, if an issue arises concerning an easement or other matter affecting title, check with the title company and your lawyer to see if a change is necessary.

Caution: If you change the title to your home, say from joint tenants to tenants in common or to a qualified personal residence trust or even a revocable living trust, you should contact your title company and obtain a confirmation that your title insurance coverage remains intact.

PREPAYING YOUR MORTGAGE

Many advisers advocate the advantages of paying off home mortgages early to save interest payments totaling hundreds of thousands of dollars. Should you make extra payments on top of your regular mortgage payment, take out a loan for 10 or 15 years instead of 30, or pay your mortgage twice a month instead of once a month. Do any of these options make sense?

Caution: Before spending much time evaluating the pros and cons of prepaying your mortgage in small increments, check your mortgage documents. If the legal documents don't permit you to prepay, you can't, regardless of the perceived benefits. Resolve this threshold legal issue before wasting time on the math!

Why might lenders not want you to prepay your mortgage an extra $100 per month? Think of the paperwork it creates. It changes the expected date at which they will receive money. Most mortgages are packaged into groups and sold as investments. If 5,000 homeowners wanted to prepay their mortgages in $25 to $300 amounts at different dates, the paperwork, calculations of new amounts due, and so on, would be staggering. So even if your mortgage documents permit prepayment, they may have some strict criteria as to when, how much, and so on.

Planning Tip: If you do opt to prepay your mortgage, be sure to check the lender's reports to you to verify that the prepayments have been properly credited.

For tax planning, all of the prepayment options are probably not good choices. But, the answer can't be based only on taxes. If paying a larger mortgage is the only way to force yourself to save then one of these methods may be appropriate for you even if from a tax and financial perspective it is not an optimal use of your money. If you may need the money, extra payments are an expensive option. It would probably be more expensive to tap your home's equity in later years with a second mortgage or home equity line. If you think you may need the money, put those extra payments in a money market fund, CD, or short-term bond.

The financial writers promoting prepayments stress how much interest you'll save over the life of the loan—and the numbers are always huge. Don't be fooled by the big dollar savings. You're paying the bank interest because you have their money working for you. If you're able to save the money without paying the bank back and invest it, you may actually be better off than prepaying. The real numbers to look at are the aftertax savings in interest (and since you're loosing tax deductions by prepaying this will hurt the comparison—saving $30,000 in interest may have only cost you $20,000) and the amount of money you would have accumulated if you had invested the money instead of prepaying the mortgage. Using this comparison, you will see that the "savings" many financial writers tout are actually minimal. Also, if you sell your home soon after prepaying, the savings from prepaying will prove minimal.

If you have a home mortgage with a low interest rate, prepayment may be very disadvantageous. On the other hand, if you have a loan with a very high interest rate, prepayment may be the best thing until you can refinance. Make sure the lender doesn't charge a penalty for prepayment.

You can only deduct interest expense on home mortgages used to acquire, construct, or substantially improve your home. If you take out a $300,000 mortgage to buy a new home, you can deduct all of the interest on it. If you refinance, you won't be able to deduct interest on the portion of the mortgage that is greater than the amount you refinanced. The only way you can ever get to deduct interest on the portion of the mortgage you prepaid is to buy a new home! So, from a purely income tax planning perspective, you're probably best off getting a mortgage for the longest period possible (probably 30 years) and paying it back as slowly as the bank will permit. Take your extra money that you would have used to prepay and invest it.

Don't forget that you can probably still borrow up to a $100,000 home equity loan and deduct the interest. But that's the limit. With soaring college and other costs, why lose the use of cheap money by prepaying? If you can deduct mortgage interest at a 35 percent tax rate, your 8 percent mortgage really only costs you 5.2 percent.

If you still want to prepay your home mortgage, read the fine print. There may be restrictions on when, how much, or in what increments you can pay. Further, the lender may not have to give you credit for partial payments immediately. Review your loan agreement first.

If you prepaid your mortgage and had to pay a penalty to the bank, the penalty is tax deductible. Prepayment penalties are deductible as interest. But penalties are subject to all the various mortgage interest deduction rules discussed in Chapter 2.

INCOME TAX BENEFITS OF HOME OWNERSHIP

Because of the tremendous desire of most Americans to own homes and the strong home lobby, the tax laws have always included many tax breaks for encouraging home ownership. Take advantage of them to the extent you can. However, you have to understand the benefits available so you can plan appropriately.

Mortgage Interest

The income tax deductions for your home mortgage were discussed in Chapter 2. The legal, tax, and financial consequences of prepaying your home mortgage were discussed earlier in this chapter.

Property Taxes

Property taxes (county, city, and other real estate taxes) can sometimes be one of the largest expenses for a homeowner. Fortunately for many homeowners, these payments are deductible so that Uncle Sam will bear part of the cost. Generally, determining how much property tax you can deduct is a simple matter. Some complications arise when you buy or sell a house. Also, some payments you make may sound deductible, but you may not be permitted to deduct them.

Deducting property taxes can be an important advantage of home ownership. Tenants generally pay for property taxes indirectly through the rent payments they make to their landlords. However, with few exceptions (check with a tax adviser in your area), tenants can't deduct property taxes.

To obtain one of the major income tax benefits of home ownership, deducting property taxes, you must first pass a hurdle. The threshold issue is to make sure you can itemize deductions on your federal income tax return. If you cannot, no deduction will be available. For the year 2000, a married couple filing a joint income tax return was entitled to a standard deduction of $7,350. So if their total itemized deductions, including property taxes, mortgage interest, medical, charity, and so on, didn't exceed this amount, there would be no tax deduction for property taxes.

Once you've passed this threshold, your property taxes will generally be tax deductible. However, as with most tax rules, the laws get quite complex when it comes to special assessments, allocations when you buy or sell your home, and so on. This section discussed many of these rules to help you maximize your property tax deductions.

Real Estate Taxes When You Buy/Sell a Home.   Real estate taxes must be prorated (divided) between the buyer and seller as of the date of the closing (transfer of ownership of the house from the seller to the buyer). Only taxes properly allocable to the buyer (or seller) can be deducted by the buyer (or seller). This follows the general rule discussed earlier—only the person liable for and paying the property taxes can deduct them. Simply, the buyer and seller are each responsible for the property taxes for the portion of the year that they own the house. Unfortunately, the calculation gets more complicated. The seller and buyer calculate their income tax on a calendar year basis—for the period from January 1 through December 31. Most property taxes are assessed on the basis of some fiscal year period, for example, July 1 through June 30 of the following year (the property tax assessment period). This is the period under local (state) law to which the tax relates. The allocation is based on the number of days in the taxing authorities' fiscal year in which the buyer and seller each owned the property.

The seller is responsible for paying (and can deduct when he pays) taxes due through the date before the sale. The buyer is responsible for paying (and can deduct when he pays) taxes from the date of sale onward. To make matters more confusing, in some places the laws may make property taxes a lien on the property, or a liability of the owner before or after the real property tax assessment year to which the taxes relate. The rule is that the taxes are deductible by the person who owns the house during the real property assessment period. If the real property taxes become a lien on the property or a liability for the seller before the property tax assessment period to which the taxes relate, and the house is sold before that assessment period begins, the seller can't deduct these taxes. Similarly, if the real property taxes become a personal liability of the buyer or a lien on the property after the end of the real property assessment period to which the taxes relate, the buyer can't deduct them.

Taxes assessed for local benefits that increase the value of the property assessed (e.g., for roads, sidewalks, sewers) will not be deductible.

Your lawyer will handle this and you should see the exact numbers on your HUD-RESPA form.

A few of the pitfalls that could jeopardize your deduction for property taxes may be apparent. Delinquent real estate taxes are treated as an acquisition cost of the property and are not deductible by the buyer. For example, when reviewing the title insurance binder, it is not unusual to find the seller's property taxes are delinquent. If the buyer pays the arrearages (which is common), the buyer *will not* be entitled to a tax deduction. A better approach is for the seller to pay the delinquent taxes directly, so that he can claim a tax deduction. A credit adjustment should then be made to the purchase price as reflected on the HUD-RESPA statement.

Watch for Tax Reassessment. Take a look at your property tax assessment. If you bought your house recently, compare what you paid to the assessment. If there is a huge difference, you could be in store for a substantial tax increase. Check with the government body that assesses and collects the tax to find out what the local law is about assessments. Some municipalities assess based on current full fair market value. Others assess based on a percentage of fair market value.

Example: If your township has a policy to assess homes at 50 percent of fair market value and your home was assessed at $40,000 to the former owner and you just bought it a month ago for $320,000, your home should probably be assessed at $160,000 (50% of $320,000). You could be looking forward to a whopping 400% tax increase.

Challenging a Property Tax Assessment. First decide whether you want to tackle the problem yourself or hire a specialist to do it.

Attorneys and property tax adjustment firms will argue for a reduction in your property tax assessment and charge you a percentage of the savings they get for you. Unless the numbers are large, it may be difficult to get an attorney or firm to help. Also, for a small case, their fees may be high. If you try it alone, contact the taxing authority (their name will be on the assessment) and indicate that you're concerned. Try to find out the facts on which the assessment was based. There may have been oversights by the appraiser who inspected your house. Perhaps he thought you had central air conditioning, aluminum siding, or other improvements which you didn't. If this is the case, bring the correct facts to the attention of the taxing authority.

Check local papers to see the prices being asked for comparable houses in your area. You may want to go to the local office that records property sales (it could be a county clerk's office) and review the available public records to see prices at which homes similar to yours, in the same general area, were recently sold. If there are differences between the sales prices of comparable homes and the assessed value of your home, bring this to the attention of the taxing authority. If you go through this process and aren't successful, take solace in the fact that your home is worth a lot more than you realized.

Your situation also raises a property tax question. The above process could take some time. Meanwhile you will have continued making payments to your bank for property taxes (or paid them directly). What should your deduction be? Do you deduct the taxes actually paid, or do you deduct the taxes you actually paid reduced by any refund? You should deduct the taxes you actually paid because they were a real liability which you were responsible for at the time. If you were successful in your challenge and get a refund report it as miscellaneous income in the year you receive it.

Which Property Taxes You Can Deduct.   What is a deductible real property tax? The answer is usually simple, but there are many exceptions and special rules.

State, county, municipal, and other local real property taxes that are deductible by taxpayers responsible for paying the tax, who actually pay the tax, and who itemize deductions on their tax returns. Deductible property taxes are taxes imposed on interests in real property (land, buildings, and improvements to either) that are assessed for the general public welfare. This includes police and fire protection and maintenance of public property.

If you paid the property tax which my children/parents/friends owed on their house, can you deduct it? Unfortunately, no. You can only deduct property taxes which are paid by you on property you own. Taxes are only deductible by the person on whom they are imposed.

Example: A taxpayer lived with his aunt in her house. A court order required him to pay the property taxes. He was not entitled to deduct the taxes, however, because he didn't own the property. The court order requiring him to pay the taxes said that the taxes he paid were rent.

A guarantor isn't allowed to deduct real estate taxes relating to a foreclosed trust property because the taxes were not imposed on him. A better approach would be to loan your children/parents/friends the money so they can pay the tax. At least that way the tax deduction won't be lost.

Special assessments can sometimes be deducted, but not always. But there are tax consequences in either situation. Special assessments can be many different things depending on what the township, county, or other taxing authority wants to call it. The first step should be to find out exactly what the "special assessment" is, what the money will be used for, whether everyone in the town or county is paying it or whether it is only being assessed against homes near yours. With this information in hand, you can figure out whether or not you have a tax deduction.

If the assessment is for improvements for the general public welfare (new streets or parks for the whole county), and is assessed against all the properties in the taxing authorities jurisdiction, you can probably deduct it. However, if the assessment is not for the general public welfare, but rather it is for improvements to your property (sidewalks for your subdivision or block, roads, sewers, and so forth), and the tax is assessed against those properties benefiting, it can't be deducted since it will increase the value of your property. If a special assessment can't be deducted, it probably represents an improvement to your home which should be added to your investment (tax basis). Put a copy of the bill and canceled check in the permanent home file you should have set up after buying your home.

A portion of a special assessment that appears to benefit only a limited number of homes may still be deductible if it is for interest and repair and maintenance type expenditures rather than capital improvements. For example, a deduction was allowed for the portion of a special assessment paid for resurfacing and repair of streets. It was not allowed for the portion used to lengthen or widen streets. You must separate the amounts that were allocable for deductible expenses.

Cooperative Apartments and Condominiums and Property Tax Deductions.   Condominiums and cooperatives, as explained in Chapter 1, are special forms of home ownership with different rules affecting the property taxes you can deduct.

Since condominiums are separately owned by each individual owner, you should pay property taxes on your unit yourself, either to the bank that has your mortgage or directly to the taxing authority. There may also be a second component to your property tax bill. If you make monthly maintenance payments to the homeowners' association, a portion of that payment is probably used to pay property taxes on the common areas that all owners share (e.g., the golf course). Your portion of these taxes is also deductible.

Most owners (tenant-shareholders) of cooperative apartments pay a monthly maintenance fee. If the cooperative corporation owns the land and building, it will pay property taxes. A portion of these property taxes will be deductible by each tenant-shareholder. If the cooperative corporation doesn't own the land and building, rather leases it, the tax paid will not be deductible by you as an owner. The cooperative should issue you a statement at the end of the year telling you your share of the deductible real estate tax. The tax laws require the cooperative housing corporation to report the interest and tax amounts to both its shareholders and the IRS. You should claim this amount as an itemized deduction. Some cooperative corporations provide the property tax data on a per share basis. Multiply the property taxes paid per share by the number of shares you own to determine your property tax deduction. Look at the contract you used to buy the apartment or the proprietary lease you received when you bought the apartment to see how many shares you own. The cooperative corporation can allocate its interest and property taxes in a manner that reasonably reflects the costs to the corporation of that apartment. Thus, if the penthouse apartment was assessed by the local property assessor at a value that was one-fifth the value of the total building, instead of the one-tenth value the share ownership indicates, this larger one-fifth ratio could be used to allocate interest and taxes. Check with your accountant.

Many cooperative corporations assess a charge for anyone selling an apartment called a *flip tax*. A flip tax is not a property tax. It's not even a tax. It's really a transfer tax that the cooperative corporation decides to charge everyone selling apartment units. It is used as a way to raise revenue for the building. The flip tax is actually part of the cost of selling your home and should be used to reduce the amount of gain realized on the sale.

Casualty Losses as a Tax Deduction

Damage to your home, a casualty loss, may generate an income tax deduction. No matter what the facts are, the tax deduction can at most ease the burden of your loss, it will never make it up. So protect yourself ahead of time. Be certain that you have proper insurance (see Chapter 4). Consider an alarm system and smoke detectors wired to a central station to report problems when you're gone. Have a good home inspection before you buy. Maintain your home properly. Take photographs and maintain records. If you still suffer a loss, plan to maximize the tax deductions you can claim as a result of that loss. This section will show you how.

Tax Rules Affecting Casualty Losses. In the event of a casualty loss, you may qualify to take a tax deduction for a portion of your loss. Insurance proceeds may also be received in certain circumstances without a tax cost.

Note: Most taxpayers assume that the insurance proceeds they receive as a result of damage to their home is always tax free. It can be, but it isn't always. Follow the rules that we discuss next to avoid an unintended tax problem.

Casualty losses are deducted on your personal income tax return, Form 1040, Schedule A, for itemized deductions. In addition, you will generally have to fill out Form 4684, Casualties and Thefts. As soon as you suffer a major loss, get a copy of the IRS Form 4684 with instructions, read it, and start keeping records.

Defining a Casualty Loss for Tax Purposes.   A casualty loss is defined for tax purposes as a loss from a fire, storm, or other similar casualty that is caused by either natural or external forces (a thief) in a sudden, unexpected, or unusual event. Disastrous floods and hurricanes are included. (It was these major natural disasters that spurred Congress to make the changes to the tax rules affecting casualty losses.) An unexpected and rapid destruction of trees due to southern pine beetles or wood borers have qualified for deduction. However, damage due to either termite infestation or Dutch elm disease, are not deductible since the damage occurs slowly over a long period of time. An accidental loss is deductible if it is caused by a sudden, unexpected, unusual, and identifiable event that damages property. A mere decline in value without physical damage is generally not deductible. If you are required to leave and abandon your home as a result of a disaster, a casualty loss can be claimed.

Determining the Tax Year in Which to Take Your Deduction. The year in which you can deduct a casualty loss can have a significant affect on the tax benefit you receive, as well as the timing of any tax refund. The cash flow provided by a tax refund can be a considerable help in financing needed repairs.

Generally you deduct your casualty loss in the year your property is damaged. But there are a number of important exceptions to this simple rule. If your house was damaged in December 2003 and you know that all but the first $200 (the amount of the deductible on your insurance policy) will be paid by your insurance company early in 2004 then you cannot claim a deduction in 2003. If you anticipate an insurance recovery, you must reduce the amount of your casualty loss deduction by that amount. If you collect less from the insurance company than you expected, deduct the loss you did not recover in the later year when you realize what you collected.

If in the later year you collect more than you thought from the insurance company, this extra amount will have to be reported as income if you claimed a tax deduction for it in the earlier year. If you deducted the amount in the earlier year but couldn't benefit from the entire deduction, because of either the 10 percent adjusted gross income limitation or the standard deduction amount, the amount for which you did not realize a benefit does not have to be treated as income.

There is a special rule if the President declares your area a disaster qualifying for federal government assistance. An election will allow you to deduct your casualty loss resulting from the disaster according to the general rules just discussed, or on your tax return for the year before the loss occurred. This is done by filing an amended income tax return on Form 1040.

The benefit of this election can be twofold. First, if your income was lower in the prior year, you will obtain a bigger deduction (this is because the deduction for 10 percent of adjusted gross income will not reduce your deduction by as much). You may get your tax benefit much sooner. If there is a major hurricane in January 2003 in your area and the President declares it a disaster area, you can claim the deduction on your 2002 tax return. If you did not make this special election, you would have to wait to claim the deduction on your 2003 tax return filed a year later in April 2004. If you've already filed your tax return for 2002 before the disaster declaration was made, you can amend it by filing a Form 1040-X to claim the casualty loss for that prior year. Thus, you can claim a 2003 flood disaster loss on your 2002 federal tax return by filing an amended tax return to get a tax refund.

Note: Because unreimbursed casualty losses can only be deducted to the extent that they exceed 10 percent of your adjusted gross income, it can be beneficial to claim your loss in the year in which your income is lower. Your decision must also consider the tax due in the year you wish to claim the loss. The safest strategy is to project the loss deduction for each year in which the deduction can be claimed and choose the best. You can have your accountant do this, or if you prepare your own returns prepare the return first with the casualty loss, and then without, and compare the numbers. If you use a computer program like Turbo Tax, this is quite simple to do.

The decision as to which year to claim the loss may be easier because of the changes made by the Taxpayer Relief Act of 2001. The tax rates in future years could be lower for you than they were in prior years. Further, the earlier you claim your loss, the quicker you receive your refund. Claim the loss as soon as you can. However, when Congress changes the law again, the decision process will also change.

Limitations and Restrictions on Deducting Casualty Losses.
There are several important limitations on deducting a casualty loss.
First, $100 for each casualty is not deductible. Next, when you add
all of your casualty losses (after deducting the $100 per casualty)
the total is deductible only to the extent that it exceeds 10 percent
of your adjusted gross income—all your earnings, less certain items
such as alimony, but before itemized deductions. This deductible
amount is added to all of your other itemized deductions. The total
of all of your itemized deductions is only deductible to the extent
that it exceeds the standard deduction. The phase-out of itemized
deductions for high-income taxpayers may reduce your deduction
further.

Example: A farmer has a gross income of $35,000 in 2000. His state in-
come taxes are $3,000 and his property taxes are $1,000. He was fortunate in that he was only on the fringes of a flood area and suffered a mere
$11,300 in damage. He wasn't insured for flood loss. His casualty loss
deduction is calculated as follows:

Casualty	$11,300
Deductible	100
subtotal	$11,200
Less 10% × Adjusted gross income	
(10% × 35,000)	3,500
Deductible Casualty Loss	$ 7,700

His total itemized deductions before casualty loss is $4,000 [$3,000 state
income taxes + $1,000 property taxes]. Assume that he is entitled to a
$7,350 standard deduction. Only the first $3,350 of casualty loss will not
provide him any additional tax benefit [$7,350 standard deduction –
$4,000]. Thus, his casualty loss will provide him an additional $3,650 tax
deduction [$7,700 – $3,350 used to meet the standard deduction
amount]. If he is in a 20 percent marginal state and federal tax bracket,
this will give him a tax savings of $730—not a lot toward a $11,300 loss.

Where you have several items of property (such as a couch, a
bookcase, and a carpet) destroyed in a fire, you do not have to
deduct $100 from each item when calculating any casualty loss de-
duction. You only have to deduct $100 per casualty. Since your
couch, bookcase, and carpet were all destroyed in the same fire,
you can add up your entire loss from that fire and subtract a single
$100 exclusion. It is a $100 exclusion per event even though many
items were destroyed. Events that are closely related can be considered a single event.

Where you have many items damaged or destroyed, the computation of any gain or loss may now be made on a pool of dollars so that you do not have to allocate insurance proceeds on an asset-by-asset basis. You compare the cost of replacing all assets (e.g., your house and your personal property such as a television, VCR, and sofa). If there are some losses and some gains, they can be offset without the requirement of calculating all gains and losses individually. This rule also gives you the flexibility to invest insurance proceeds in a ratio that differs from the ratio in which you were paid. If your insurance distribution was based on a ratio of 75 percent for the value of the real estate and 25 percent for the value of the personal property, you can now reinvest those distributions in any other ratio. A reinvestment of 60 percent in real estate and 40 percent for personal property could be made with no adverse tax consequence.

Example: Assume your insurance policy paid you $95,000 for your home and $31,500 for personal property, for a total of $126,500. If you reinvest these insurance monies (according to the rules described next) fully in a replacement home, even in different proportions, there will be no taxable gain. Thus, if you spent $105,000 towards your new home and only $21,500 (or more) for personal property, there would be no taxable gain.

If you refuse to file an insurance claim (e.g., you are afraid your rates will go up), you cannot deduct the casualty loss. If the property was insured, you must file a timely insurance claim in order to claim a tax deduction.

How the Loss Is Calculated for Tax Purposes.   The manner in which you calculate how much your casualty loss deduction is can be quite complicated. Your casualty loss is the lower of the following two amounts: (1) the decrease in the value of your property as a result of the casualty; or (2) your adjusted basis in the property. The decrease in value is the fair market value of your property before the casualty loss minus the fair market value of your property after the casualty loss. Your adjusted basis in the property is the price you paid for your house less any depreciation you deducted on a home office or rental apartment which was part of your house. After you determine the amount of the loss, you must subtract $100 per casualty, 10 percent of your adjusted gross income from all of your casualty losses, and expected insurance recoveries, and consider your standard deduction.

How to Prove Your Loss to the IRS.   There are several ways to prove the amount of your casualty loss. If the casualty was from a theft, or a car crashing into your property, or a similar event, file a police report immediately. The best evidence you can have is an independent police report. This will probably also help you in recovering from your insurance company as well. Call your insurance agent as soon as possible and advise him or her of the damage. As soon as possible after it occurs, shoot photographs of the damage to your property. The comparison of these damage photos with the photographs you took as part of your household inventory before any damage was done will highlight your loss. At the first opportunity, confirm your earlier phone call to your insurance agent in writing. Save copies of everything for your tax return as well.

Try to collect receipts, cancelled checks, invoices, and so forth to prove the following information for your casualty loss: nature of the loss, evidence that the loss was the direct result of the casualty, cost of the property destroyed, any depreciation claimed on the property (for example, if you had a home office), the value of the property before and after the casualty, any insurance recovery.

If your property was damaged by a tornado, save a copy of the next days local newspaper discussing the damage to your area. This could be a great help if you are audited by the IRS and the agent questions your deductions. If the damage is extensive and your loss is large, consider getting an appraisal of your property.

If you cannot prove the cost of the property destroyed and it's fair market value, than the IRS will sometimes accept your repair bills as an estimate of the damage that was done. You should be prepared to show that the repairs were necessary to restore the property to the condition it was in before the casualty. This is where a picture can be worth a thousand words.

How to Avoid Tax on Insurance Proceeds Received as a Result of a Disaster.   Where property, such as your home, is destroyed and insurance proceeds are received you may have to report a taxable gain as if you had sold the house, unless you reinvest the insurance proceeds in qualifying replacement property within the specified time period.

Any gains on insurance proceeds received as a result of a disaster under the old law had to be reinvested within two years of the close of the tax year in which the gain was realized to avoid any tax cost.

The new law provides a four-year period to reinvest insurance proceeds on gain from sale of a principal residence without any tax consequences.

Example: A rancher suffered a flood loss to his home in July 2003. The tax year ends December 31, 2003. Insurance proceeds are received in November 2003. The rancher has until four years after December 2003 (i.e., until December 2007) to reinvest in a replacement property to avoid any tax cost.

A special rule permits renters to be treated as if they owned property for purposes of this reinvestment rule.

Planning Tip: If your principal residence was affected by a significant natural disaster, and insurance proceeds created a taxable gain, review your recent tax filings to see if there is an opportunity to file a refund claim by filing an amended tax return on Form 1040-X.

HOME-BASED BUSINESSES

Tens of millions of Americans operate home-based businesses. There are a host of legal and tax issues to consider in operating such businesses. This section explores some of them.

Legal Issues

Most home-based business owners mistakenly assume that everything is quite simple; it's only a small home business. The size and location of your business don't give you any assurance that the liabilities and lawsuits you face won't be large.

Meet a Business Lawyer—Now! If you're starting a business, or have one, pay for a consultation with a lawyer who specializes in closely held business matters. There are always issues unique to each business of which you need to be aware. Make the meeting productive by preparing. The tip below tells you how.

Planning Tip: Issues to address:

- How should the business be organized?
- What special insurance coverage do you need?
- What contracts are you using or should you be using?
- What liability risks do you face and what can be done about them?
- What bank accounts do you need?
- Review any standard or common correspondence and a typical business transaction so that legal, tax, and other issues can be identified.
- What issues should you seek legal help for? (Most home-based businesses won't need a lawyer's help often, but you don't want to overlook the times you should.)
- Bring several years' tax returns for the business, copies of correspondence, contract forms, and key contracts you've signed (e.g., with a distributor), and so on.

Zoning Issues May Affect a Home Business.   Before you begin your home-based business, it is important to consult any applicable zoning laws for the land in question. There are many zoning considerations. These include limits placed on the use of the land (i.e., it may only be used for residential purposes, but not commercial) and limits placed on the percentage of land that may be built up. (To preserve the appearance of a community, zoning laws often prohibit landowners from building on more than a certain percentage of the property.)

Note: Many towns require a special approval or certificate for operating a home-based business. Call your town, find out the requirements, and if you qualify, obtain the appropriate certificate.

If your home is a cooperative or condominium, check the bylaws and rules for requirements or prohibitions.

Observe the Legal Formalities of a Business.   Home-based businesses have various requirements to meet for the business to qualify as a business, thereby allowing you to take advantage of any applicable tax deductions or other benefits. These requirements and benefits will be discussed next.

- Businesses maintain separate bank accounts from their owners. Transactions between the business and you as an owner should be as if you did not control the business.

- If you lend or borrow money, sign a loan agreement with fair interest (see Chapter 2 for a sample note). You can be paid a salary or receive a distribution. Do not pay personal expenses from a business account. If you do, reimburse right away and don't make a habit of it. If you commingle business and personal transactions, don't expect any court or IRS to respect the business as a business.

- Businesses may not be covered under your regular insurance. Consult an insurance agent and find out what special coverage you need. Often, it may not be more than an inexpensive rider on your homeowners policy. However, if you have customers coming to your home (employees, or others), you may have substantial insurance requirements that are not addressed by personal insurance. Your business may require its own liability, auto, and other insurance.

- Businesses should conduct business in the name of the business, not in your personal name.

- If you have a trade name, logo, slogan, web site, or so on, be certain to consult with an intellectual property (IP) attorney to safeguard these rights. For many businesses, the most important assets are intangible assets like a name or logo. Don't assume you can use it unless an attorney has done the necessary searches and registered the name for you. This protects you against others also using the name.

Caution: Simply filing a corporation, limited liability company, or tax identification number with the IRS will not give you any assurance that your business can use the name, slogan, or logo. These filings are unrelated to the right to use intangible assets.

Structuring the Business: LLC for the Business. The Limited Liability Company, or LLC, has become a popular form for organizing business and investment activities. An LLC is taxed as a flow-through entity for tax purposes (i.e., it shouldn't have any significant tax impact on you). But most importantly, it provides limited liability. If the business formalities of the LLC are observed (all contracts and transaction completed in the LLC name, separate bank, and other records) a customer or vendor suing the business should not be able to reach your personal assets.

Note: Although there are many exceptions, any level of asset protection that is relatively easy to administer and not expensive to maintain is worth consideration. An LLC fits that profile.

For tax purposes, if you are the sole owner, the business is treated as a "disregarded entity" for tax purposes. This means you would continue to report income from your home business on Schedule C of your Form 1040 and no special tax return would have to be filed. If your business is a rental property, it would be reported on Schedule E. If there is no extra tax return each year, then forming the LLC may, other than the initial one time set-up costs, not entail any more cost than not having such an entity. You should carefully evaluate the benefits versus the costs of an LLC.

In most cases, if you are serious about your home-based business, set it up as an LLC from inception. Talk to your attorney. In some states the rules may differ and there may be an advantage to using another form of ownership.

Note: If you transfer your home-based business to an LLC for asset protection reasons, you will also need to have your lawyer assist you in assigning any contract rights you had pertaining to the business to the LLC. This can be done by using a modified version of the assignment form illustrated on page 64.

Tax Considerations

Is a home-based office tax deduction worth claiming? Supplies, travel, and pure business costs are not the issue. If you buy equipment, it can be depreciated or deducted. The cost of stationery, paper, and other supplies can be deducted. Expenses relating to your home that are part personal and part business, are the issue. These are a share of utility costs, depreciation of your home, and so forth. This is a question rarely asked by taxpayers. But because of the abuse of home-based office deductions, the requirements, reporting, and tax audits have become so tough, you should consider this question before planning further. Most home-based business operators assume that they will qualify for a significant tax deduction for running a business in their home. In most cases, the deduction is not nearly as large as anticipated. It creates a lot of record keeping and tax filing requirements and is an audit point (red flag) for the IRS. Before counting your tax benefits, meet with an accountant and review the net benefits. In some cases, you may just be better off forgetting the tax deduction even though you meet the requirements and qualify. While it's not easy to give up a legitimate tax deduction, make sure the break is worth the effort if you claim it. Discuss it with your accountant.

Requirements for Home-Based Office Tax Deductions.   Once you've decided to claim a home-based office tax deduction, you must then identify what kind of deductions you can claim. You may qualify to claim part of the cost of your home, cooperative apartment, or condominium. This entitles you to depreciate a portion of the cost. A similar portion of your gas, electric, and other utility and home maintenance expenses can also be deducted.

Significant limitations and restrictions apply to home-based office deductions. To claim a deduction for a home-based office, a room or the portion of your home used as an office must be used exclusively and on a regular basis for:

- Meeting clients or dealing with customers and patients in the ordinary course of your business.
- As the principal place of any business which you conduct. You can have more than one business for purposes of this test. Thus, you can be an employee and can moonlight and claim a home-based office deduction for your moonlighting business, so long as the other tests are met. A principal place of business can be a place where management or administrative functions are performed if there is no other fixed location to conduct such activities.
- A separate structure used in connection with your business that is not attached to your home. For example, a garage converted to an office or a small guest house on the same lot as your home.

To be used exclusively, the home-based office must not be the same area where your children watch television while you work. The room or portion of a room must be used solely for business use. An exception to this strict rule applies if your business is a wholesale or retail business. You can then deduct the expense allocable to the portion of the home used for storage of inventory or samples.

If you are an employee, the portion of your home used for business must be so used for the convenience of your employer. This is a tough test to meet. It generally requires that the home be the focal point of your work for your employer. Alternatively, it can be a practical necessity for you to use an office in your home.

The requirement that the home be used regularly means that the room or portion of your home for which you claim a home-based office deduction must be used regularly in the pursuit of your business. For professionals, clients will generally have to meet or deal with you in the home office. Contact by telephone will generally not suffice. Keep a log or diary. If you keep an appointment book where you note all of your appointments, this should be a big help. If it's appropriate to your type of business, keep a guest log where all visitors can sign in. A good chronological file of all mail, bills, and other correspondence may also help trace your use of the home office on a regular basis. In one case, a college professor was provided the opportunity to use a space on the college campus that consisted of a shared office in a room with 20 professors. A communal phone for on-campus calls was provided. Each work space also had a writing shelf and locker space. The professor felt this was inadequate and maintained an office at home. The court decided that his home office was for his convenience and not required for his job so his deductions were denied. To qualify, the home office should, as a practical matter, be essential to your being able to perform your employment-related duties. Your position will be supported if the home office expenses are entirely separate from your personal living expenses.

Planning Tip: Insurance requirements, municipal ordinances, and similar administrative matters discussed earlier in this chapter will have an important beneficial side effect: All help demonstrate that you're really running a serious business out of your home, helping you prove to the IRS that the home-based office is a real business and that your tax deductions should be allowed.

If you've decided to go for a home-based office deduction, obtain Form 8829 from the IRS and read the instructions. Begin keeping appropriate records.

Restrictions on Deductions.   Once you've surmounted the complex hurdles and can qualify for the home-based office deduction, you face a host of limitations on how much you can deduct. The tax regulations specify how your home-based office expenses must be allocated between personal and business and the order in which you can claim them. The deductions attributable to your home-based office (depreciation, insurance, utilities, and so on) are only allowed to the extent of the amount of the net income from the business conducted out of the home-based office. This limitation does not apply to business expenses that have no particular connection to your having a home-based office (supplies, travel, consultants, and so forth).

If you're an employee and claim deductions for home-based office expenses relating to your employment, these expenses are deductible as miscellaneous itemized deductions. This means that they will be subject to the same limitation that all miscellaneous itemized deductions are subject to. Namely, a deduction will only be allowed to the extent that total miscellaneous itemized deductions exceed 2 percent of your adjusted gross income.

Affect of Home Office on Sale of Your Home. If you qualify a portion of your home for the home office tax deduction, that portion of your home will not qualify for the favorable tax break on selling your home described in Chapter 6. Consider this detriment before opting to claim a deduction.

HOME IMPROVEMENTS

Major home improvements are rarely easy. They are expensive. They almost always cost more than anticipated—there are always extras. If you're living in the house at the same time, the noise and dirt, even with the best of contractors, can be tough. This section provides some basic information as to the legal and tax issues to consider in making home improvements.

Dealing with Contractors

The key legal advice for the contract you sign with a home contractor is the same as the advice given for a contract with a moving company. Focus on picking a reputable contractor who wants you to be a good referral source in the neighborhood when the work is done. Once you've done that, you can consider the contract. But remember that there is much to the old adage that a contract is only as good as the person signing it.

How do you pick a good contractor? Ask around the community for reliable contractors. Ask local realtors, real estate attorneys, home improvement and hardware stores. The people who deal professionally with home improvement contractors are likely to know the quality of their work. Inquire about the contractor's price, reliability, work ethic, and the quality of the work. Seek out home owners who have used that contractor, and ask for a candid assessment.

Here are some other tips to consider when choosing a contractor:

- Drive around your neighborhood and look for construction. When you find contractors, ask them for business cards and any other relevant information.
- Ask around the local lumber yard, hardware store, or any other place that contractors are likely to frequent.
- Ask a contractor who you know and trust about other types of contractors.
- Make inquiries at the local builders' association or traders' association.
- Make sure that you have policies, scheduling, and other important information worked out between you and the contractor prior to construction. Ask questions and make sure the contractor answers them sufficiently. This can help avoid many problems.
- Get a credit report on the contractor.
- Contact the better business bureau for comments filed on the contractor.
- Try to get everything in writing, from the actual agreement to the work schedule.

Once you've selected a contract and agreed on terms and price, review the contract carefully. Often contractors will use standard American Institute of Architect (AIA) forms. Have your architect and lawyer review the contract as well. Consider the following:

- Who is signing the contract? Is the contract in the name of the company you negotiated with or is it an unknown name.

The latter may mean that the contract is with a small corporation formed with few assets so that it is immune to lawsuits.

- What is the schedule and how much of a guarantee is there?

- What limitations does the contract place on the contractor's liability? Does the contract disallow any claim you have if the contractor is late or uses inferior materials?

- Does the contract and detailed schedule clearly reflect the work you agreed to, the price agreed to, the quality and nature of the materials?

- Does the contract clearly specify what you are providing at your expense versus what items the contractor is providing? These should match what you agreed to with the contractor during the negotiations.

- Are items to be provided by the contractor specified in detail? If not, you may get the least expensive (poorest quality) of that item.

- Are painting, cleaning, garbage removal, and other assumed activities specified?

- Does the contractor have appropriate licenses and insurance? The contract should specify this and the exhibits to the contract should have certificates attached.

Example: Your contractor is billing you for extras you never heard of or agreed to. Ask your lawyer about local laws pertaining to such changes. In one case, a construction contractor was denied the right to collect for additional work done in response to changes in the contract since he did not comply with laws that required that extras should have been reduced to a signed contemporaneous writing. The court took a very strict view of the statute, even where its protections were not explicitly sought. The court believed that this approach was necessary to prevent unscrupulous acts against consumers who were to be protected by the law.

Income Tax Considerations

There are a number of income tax considerations of a home improvement, including:

- Keep records of all costs of improvements since these will add to your investment (tax basis) in the home. Remember that you can save capital gains when you sell the home if your gain exceeds the amount the tax laws let you exclude (see Chapter 6).

- Your town will likely reassess your home after improvements. See the earlier discussion in this chapter about fighting the reassessment, and being able to deduct the taxes involved.

- Your home mortgage to finance the improvements may qualify as acquisition indebtedness and be tax deductible (see Chapter 2).

Zoning, Deed, and Related Legal Issues

Before engaging in any significant construction or home improvement, consult with a local real estate attorney about any zoning (local laws governing property use) and other requirements. There are a host of rules that could affect what you do. If you are in a condominium association, the bylaws should be reviewed. Even if you live in a single-family residence, you should have your attorney check the deed. There could be restrictions. It's always cheaper and easier to deal with the restrictions up front, not after you've paid for architectural plans and taken other steps toward construction. The homeowner in the following example learned the hard way.

Example: An action was brought to enforce a restrictive covenant in a deed to prevent a property owner in the subdivision from subdividing his lot so a second house could be built. The court noted that the key factor was the intent behind the restrictive language contained in the deed which would be determined by reading the subdivision deeds in light of all surrounding circumstances. The court was persuaded that the original grantor intended to impose a uniform plan of development on the particular tract in issue. The court reviewed a number of factors, including the common grantor's intent to sell the entire tract and exhibition of a map or plat of the entire tract at the time of sale and whether development actually occurred in accordance with the uniform plan. Less weight was given to deviations occurring after the last parcel was conveyed by the common grantor. The court noted that every deed explicitly restricted the burdened property to residential use. The language in the various deeds, however, differed slightly (e.g., one dwelling house, dwelling house, one-family house). Defendants argued that such descriptions limit the type, but not the number, of dwelling houses that can be built on their property. The court found that the language was intended to restrict both. The result: The homeowner could not subdivide and build a second house.

Easements

A related property issue is easements. These are rights of access through another's property. They are not ownership rights, but rather a more limited right to use another person's property, a privilege. The simplest example is that the back portion of your property is near a major road, but does not have access without crossing a neighbor's drive. If the neighbor grants you limited access to use that back road, the arrangement can be documented as an easement.

Internet Sites to Help You Get the Home Improvements You Want

There are a host of home improvement web sites. In addition to commencing a general search through the various search engines, try the following sites:

- http://www.improvement.com provides a nationwide team of home improvement experts to make the home remodeling process more successful for both homeowners and service providers. Services include finding a contractor, finding a lender, finding maintenance and repair services, and more.

- http://www.myhomekey.com provides information and links to help you obtain home services and solve problems in your home. You can schedule an appointment with repair, service, and home improvement professionals in your area, purchase brand-name appliances and arrange to have them installed, obtain energy savings advice, connect with your community, organize vital home information, and more. Services include repairs, maintenance, improvements, and more.

- http://www.ourhouse.com is a web site that claims to have over 30,000 home products, expert advice in home decor and home improvement, plus information or links to reliable service professionals. The site is in partnership with Ace Hardware, a company with over 75 years of home improvement experience. The web site includes shopping for home products, a real estate center (find a home, an agent, a mover, a loan, insurance, and get a credit report), indoor and outdoor services (fencing, pool servicing, pest control, etc.), information and links to subcontractors (e.g., electrical, carpentry), links to cleaning services, information on using and finding contractors, and more.

INCOME TAX DEDUCTIONS RELATING TO THE PRINCIPAL RESIDENCE IN DIVORCE

Divorce raises a host of tax and legal issues concerning your home. The following discussion highlights a few of the tax questions that arise concerning expenses paid to operate a home when the couple is divorcing or divorced. See also Chapter 6 concerning the sale of a home and divorce.

It is common for one spouse to remain in the marital residence, typically with the children and the second spouse to vacate and establish a residence elsewhere, the non-occupant spouse. Where the non-occupant spouse pays some or all of the mortgage interest, property taxes, and other expenses, a number of issues arise as relating to who is entitled to claim the tax deductions.

For simplicity, let's assume the wife stays in the home and the husband moves to another residence. Is the husband who paid the expenses credited with having paid the taxes, interest, and other expenses?

If the husband is so credited, is he entitled to deduct the amounts so paid as taxes and interest? Will he receive a tax benefit for such deductions? Does the standard deduction, home mortgage interest, or some other limitation prevent him from realizing a tax benefit? Principal payments on a mortgage or rent on a residence are not deductible.

If the husband is not treated as having paid taxes, interest, or other payments, he could be treated as having paid alimony, child support, or a property settlement. Each of these items has a substantially different tax result.

Where the wife has paid the interest, taxes, or other expenses directly, is she entitled to deduct the amounts so paid as taxes and interest? Will she receive a tax benefit for such deductions? Does the standard deduction, home mortgage interest, or some other limitation prevent her from realizing a tax benefit? Principal payments on a mortgage or rent on a residence are not deductible.

The tax results to the parties can differ substantially depending on the resolution of these questions.

Example: Assume that the husband pays $1,500 to the mortgagee of the marital residence. If most of this payment is for deductible mortgage interest, the tax deduction for the husband, if he is deemed to have incurred such expense, could be worth approximately $500. Thus, the after-tax cost to the husband will be $1,000. If the husband transferred his entire interest in the house to his wife as part of the divorce settlement, the $1,500 payment could be characterized as alimony payments by the husband. Thus the amount would be deductible by him. The wife would report the $1,500 as alimony income and claim the deduction for the mortgage interest. If the wife, for example, had insufficient other itemized deductions, she may not gain any additional benefit for the mortgage interest deduction. Thus in this second scenario, the overall tax results for the two parties are quite different. If the divorce decree provided that the husband would only be obligated to pay the mortgage amount until his youngest child comes of age (18 years), then his payment would be nondeductible child support. The husband would not qualify to deduct the payment as either alimony or interest. The wife would not be taxed on the amount paid by the husband. She might, however, qualify for a home mortgage interest deduction.

In many matrimonial cases, the husband moves out of the marital residence but continues to pay some or all of the mortgage payments. Will the husband still qualify to deduct the mortgage interest payments? To qualify for a home mortgage interest deduction, the residence must be the taxpayer's principle residence. Where the couple is still married, even if they file separate tax returns, the husband will be treated as meeting this test since the tax law treats both spouses as one taxpayer for the purposes of this test. However, once the parties divorce, this exception will no longer be applicable. You may want to consult a tax accountant to see if there is any way to salvage the deduction.

If the marriage has not been terminated, the husband owns an interest in the marital residence, and is obligated on the mortgage, he will be treated as having made whatever interest and tax payments that he paid for. Therefore, he should be entitled to a tax deduction (subject to the home mortgage interest, standard deduction, and other rules).

Where the husband pays for mortgage, taxes, or other expenses, pursuant to either a separation agreement or a divorce decree, and the wife owns the entire interest in the former marital home (presumably, the husband transferred his interests in the marital residence to the wife as part of the property settlement), the husband's payments cannot be characterized as interest or taxes. They must be classified as either alimony, child support, or property settlement.

For payments to be characterized as alimony (and hence deductible by the payor), they must be made pursuant to a divorce decree or separation agreement. A verbal agreement will not suffice. The wife would report the amounts paid as interest or property taxes and claim the applicable deductions on her tax return. Payments to third parties on behalf of the wife (payee spouse) can qualify as alimony if made under a qualifying divorce instrument.

If the husband (payor spouse) owns the property and the wife (payee spouse) is permitted use of the property, the payment of these housing expenses cannot be deducted by the payor as alimony.

Where the ownership is as joint tenants or tenancy by the entirety, the husband's payments should be treated as interest, taxes, and other payments.

Where the husband pays for utilities or rental payments for the wife, these payments will be characterized as alimony, child support, or property settlement, depending on the agreement.

CHAPTER SUMMARY

Owning and operating a home is expensive and complex. The legal and tax issues are considerable. To secure the most tax benefits, avoid lawsuits and other legal pitfalls, you have to have some background about the issues and risks involved so you can hire the appropriate professionals to help you.

FOR YOUR NOTEBOOK

SAMPLE HOME BUILDING/IMPROVEMENT CONTRACT FORM TO DISCUSS WITH YOUR ARCHITECT AND ATTORNEY

Note: Determine who the parties are and make sure the name of the contractor is the exact name of the company that advertised and that you investigated.

AGREEMENT made this January 3, 2002 between Harry Homeowner (hereinafter referred to as the "Owner") and General Contractors Co., Inc. (hereinafter referred to as the "Contractor") as to the Addition on 5 North Avenue, Big City, USA (hereinafter referred to as the "Project" or "Work"). The Owner and Contractor agree as set forth below.

a. The Work

Note: Most contracts define the job by attaching exhibits listing various materials, steps, architectural plans, and the like. Be sure that the listing matches what is attached, and that it includes everything necessary to the job.

The Contractor shall perform all the Work required by the Contract Documents for Addition on 5 North Avenue.

b. Time of Commencement and Completion

Note: "On or about" is common language. It doesn't assure you that the work will be done within a few weeks of the target date. Review this issue with the architect and contractor. No contractor can guarantee whether, no union problems, materials being available, and so on. Determine what is reasonable to expect.

The Work to be performed under this Contract shall be commenced on or about October 1, 2002, and completed on or about December 15, 2002.

c. Contract Sum

Note: The contract price should cover everything listed in the contract. Be cautious for items listed as excluded, how extra items or changes will be handled, what you must provide, and so on.

The Owner shall pay the Contractor for the performance of the Work, subject to additions and deductions by Change Order as provided in the General Conditions, in current funds, the Contract Sum of Ninety Thousand Dollars ($90,000.00). The Owner shall pay or reimburse the Contractor, in current funds, for all local taxes imposed on the Project.

d. Progress Payments

Based on Applications for Payment submitted to the Owner by the Contractor, the Owner shall make progress payments on account of the Contract Sum to the Contractor as follows:

Note: Ideally every contractor wants to be ahead of the homeowner. They would like to have more money from you than what they've spent on the job. As a homeowner you want the opposite. The end result should be a payment structure that approximately tracks what the work is that has been completed. Another approach is to have the architect as an independent professional certify the portion of the job completed before you make progress payments. Also discuss how much you can hold back until the work is completed.

---

1. $33\frac{1}{3}$ percent on commencement;
2. $33\frac{1}{3}$ percent on completion of foundation, meaning 8-foot foundation wall and waterproofing;
3. $16\frac{2}{3}$ percent on commencement of interior work, meaning prior to installing doors, windows, and interior work.

Note: "Substantial" completion doesn't mean that everything is done. You may want to negotiate a final agreed hold back of the value of a punch list of final items.

---

4. $16\frac{2}{3}$ percent final payment on substantial completion.

The Owner shall make payment of all local taxes when taxes are due.

Owner agrees to pay to Contractor in monthly progress payments of _____ percent (_____%) of labor and materials that have been placed in position, with funds received by Contractor from Owner for work performed by Contractor as reflected in Contractor's applications for payment. Such monthly progress payments shall be made ten (10) days after receipt of payment from the Owner by Contractor. Final payment to Contractor shall be made ten (10) days after the entire work required by the Prime Contract has been fully completed in conformity to the Contract Documents and has been delivered to and accepted by Owner, Architect, and Contractor, with funds received by Contractor from Owner in final payment for work under the prime contract. Contractor agrees to furnish, if and when required by Homeowner, payroll affidavits, receipts, vouchers, releases of claims for labor, material, and from his Contractors performing work or furnishing materials under this Agreement, all in form satisfactory to Owner, and it is agreed that no payment hereunder shall be made, except at Owner's option, until and unless such documents have been furnished. Owner, at his option, may make any payment due hereunder by check made payable jointly to Contractor and any of his contractors, suppliers, and materialmen who have performed work or furnished materials under this Agreement. Any payment made hereunder prior to completion and acceptance of the work, as referred to above, shall not be construed as evidence of acceptance or acknowledgement of completion of any part of any Contractor's work.

e. Final Payment

The Owner shall make final payment three days after completion of the Work, provided the Contract be then fully performed, subject to the provisions hereof.

f. Enumeration of Contract Documents

Note: You must be certain all documents relating to the work are attached or referred to in the contract (the legal phrase is "incorporated by reference." Thus, the architectural plans are too long to attach, but specific plans by a named architect, as of a specified date, can be referred to.

The Contract Documents are as noted in the General Conditions and are enumerated as follows:

This Agreement (which includes the General Conditions), Supplementary and other Conditions, the Drawings, the Specifications, all Addenda issued prior to the execution of this Agreement and attached hereto, Change Orders.

g. Contract Documents

The Contract Documents consist of this Agreement (which includes the General Conditions), Supplementary and other Conditions, the Drawings, the Specifications, all Addenda issued prior to the execution of this Agreement and attached hereto, and Change Orders. These form the Contract and what is required by any one shall be as binding as if required by all. The intention of the Contract Documents is to include all labor, materials, equipment, and other items as provided in Exhibit _____ necessary for the proper execution and completion of the Work and the terms and conditions of payment therefor, and also to include all Work which may be reasonably inferable from the Contract Documents as being necessary to produce the intended results.

The Contract Documents shall be signed by the Owner and the Contractor. By executing the Contract, the Contractor represents that he has visited the site and familiarized himself with the local conditions under which the Work is to be performed.

The term Work as used in the Contract Documents includes all labor necessary to produce the construction required by the Contract Documents, and all materials and equipment incorporated in the construction.

h. Owner

1. The Owner shall furnish a survey.
2. The Owner shall secure and pay for easements for permanent structures or permanent changes in existing facilities.

3. The Owner shall pay all sales, consumer, use, and other similar taxes required by law.

i. Contractor

Note: The contract should be very clear as to what the contract is obligated to do.

The Contractor shall supervise and direct the work, using his best skill and attention. The Contractor shall be solely responsible for all construction means, methods, techniques, sequences, and procedures and for coordinating all portions of the Work under the Contract.

Unless otherwise specifically noted, the Contractor shall provide and pay for all labor, materials, equipment, tools, construction equipment and machinery, water, heat, utilities, transportation, and other facilities and services necessary for the proper execution and completion of the Work.

The Contractor shall at all times enforce strict discipline and good order among his employees, and shall not employ on the Work any unfit person or anyone not skilled in the task assigned to him.

Note: The following paragraph language is common, but not sufficient as there are many grades of materials that could meet the requirements below. You must have your architect specify the grades and quality of each item to be used in the job. Often a major difference between the prices bid by different contractors is the more expensive contractor may be assuming better quality materials.

The Contractor warrants to the Owner that all materials and equipment incorporated in the Work will be new unless otherwise specified, and that all Work will be of good quality, free from faults and defects and in conformance with the Contract Documents. All Work not so conforming to these standards may be considered defective.

Note: Who should pay for fees? In some towns, they can be quite expensive.

The Contractor shall secure all permits, fees and licenses necessary for the execution of the Work.

The Contractor shall give all notices and comply with all laws, ordinances, rules, regulations, and orders of any public authority bearing on the performance of the Work and shall notify the Owner if the Drawings and Specifications are at variance therewith.

The Contractor shall be responsible for the acts and omissions of all his employees and all subcontractors, their agents and employees and all other persons performing any of the Work under a contract with the Contractor.

The Contractor at all times shall keep the premises free from accumulation of waste materials or rubbish caused by his operations. At the completion of the Work, he shall remove all his waste materials and rubbish from and about the Project as well as his tools, construction equipment, machinery and surplus materials, and shall clean all glass surfaces and shall leave the Work "broom clean" or its equivalent, except as otherwise specified.

The Contractor shall indemnify and hold harmless the Owner from and against all claims, damages, losses and expenses including attorneys' fees arising out of or resulting from the performance of the Work, provided that any such claim, damage, loss or expense (1) is attributable to bodily injury, sickness, disease, or death, or to injury to or destruction of tangible property (other than the Work itself) including the loss of use resulting therefrom, and (2) is caused in whole or in part by any negligent act or omission of the Contractor, any subcontractor, anyone directly or indirectly employed by any of them or anyone for whose acts any of them may be liable, regardless of whether or not it is caused in part by a party indemnified hereunder. In any and all claims against the Owner by any employee of the Contractor, any subcontractor, anyone directly or indirectly employed by any of them or anyone for whose acts any of them may be liable, the Indemnification obligation under this Paragraph x.x shall not be limited in any way by any limitation on the amount or type of damages, compensation or benefits payable by or for the Contractor or any subcontractor under workmen's compensation acts, disability benefit acts or other employee benefit acts. The obligations of the Contractor under this provision shall not extend to the liability of the Architect, his agents or employees arising out of (1) the preparation or approval of maps, drawings, opinions, reports, surveys, change orders, designs, or specifications; or (2) the giving of or the failure to give directions or instructions by the Architect, his agents or employees provided such giving or failure to give is the primary cause of the injury or damage.

j. Subcontracts

Note: Most jobs have the contractor hiring one or more other contractors. These are called subcontractors since they work for the contractor you hired. You want to be sure that "subs" are properly licensed and that your contractor is responsible for their work. You don't want to have to fight with a sub you've never met or spoken with.

A subcontractor is a person who has a direct contract with the Contractor to perform any of the Work at the site.

The Contractor shall not employ any subcontractor to whom the Owner may have a reasonable objection. The Contractor shall not be required to employ any subcontractor to whom he has a reasonable objection. Contracts between the Contractor and the subcontractor shall be in accordance with the terms of this Agreement and shall include the General Conditions of this Agreement insofar as applicable.

k. Separate Contracts

Note: The following paragraph is often objectionable to contractors who want full control of the job site if they are to be responsible. You may be better off having the one contractor hire and coordinate everyone. Also, consider whether you really want to insist on your contractor using a sub you pick rather than a sub the contractor has worked with before.

The Owner reserves the right to award other contracts in connection with other portions of the Project or other work on the site under these or similar Conditions of the Contract.

The Contractor shall afford other contractors reasonable opportunity for the introduction and storage of their materials and equipment and the execution of their work, and shall properly connect and coordinate his Work with theirs.

Any costs caused by defective or ill-timed work shall be borne by the party responsible therefor.

l. Arbitration

All claims or disputes arising out of this Contract or the breach thereof shall be decided by arbitration in accordance with the Construction Industry Arbitration Rules of the American Arbitration Association then pertaining unless the parties mutually agree otherwise. Notice of the demand for arbitration shall be filed in writing with the other party to the

Contract and with the American Arbitration Association and shall be made within a reasonable time after the dispute has arisen.

m. Time

All time limits stated in the Contract Documents are of the essence of the Contract.

If the Contractor is delayed at any time in the progress of the Work by changes ordered in the Work, by labor disputes, fire, unusual delay in transportation, unavoidable casualties, causes beyond the Contractor's control, then the Contract Time shall be extended by Change Order for such reasonable time as the Contractor and Owner may mutually determine.

Contractor shall have complete control of the premises on which the work is to be performed and shall have the right to decide the time and order in which various portions of the work shall be installed and the relative priority of the work of Subcontractor and other subcontractors, and, in general, all other matters pertaining to the timely and orderly conduct of the work or neglect or default of Owner, Architect, or Contractor, or should a subcontractor be delayed waiting for materials, if required by this Contract to be furnished by Owner or Contractor, or by damage caused by fire or other casualty for which Subcontractor is not responsible, or by the combined action of the workmen, in no way caused by or resulting from fault or collusion on the part of a subcontractor, or in the event of a lock-out by Contractor, then the time herein fixed for the completion of the work shall be extended by the number of days that a subcontractor has thus been delayed, but no allowance or extension shall be made unless a claim therefor is presented in writing to Contractor within 48 hours of the commencement of such delay, and under no circumstances shall the time of completion be extended to a date which will prevent Contractor from completing the entire project within the time allowed Contractor by Owner for such completion.

n. Payments

Payments shall be made as provided in this Agreement.

Payments may be withheld on account of (1) defective work not remedied; (2) claims filed; (3) failure of the Contractor to make payments properly to subcontractors or for labor, materials, or equipment; (4) damage to another contractor; or (5) unsatisfactory prosecution of the Work by the Contractor.

Final payment shall not be due until the Contractor has delivered to the Owner a complete release of all liens arising out of this Contract or receipts in full covering all labor, materials, and equipment for which a lien could be filed, or a bond satisfactory to the Owner indemnifying him against any lien.

The making of final payment shall constitute a waiver of all claims by the Owner except those arising from (1) unsettled liens, (2) faulty or defective Work appearing after Substantial Completion, (3) failure of the Work to comply with the requirements of the Contract Documents, or (4) terms of any special guarantees required by the Contract Documents. The acceptance of final payment shall constitute a waiver of all claims by the Contractor except those previously made in writing and still unsettled.

o. Protection of Persons and Property

The Contractor shall be responsible for initiating, maintaining, and supervising all safety precautions and programs in connection with the Work. He shall take all reasonable precautions for the safety of, and shall provide all reasonable protection to prevent damage, injury or loss to (1) all employees on the Work and other persons who may be affected thereby, (2) all the Work and all materials and equipment to be incorporated therein, and (3) other property at the site or adjacent thereto. He shall comply with all applicable laws, ordinances, rules, regulations, and orders of any public authority having jurisdiction for the safety of persons or property or to protect them from damage, injury, or loss. All damage or loss to any property caused in whole or in part by the Contractor, any Subcontractor, or anyone directly or indirectly employed by any of them, or by anyone for whose acts any of them may be liable, shall be remedied by the Contractor, except damage or loss attributable to faulty Drawings or Specifications or to the acts or omissions of the Owner or Architect or anyone employed by either of them or for whose acts either of them may be liable but which are not attributable to the fault or negligence of the Contractor.

p. Contractor's Liability Insurance

Note: Obtain a certificate of insurance. Also as owner you should speak with your homeowners insurance company to be sure you have all the appropriate insurance for construction.

The Contractor and each separate Contractor shall purchase and maintain such insurance as will protect him from claims under workmen's compensation acts and other employee benefit acts, from claims for damages because of bodily injury, including death, and from claims for damages to property which may arise out of or result from the Contractor's operations under this Contract, whether such operations be by himself or by any Subcontractor or anyone directly or indirectly employed by any of them. This insurance shall be written for not less than any limits of liability specified as part of this Contract, or required by law, whichever is the greater, and shall include contractual liability insurance as applicable to the Contractor's obligations under Paragraph xx. Certificates of such insurance shall be filed with the Owner and each separate Contractor.

q. Owner's Liability Insurance

The Owner shall be responsible for purchasing and maintaining his own liability insurance and, at his option, may maintain such insurance as will protect him against claims that may arise from operations under the Contract.

r. Property Insurance

Unless otherwise provided, the Owner shall purchase and maintain property insurance on the entire Work at the site to the full insurable value thereof. This insurance shall include the interests of the Owner, the Contractor, Subcontractors, and Sub-subcontractors in the Work and shall insure against the perils of Fire, Extended Coverage, Vandalism, and Malicious Mischief.

Any insured loss is to be adjusted with the Owner and made payable to the Owner as trustee for the insured, as their interest may appear, subject to the requirements of any mortgagee clause.

The Owner shall file a copy of all policies with the Contractor prior to the commencement of the Work.

The Owner and Contractor waive all rights against each other for damages caused by fire or other perils to the extent covered by insurance provided under this paragraph. The Contractor shall require similar waivers by Subcontractors and Sub-subcontractors.

s. Changes in the Work

Note: Changes are probably the biggest source of disputes. The key to avoiding this is think through everything possible in advance. Attach all agreements or incorporate them by reference in the contract. Work with reputable professionals (contractor, architect, and lawyer) and be sure all changes are agreed to in writing.

The Owner without invalidating the Contract may order Changes in the Work consisting of additions, deletions, or modifications, the Contract

Sum and the Contract Time being adjusted accordingly. All such Changes in the Work shall be authorized by written Change Order signed by the Owner.

The Contract Sum and the Contract Time may be changed only by Change Order.

The cost or credit to the Owner from a Change in the Work shall be determined by mutual agreement.

t. Correction of Work

The Contractor shall correct any Work that fails to conform to the requirements of the Contract Documents where such failure to conform appears during the progress of the Work, and shall remedy any defects due to faulty materials, equipment, or workmanship which appear within a period of one year from the Date of Substantial Completion of the Contract or within such longer period of time as may be prescribed by law or by the terms of any applicable special guarantee required by the Contract Documents. The provisions of this contract apply to Work done by Subcontractors as well as to Work done by direct employees of the Contractor.

u. Liens

In case suit is brought on any claim or liens for labor performed or materials used on or furnished to the project, Subcontractor shall pay and satisfy any such lien or judgment as may be established by the decision of the court in said suit. Subcontractor agrees within ten (10) days after written demand to cause the effect of any such suit or lien to be removed from the premises, and in the event Subcontractor shall fail so to do, Contractor is authorized to use whatever means in its discretion it may deem appropriate to cause said lien or suit to be removed or dismissed and the cost thereof, together with actual attorneys' fees, shall be immediately due and payable to Contractor by Subcontractor. Subcontractor may litigate any such lien or suit provided he causes the effect thereof to be removed, promptly in advance, from the premises, and shall further do such things as may be necessary to cause Owner not to withhold any monies due to Contractor from Owner by reason of such liens or suits.

v. Termination by the Contractor

If the Owner fails to respond to an Application for Payment for a period of four days through no fault of the Contractor, or if the Owner fails to make payment thereon for a period of seven days, the Contractor may, upon four days' written notice to the Owner, terminate the Contract and recover from the Owner payment for all Work executed and for any proven loss sustained upon any materials, equipment, tools, and construction equipment and machinery, including reasonable profit and damages.

w. Termination by the Owner

If the Contractor defaults or neglects to carry out the Work in accordance with the Contract Documents or fails to substantially perform any provision of the Contract, the Owner may, after seven days' written notice to the Contractor and without prejudice to any other remedy he may have, make good such deficiencies and may deduct the cost thereof from the payment then or thereafter due the Contractor or, at his option, may terminate the Contract and take possession of the site and of all materials, equipment, tools, and construction equipment and machinery thereon owned by the Contractor and may finish the Work by whatever method he may deem expedient, and if the unpaid balance of the Contract Sum exceeds the expense of finishing the Work, such excess shall be paid to the Contractor, but if such expense exceeds such unpaid balance, the Contractor shall pay the difference to the Owner.

This Agreement executed the day and year first written above.

[Signature lines and notary forms omitted.]

SAMPLE RECORD KEEPING FORM FOR PROPERTY IMPROVEMENTS

You should maintain detailed records of the cost of your home, capital improvements that add to your tax basis, and so on. These records are helpful in the event of a zoning change, casualty loss, fire, theft, and so on. They can demonstrate to the IRS, and insurance company or court what you've spent and the condition of your home. Further, although $250,000/$500,000 exclusions sound high, inflation may erode their value. You can never be certain whether you will meet all of the requirements of the exclusion.

Note: For more information and many detailed template and record keeping instructions, see Shenkman, *The Beneficiary Handbook* (John Wiley & Sons, Inc.).

REAL ESTATE IMPROVEMENTS				
Property: _____				
Date	Description	Reference	Cost	Copy Attached

SAMPLE HOME MAINTENANCE
RECORD KEEPING FORM

Use copies of this form to track home repairs. This can be helpful to identify when routine maintenance should be ordered, whether repairs were properly made, as a record if you are selling your home, qualifying for warranties, and so forth. Number the receipts sequentially and keep them in a file or loose leaf binder behind the home maintenance form. While some computer programs help you track maintenance, you should still maintain a paper file so that you have your receipts organized.

Note: If you use a check paying program on your computer, you will have a separate account for home repairs. Periodically print out the detail report of that account and file with your template and bills.

Date of Repair (Number of Bill Attached)	System Repaired (e.g., "Roof")	Contractor: Name, Address, Telephone Number	Description of Repair	Payment (Check Number, Credit Card, etc.)	Date for Next Service Call or Follow Up

SAMPLE EASEMENT TO DISCUSS WITH YOUR REAL ESTATE ATTORNEY

This Easement agreement made [Month, Day, Year] between [Your Name], as user (Tenant, or User), whose address is [Your Address], and [Neighbor/Name], as provider (Dominant Tenant, or Provider), whose address is [Neighbor Address].

Note: If you are to pay a one time or periodic fee, this should be reflected in the agreement.

NOW THEREFORE, for $1.00 and other good and valuable consideration receipt of which is acknowledged, the User and Provider agree as follows:

The Provider, for himself, his heirs and assigns, grants and conveys unto the User, and the User's heirs and assigns, an easement in and to and upon and over that parcel of property described in Schedule A attached hereto [have a survey company prepare, and your attorney review, a legal description of the area of the easement. The description should include a schematic as well as a metes and bounds legal description], located on the [Property Address], in [County, State].

This Easement is granted for the sole purpose of providing routine, normal and typical residential real estate ingress and egress to [Your Address] residence [describe other permitted uses if applicable]. Access is expressly limited to automobile, delivery and pedestrian traffic, but expressly excluding construction, commercial or other vehicles [describe other limits or restrictions, if any].

User covenants that User or User's heirs, successors and assigns, will maintain and repair the roadway subject to this Easement in reasonable fashion and hold Provider and Provider's heirs and assigns, harmless from any suit or claim relating to the User's use or maintenance of the Easement.

The term of this easement shall end on [indicate date or event of termination].

IN WITNESS WHEREOF, the parties have set their signatures below, as of the date first above written:

[Signature and notary forms omitted.]

4 PROTECTING YOUR HOME

Your home, as mentioned many times in this book, is likely to be your largest, or one of your largest assets. Therefore, protecting your investment is an obviously important step to take. This is not as simple as taking photographs and purchasing insurance or having fire extinguishers on each level. There are many risks to protect your home from, often risks which the typical homeowner overlooks. This chapter will highlight many of them and give you practical advice as to how to protect your home.

PROTECTING YOUR HOME IF YOU BECOME DISABLED

Disability is a major risk. Most homeowners, especially younger ones, likely have life insurance. But at most ages, disability is a far greater risk than death. If you are sick or injured and can't work for six months, how will you make your mortgage payments and cover the other costs of home ownership? The answer is you have to plan or you could lose your home.

Insurance Protection

Insurance protection can come in several forms. Everyone who is working and relying on their income to support them should consider disability insurance. This pays some portion (often 60 percent or less) of what you earned while you are disabled. Disability insurance can be expensive. You can control the costs by joining a group plan (e.g., a fraternal or professional group you belong to may have a cheaper rate for members). Your employer may make coverage available. If you have to buy your own coverage, consider eliminating some of the frills and structuring a policy to obtain the coverage you need at the least cost. For example, if you have sufficient savings to tide you over for three months, you could take a three-month waiting period on the policy. This means that the policy won't pay until you've been disabled at least three months.

Business overhead insurance should be considered by self-employed business owners who need to protect a business and their home. If you are disabled or have a casualty at your business, you may still have to pay for expenses to keep your business going. If these expenses eat up your savings, how will you provide for your home? The answer may be to obtain business insurance.

Other Financial Resources to Protect Your Home

Lines of credit, home equity lines, and cash reserves all provide for meeting your expenses in the event of an emergency. Investigate them all. If you can obtain a home equity line at no or nominal cost for your house, why not do so? In the event of any emergency, disability or otherwise, you can tap that line of credit to meet expenses while you sort things out or recover. Every financial planning magazine and book on disability planning suggests some level of emergency funds or savings.

Durable Power of Attorney

Having adequate cash resources is only one step in protecting your home. If you are ill, someone may have to handle any of the many legal matters discussed in this book for you. They won't have any authority to do so unless you grant them a power of attorney to deal with your home. This is a legal document in which you, as the principal, authorize another person, called your agent, to transact business and legal matters on your behalf. If, for example, your illness is so severe that your home needs to be sold, you need someone to have the authority to do this. If you do not have a durable power of attorney (durable means it will continue to be valid even if you are disabled), your family or others will have to hire a lawyer and may have to have someone appointed as your legal guardian to handle these matters. This is an expensive and time-consuming process.

PROTECTING YOUR HOME FROM MEDICAID

Many, if not most, elderly homeowners fear losing their homes, and other assets, to cover medical care and nursing costs. The rules are a complex web of federal and state statutes and regulations and vary tremendously depending on what state you reside in. Planning can be further complicated by the wide array of private insurance and other arrangements. You really should consult with an elder law specialist in your area. This is not a tax or estate specialist, but rather someone who devotes a substantial part of their time to planning for the elderly and who has familiarity with the state laws, insurance programs, and other factors that will affect your planning.

If your income and assets don't fall below some rather low hurdle rates, Medicaid won't pay the nursing home bills. Meeting these tests while conserving your house and other assets for your spouse and children or other heirs is the focus of the planning. Certain assets, depending on your state's laws, are excluded from these tests to determine Medicaid eligibility. This means these assets can be owned and won't be depleted to pay costly nursing home bills in lieu of Medicaid covering the costs. Your house may be protected if it was your principal home and was occupied by you, the patient, or your spouse. However, if both you and your spouse are absent from the home for more than six months, the law may presume that the home is no longer a principal residence, and it would therefore no longer be protected.

Caution: The specific rules differ by state, and there are a host of technical details and rules beyond the scope of this brief discussion. Be certain to consult an elder law specialist (not a general estate planner) in your area well in advance of any needs arising.

A look-back rule requires that the state authorities look at assets transferred within some time period, say 36 to 60 months before you entered a nursing facility. So if you transfer assets to your children, for example, 20 months before entering a nursing facility, those assets may be reached to pay for your care. Alternatively, those assets may be used in a state-mandated calculation that determines how many months of care must be paid for by your assets before state programs will be available to cover the cost to you. You may be permitted, as a patient, to transfer the home to a spouse, minor or disabled child, a child who has lived in the home for two years caring for the parent, or to certain siblings.

The planning that the elderly often consider is transferring their house more than the requisite number of months before they anticipate applying for Medicaid, transferring their house to excluded persons, or converting a nonexcluded resource into an excluded resource (e.g., a renter can use liquid funds, which aren't an excluded resource, to buy a house that may be an excluded resource under your state's laws).

A classic approach is for you as the parent to gift the house to the children and reserve a life estate in the property. This gives you as the parent the right to live in the home and assures that the full value of the home will be included in the parent's estate. This will provide a step-up in tax basis (since the house is included in your estate for federal estate tax purposes) and save the heir income tax on their eventual sale of the property (because of the step up in basis, see Chapter 6). Although it could be argued that the life estate has value, Medicaid seems at present to accept this as having no value for eligibility purposes.

Planning Tip: See the sample deed with a life estate on page 179.

Another approach is to gift the entire interest in the house and execute a lease for use of the property. There are also ways to transfer assets to trusts to accomplish these objectives. Estate, gift, and other transfer taxes must be considered in such planning. However, with the increase in the exclusion (amount you can gift or bequeath tax free is $1 million in 2002) most people won't have to worry about estate and gift taxes when engaging in this type of planning.

HOW TO PROPERLY INSURE YOUR HOME

Homeowners' Insurance Basics

It is important for you, as a homeowner, to be aware of the many risks to your property and whether or not these risks need insurance. Basic homeowner's policies usually will cover normal problems like fire damage, water damage, and theft, in addition to more unusual occurrences like plane crashes and civil riots. This will prove sufficient for many homeowners. However, there are a few issues that must be dealt with separately depending on geographical location.

One risk that may not be covered by basic insurance is the risk of earthquakes, volcanoes, and other natural disasters. For many people, these risks don't apply. However, if you live in a natural-disaster prone area, it is important to make sure that you are properly insured and understand the limits of your insurance coverage. You should understand how large a deductible there is on the insurance and how this affects costs. The *deductible* is the amount that the insurance company won't pay. If you have a $500 deductible, the insurance company won't pay the first $500 of any loss. The larger the deductible, the less the premium.

Not all insurance policies are created equal. Review the policies you are considering and answer the following questions:

- Is the amount of coverage reasonable in light of the value of your home? Personal property (furniture, clothes, etc.) is sometimes covered as to a percentage of the value of the home coverage. Are the figures adequate? Most policies include special limits for certain types of property such as cash, jewelry, art work, and so on. If these limits are not sufficient (and they almost never are), you need the additional protection offered by a *floater* or *rider* for that property.

- What are the deductibles? Don't assume that the main deductible is the *only* deductible. There are often separate deductibles for different types of items. Be sure to review them all.

- What is the basis on which payment is determined? Even if you have adequate coverage, if the insurance policy will pay only the value of your home up to its depreciated value, or fair market value, that amount may not be enough to rebuild your home if it is severely damaged. If the replacement cost to rebuild your house is more, then you will be short of funds. Review the payment basis in the policy as well as the policy limits to be sure you really have the coverage you need.

- What types of limitations are included in the policy? For example, the policy might require that you commence or even complete rebuilding your house within a specified time period of the damage. If the time period is too short to be reasonable,

even a payment basis that sounds liberal may not be. Policies
can include a host of other limitations. You have to read your
policy thoroughly to understand what you are getting.

- Most policies require that you insure a minimum percentage
  of the value of the house for full coverage to be available. Be
  sure that you meet that requirement.

- What losses will the policy protect you against? These are
  called *covered losses*. Does it include all risks you are concerned
  about? What risks are excluded? Often flood and earthquake
  damage is excluded. If these are real risks, you may need additional coverage. Many policies will say "all risks, except as
  otherwise provided." Read the fine print of what is otherwise
  provided. It could be significant.

- Does the policy cover other permanent structures such as
  garage, utility hut, and so on? Are the limits reasonable?

- Are living expenses covered? If your house is severely damaged
  you may not be able to live there until it is repaired. The costs
  of temporary housing could be as great as the repair costs in
  some instances. Will your policy cover your living expenses?
  Under what circumstances? With what limits?

- Is landscaping, tree removal, fire department charges, debris
  removal, and other items covered? Many policies do not cover
  these potentially expensive "extras."

- Will the policy cover rebuilding or repairs up to the current
  town code standards? If your house is old, the building codes
  were likely less stringent when your house was built. However,
  if a major repair or rebuilding is to be undertaken, the current
  building codes apply. If your policy limits the payments to
  those based on the existing house, it may not provide the
  money you need to be able to rebuild.

- Does the policy cover business property? This is important for
  many homeowners even if they don't have a formal home office. Many homeowners have computer and other electronic
  equipment at home which they use for work. See the discussion in Chapter 3 about home offices.

- Does the policy cover breakage of fragile items? If not, and
  you are moving, verify that your mover's contract covers any
  potential damage. See Chapter 3 about moving expenses.

- What type of personal liability coverage does the policy include? What is covered? What is excluded? Does the coverage include the costs of legal fees to defend you against a claim? Legal fees can be as expensive as the amount you are ultimately required to pay, sometimes more.
- What types of medical coverage are provided?

Business, Rental, and Other Special Risks

If you operate a business in your home, you at minimum will need to check with your insurance agent about special riders to extend your homeowners coverage to apply to the business. In many cases, as explained in Chapter 3, you will need special insurance.

Umbrella or Personal Excess Liability Insurance

To cover personal injury and similar claims that may occur in amounts greater than the limits available under your general property insurance, it is important to have an additional liability coverage policy. Basic liability coverage under most homeowners' insurance policies is not enough to protect you in case of serious personal injury. Typically, this type of insurance may only cover $300,000 in damages (the amounts vary by policy and insurer). If, however, a personal injury were to occur and the resulting lawsuit was for $1 million, you would be left to pay the balance by yourself (i.e., $700,000). Therefore, it is prudent to consider and often purchase additional coverage which is typically called an *umbrella policy* or personal excess liability policy. This would increase the amount of the coverage over the amount of liability coverage offered under your general homeowners policy. Amounts are typically $1 million and greater.

Title Insurance

Title insurance, which protects your ownership interest in your home, was discussed in Chapter 1.

Web sites That Provide Insurance Information

There are a number of good web sites that can help you with home-owners insurance issues. Consider the following as a starting point:

- http://www.insurance.com can guide you through the entire process of buying insurance, from choosing the right products to selecting from multiple quotes to ultimately, purchasing insurance. Insurance.com offers access to auto insurance (usually covered under the same umbrella or excess liability policy as your home), term life insurance (a better way to address insurance to repay your mortgage on death than mortgage insurance), homeowners insurance, and more. This site provides a "Get a Quote" feature where you enter the state in which you live, and you are linked to an insurance company that can give you a free quote. In addition, this web site provides a basic introduction to home insurance, as well as answers to frequently asked questions associated with home insurance.

- http://www.insweb.com operates an online insurance marketplace that enables consumers to shop for a variety of insurance products, including automobile, term life, homeowners, and other insurance.

- http://www.insweb.com is a resource that can provide homeowners insurance quotes through several partnership companies. However, there are a limited number of states for which you can get an insurance quote. In addition, insweb.com provides a learning center that features up-to-date articles on issues that may concern homeowners.

PRACTICAL SECURITY FOR YOUR HOME AND ITS CONTENTS

This book has focused on legal issues for your home. Taking legal steps to protect your home or vacation home and tax planning steps alone are not enough. You need to take basic steps to protect your home physically as well. The following discussion highlights some of these issues so that you don't overlook them.

Lights, Camera, Action

Let's shed a little light on home security. Every survey you read lists lighting near the top of the steps you can take to safeguard your home. If your home isn't well illuminated at night, add outdoor spot lights. Inside have several lights on timers so that the home always, at least to an amateur burglar, appears occupied. Consider installing emergency lights that are activated when the power fails. They can help prevent injury as you look for the flashlights and candles you keep on hand for such emergencies.

A picture is worth a thousand words. Take photographs and keep them in your safe deposit box at the bank. There is no cheaper, simpler, and easier method to demonstrate what was in your home and the condition of your home in the event of a casualty loss, robbery, or other problem. Photographs can remind you what was lost or damaged in a flood, or show an IRS agent that you really suffered the losses deducted on your tax return. Take photographs of every room, from every possible angle. Before shooting, be certain to open every drawer and closet so that the contents are visible. Buy a permanent marker and note on the back of the photographs key content items and the date of the photograph.

Get an Alarm

Good locks on your doors, secure windows, and lights are the first step to physically protecting your home. The next step is a home alarm. These can range from modestly priced, simple systems to complex, costly arrangements. Consider what is best for you. Fire and smoke detectors are a must. You can have them wired through an alarm to a monitoring station so that they will safeguard your home even when you're gone. A good starting point for your research is the Internet. You can consider the following web sites:

- http://www.go2homeprotect.com provides security information for your home, family, valuables, or business from Alliant Energy Resources Home Protection.
- http://www.respond.com/apps can help you with everything from a basic security system for your home to an all-inclusive

system to monitor your home or other building. The site provides products and services that will keep you safe and put your mind at ease.

- http://www.adt.com is the web site for one of the largest and best-known security firms—ADT.

CHAPTER SUMMARY

Protecting your home is more complex and requires much broader planning than most people anticipate. Protecting your home includes the obvious things like an alarm system and proper insurance. But it also includes operating your business and investment assets in the correct form using an entity to limit liability so that a claim against your business will not enable someone to seize your house or other personal assets to satisfy a claim. Proper disability planning to protect your home if you cannot work is just as essential. This chapter has reviewed these and other planning steps you should consider to protect your most valuable asset.

FOR YOUR NOTEBOOK

SAMPLE DEED LANGUAGE GIVING AWAY YOUR HOME WHILE RETAINING A LIFE ESTATE TO DISCUSS WITH YOUR ELDER LAW ADVISER AND ATTORNEY

Prepared By:

_____

Attorney Signature

a. Date of Deed; Parties

This Deed is made on [Month, Day, Year] between [Your Name], whose post office address is [Your Address], referred to as the Grantor; and [Grantee Names] [e.g., typically your children], whose post office address is [Grantee Address], referred to as the Grantee. The words "Grantor" and "Grantee" shall mean all grantors and all grantees listed above.

b. Property

1. The address of the property is [Property Address].
2. [Map Reference]. Municipality of [Town Name].
3. The Block Number is [Block Number]. The Lot Number [Lot Number]. Account No. [   ].
4. The property consists of the land and all the buildings and structures on the land in the Township of [   ], County of [   ] and State of [   ].

Note: The legal description is often quite lengthy and can be attached as a schedule to the deed.

---

5. The legal description is: [Legal Description].
6. A tax identification number for the property is [Tax Number].

c. Transfer of Ownership

> **Note:** The deed used for elder law planning is often structured as a gift. When this is done there is no indication of the real value of the house being transferred as there would be in a deed used to purchase a house.

1. The Grantor grants and conveys (transfers ownership of) the property described below to the Grantee. This transfer is made for the sum of One ($1.00) Dollar and 00/100.
2. The Grantor acknowledges receipt of this money.
3. The Grantee, and Grantee's heirs and assigns, is to have and to hold the Property transferred herein, forever, excepting and reserving from this transfer the life estate reserved to the Grantor, below.

d. Promises of Grantor to Grantee Relating to Transfer

The Grantor promises that the grantor has done no act to encumber the property. This promise is called a "covenant as to grantor's acts" as defined under applicable state law. This promise means that the Grantor has not allowed anyone else to obtain any legal rights that affect the property (such as by making a mortgage or allowing a judgment to be entered against the Grantor).

e. Transfer Subject to Life Estate

> **Note:** The following is a key provision in using a gift of your house to protect it from medical costs. You retain a life estate. This enables you to live in the house and enables your heirs to obtain a step up in the investment (tax basis) in the house on your death.

The transfer herein is expressly made subject to a life estate, to the grantor for and during the natural life of Grantor. This reserved life estate includes the exclusive enjoyment, possession, and use of the premises, and the exclusive rights to all rents and profits from, or attributable to the property.

f. Witnesseth

That in consideration of One Dollar and no 00/100, the said [Grantor Name], the grantor does grant and convey unto the said [Grantee Names], grantees, the interests in the Property.

The grantor signs this Deed as of the date first above written.

_____
Grantor Name

Witnessed By:

Witness Name: _____

Witness Signature: _____

State of [State Name]

ss:

County of [County Name]

I Certify that on [Date, Grantor Name], personally came before me and acknowledged under oath, to my satisfaction, that this person (or if more than one, each person), was the maker of this Deed; executed this Deed as his or her act and deed; and made this Deed for $1.00 as the full and actual consideration paid or to be paid for the transfer of title.

Record and Return to:
[Attorney Name]

_____
[Attorney Name]
An Attorney at Law in the State of [State Name].

SAMPLE DURABLE POWER OF ATTORNEY WITH PROVISIONS CONCERNING YOUR HOME TO DISCUSS WITH YOUR ATTORNEY

Note: If your house closing is scheduled and you will be out of town, say on vacation or attending to a personal emergency, you can use a special power of attorney to authorize someone to handle the closing for you. If this is done, the power of attorney form has to be modified substantially so that all powers given the person you are designating to act ("agent") are restricted so that they only pertain to the closing. This sample form, in contrast, is a general power authorizing your agent to take action in most situations.

For a more comprehensive general power of attorney form, with annotations, see the website: www.laweasy.com. For a detailed power of attorney with comprehensive tax and economic commentary see: Shenkman, *Tax Practitioner's Guide to Reviewing Legal Documents* (Practitioner's Publishing Company, Inc.).

KNOW ALL PERSONS BY THESE PRESENTS, that I [Your Name] (the Grantor) (Social Security Number: [Social Sec]), residing at [Your Address], being of the age of majority under the laws of [State Name], and of sufficient capacity to conduct my business and financial affairs, in order to provide for management of Grantor's financial, legal and related, affairs in a more orderly fashion, hereby declare as follows:

Appointment of Agent

Note: Determine who to appoint as agent. Be sure it is someone trustworthy. You can name co-agents but it may make it impossible to obtain quick action in an emergency.

Grantor hereby makes, constitutes, and appoints (Grant) [Agent 1 Name] residing at [Agent 1 Address], as Grantor's true and lawful Attorney-in-Fact and agent (the Agent) for Grantor and in Grantor's name, place, and stead and for Grantor's benefit, or any alternate appointed in accordance with the provisions of this Power of Attorney (the Agent).

Alternate Agent

If [Agent 1 Name] is unwilling or unable to act as Agent, Grantor appoints the first person able and willing to serve from the following list, as Grantor's Agent (the Alternate Agent):

Note: Name several successors.

---

a. [Agent 2 Name], who resides at [Agent 2 Address].

b. [Agent 3 Name], who resides at [Agent 3 Address].

c. [Agent 4 Name], who resides at [Agent 4 Address].

Such person shall serve as Grantor's Agent. The timing of the appointment of the Alternate Agent shall be governed by the provision below, "Effective Date." Any rights or powers granted to the Agent are granted to the Alternate Agent, unless specifically provided to the contrary.

Note: If this were to be a special power of attorney solely used for a closing, the next provision would be deleted.

Direction to Agent to Support
Grantor and Named Persons

a. The Agent is hereby authorized and directed to perform all acts reasonable and necessary to maintain Grantor's customary standard of living: to provide living quarters by purchase, lease, or other arrangement, or by payment of the operating costs of Grantor's existing living quarters, including interest, amortization payments, repairs, taxes, and so forth; to provide for the retention and payment of reasonably necessary domestic help for the maintenance and operation of Grantor's household; to finance or arrange for the purchase of other necessaries, including but not limited to clothing, transportation, entertainment, and incidentals; and to provide medical care.

b. The Agent is further authorized and directed to provide for the health, education, support, and maintenance of Grantor's spouse, and Grantor's children (whether or not such children are minors or dependents, and even if above the age of majority), in accordance with an ascertainable standard as defined in Code Section 2041 and the Regulations thereunder. Grantor recognizes that such transfers to or for the benefit of persons other than Grantor may constitute gifts and authorizes that such transfers be permitted and that such transfers not be restricted by the provisions below under the caption "Gifts."

Powers of Agent

Note: The italicized language illustrates one of the many types of modifications your attorney might make to a general power of attorney form so that it could only be used to consummate a real estate closing in your absence. Other modifications necessary for this limited use or special power of attorney are not illustrated.

The Agent is hereby granted all the powers and rights necessary to effect Grantor's wishes *pertaining solely to the consummating of the closing of the purchase of the single family residence located at 123 Main Street, Anytown, USA, in accordance with a Contract of Sale, Form X-3, dated January 2, 2003, including matters pertaining to the title of said house and the closing of the mortgage financing with First State Bank in accordance with a commitment dated January 23, 2003,* including, in addition to any power authorized by the laws of [State Name] for an agent, the following:

a. General Financial Matters

Request, ask, demand, sue for, recover, sell, collect, forgive, receive, and hold money, debts, dues, commercial paper, checks, drafts, accounts, deposits, legacies, bequests, devises, notes, interests, stocks, bonds, certificates of deposit, annuities, pension and retirement benefits, insurance proceeds, any and all documents of title, choses in action, personal and real property, intangible and tangible property and property rights, and demands whatsoever, liquidated or unliquidated, as now are or may become owned by, or due, owing, payable, or belonging to Grantor, or in which Grantor has or may hereafter acquire interest. Agent may use and take all lawful means and equitable and legal remedies, procedures, and writs in Grantor's name for the collection and recovery of the above; and may adjust, sell, compromise, and agree for the same; and to make, execute, and deliver for Grantor, on Grantor's behalf and in Grantor's name, all endorsements, acceptances, releases, receipts, or other sufficient discharges for the same.

b. Social Security and Government Benefits

Apply to any governmental agency for any benefit or government obligation to which Grantor may be entitled; endorse any drafts or checks made payable to Grantor from any such agency. To serve as a representative payee for Social Security or other governmental payments. The Agent is expressly authorized to execute vouchers on Grantor's behalf for reimbursements properly payable to Grantor by the United States government or any agency thereof or any state agency. The Agent is expressly authorized to change Grantor's address for the purpose of receiving checks, mail, or other matters from the Social Security Administration or any other governmental agency.

Note: The following paragraph would be included in a general and special power if the special power is to deal with real estate, such as your home. However, if the special power of attorney is to be limited solely to enabling your agent to buy or sell a particular house, this provision would be restricted to that transaction and for the particular property involved.

---

c. Contract, Real Estate, and Other Matters

Exercise or perform any act, power, duty, right, or obligation that Grantor now has, or may acquire, including the legal right, power, or capacity to exercise or perform in connection with, arising from, or relating to any person or property, real or personal, tangible or intangible, or matter whatsoever, including, without limiting the foregoing, the right to execute a deed or security agreement; to release a security agreement; to enter into a lease, option, mortgage or similar arrangement; to enter into a contract of sale and to sell or purchase any real, personal, tangible, or intangible property on Grantor's behalf, including but not limited to the property located at [Your Address] and [Other Property].

d. Securities and Investments

Make, receive, sign, endorse, acknowledge, deliver, and possess documents of title, bonds, debentures, checks, drafts, stocks, proxies, or warrants, relating to accounts or deposits, or certificates of deposit, other debts and obligations, and such other instruments in writing of whatever kind and nature as may be necessary or proper in the exercise of the rights and powers herein granted. Sell, or purchase any and all shares of stocks, bonds, or other securities now or later belonging to Grantor that may be issued by any association, trust, or corporation, whether private or public; and make, execute, and deliver any assignment, or assignments, of any such shares of stocks, bonds, or other securities.

e. Legal Actions

Settle, adjust, compromise, or submit to arbitration any accounts, claims, debts, demands, disputes, or other matters between Grantor and any other person or entity, or which concern any property, right, title, interest, or estate. Begin, prosecute, enforce, abandon, defend, or settle all claims or judicial or administrative proceedings. Execute and file documents to toll any statute of limitations. Grantor recognizes that the inclusion of the latter phrase may serve to prevent the tolling of a statute of limitations or other deadline which would otherwise be tolled pending Grantor's disability.

Note: Should gifts be permitted to be made of your residence? What about your vacation home? Should there be limits? What about the authority to transfer your house to a Qualified Personal Residence Trust or by-pass trust to save estate taxes? What about a gift deed reserving you a life estate?

---

f. Gifts

1. Make outright gifts of cash or property to an adult, or to a person under the age of majority according to applicable State law under the State Gifts to Minors' Act or Transfers to Minors' Act in custodial form, or to a trust for the benefit of any such minor. If an irrevocable trust exists for such person, and such person is the sole current beneficiary of such trust, the gift may be made to such trust for the benefit of such person.

2. Gifts made under this authority to each donee in any calendar year shall not exceed the maximum amount that is excluded as a taxable gift under Code Section 2503(b) and 2503(e), or any successor statute, effective as of the date of any gift. Although this amount is presently limited to $10,000 ($20,000 for gifts split with Grantor's spouse), as indexed, and amounts paid for educational or medical expenses (as defined under Code Section 2503(e)), Grantor understands that this amount may be changed by legislation following the execution of this Power of Attorney, and indexing, and such changed or indexed amounts shall apply. However, gifts to Grantor's spouse may be unlimited so long as no federal gift tax is incurred.

Note: Who can your agent make gifts to? If your house is involved as part of your assets which your agent may give away, carefully consider who the agent can make the gifts to.

---

3. Permissible donees ("Authorized Donees") hereunder shall include Grantor's spouse, any child of Grantor and their descendants, as well as any person who shall be married to any of the foregoing. In addition, permissible donees shall include any person to whom Grantor has had a longstanding practice of making annual gifts.

4. The power granted in this paragraph may be exercised by the Agent without regard to any laws concerning self-dealing. Grantor specifically grants to the Agent the right to make gifts to himself or herself, his or her spouse, and their issue if such persons are within the class of permissible donees as defined in this paragraph. Grantor grants to the Agent the power to prepare, sign, and file gift tax returns with respect to gifts made by Grantor, or by the Agent on Grantor's behalf, for any year or years; to consent to any gift and to utilize any gift-splitting provision or other tax election relating thereto. This power is in addition to and not in limitation of the specific tax powers granted below.

g. Disclaimers

Note: Disclaimers can be an extremely important part of asset protection and estate planning. Be sure your agent is authorized to disclaim assets.

Execute a qualified disclaimer without court approval under State law, and/or under Code Section 2518. A disclaimer may be exercised as to part or all of any asset, interest, gift, or transfer of any kind or nature that may pass to Grantor under any instrument or transaction.

h. Transfer of Property to Trust

Note: A common transaction is the transfer of a residence to a living trust. Be sure your power of attorney permits this.

---

1. With respect to a revocable living trust for the benefit of Grantor:

(a) Convey, transfer or assign any cash, real estate or other tangible or intangible property in which Grantor shall own any interest to the trustee or trustees of any trust that Grantor may have created during Grantor's lifetime, provided that such trust is subject to Grantor's power of revocation.

(b) The Agent may direct the trustee of any such revocable living trust to distribute amounts to the Grantor in any taxable year not in excess of the amounts authorized below to be transferred as gifts in such calendar year, and which will, in fact, so be transferred by Agent as gifts under the provision below "Gifts."

(c) Form a revocable living trust, in the event of Grantor's disability, under the following terms and conditions:

  i) Grantor shall be the sole beneficiary of such trust during Grantor's lifetime.

  ii) Distributions shall be made from the trust for Grantor's care and comfort without any limitation whatsoever and in a manner which provides for Grantor without concern for any remainder beneficiaries of said trust.

  iii) The co-trustees of such trust shall be the first two persons named and appointed above as Agent or Alternate Agent under this Durable Power of Attorney. If there is only one such Agent able and willing to act then such Agent shall select an institutional co-trustee to serve with such Agent. No person who has previously divorced or legally separated from Grantor shall serve as such a co-trustee.

2. With respect to any irrevocable inter-vivos trust:

Note: There can be benefits to transferring your house to an irrevocable trust, such as the Qualified Personal Residence Trust, discussed in Chapter 7.

(a) Transfer any assets to any irrevocable trust heretofore or hereafter established by Grantor as grantor not in excess of the amounts authorized to be transferred as gifts in any calendar year under the provision below "Gifts."

(b) Agent may form and execute an inter-vivos trust to hold Gifts by or on behalf of the Grantor made to any of the Authorized Donees if such Authorized Donees are beneficiaries (contingent, or otherwise) of any trust formed under Grantor's last will and testament, and the terms of the trust so formed are similar to the terms of such trust under Grantor's last will and testament.

Compensation of Agent

Note: If an agent is to manage property or take on other time-consuming tasks, some compensation should be provided for. Most standard forms don't address this.

Any Agent or Alternate Agent hereunder shall be entitled to reasonable compensation for the services rendered. A bill estimating the hours spent, services performed and charges paid, shall be provided to any joint Agent acting hereunder with such Agent, if any, or if not to the next succeeding Agent named herein.

Approval of Agent's Acts

Grantor hereby approves and confirms all acts performed by Grantor's Agent on Grantor's behalf. Grantor hereby confirms all that the Agent shall do or cause to be done, by virtue of this Power of Attorney.

Disability of Grantor

Note: Almost every power of attorney, perhaps with the exception of a special power to be used for a limited purpose such as purchasing your home while you are on vacation, should be durable. This means the grant of authority to your agent will remain valid even if you are disabled.

This Power of Attorney shall not be affected by Grantor's subsequent disability as principal. Grantor does hereby so provide, it being Grantor's intention that all powers conferred upon the Agent herein shall remain at all times in full force and effect, notwithstanding Grantor's subsequent incapacity, disability, or any uncertainty with regard thereto.

Third Party Reliance

Third parties may rely upon the representations of the Agent for all matters relating to any power granted to the Agent, and no person who may act in reliance upon the representations of the Agent or the authority granted to the Agent shall incur any liability to the Grantor or Grantor's estate as a result of permitting the Agent to exercise such power. Any third party may rely on a duly executed counterpart of this instrument, or a copy thereof, as fully and completely as if such third party had received the original of this instrument. Any third party may rely on the authority of any Alternate Agent when such Alternate Agent presents an original executed copy of this Power of Attorney. Such third party need not request proof, other than an affidavit of the Alternate Agent, under oath, that any prior named Agent is unable or unwilling to serve in such capacity.

Construction

a. This instrument is to be construed and interpreted as a durable general [limited (if only to say sell your home)] power of attorney. The enumeration of specific items, rights, act, or powers herein is not intended to nor does it limit or restrict, and is not to be construed or interpreted as limiting or restricting, the general powers herein granted to the Agent.

b. Should any provision or power in this document not be enforceable, such enforceability shall not affect the enforceability of the rest of this document.

c. Any references to the Code or any Sections of the Code are references to the Internal Revenue Code of 1986 and shall include any successor or amended Code, statute, or applicable Treasury Regulation.

d. Captions, titles, and section numbers (and letter designations) are inserted for convenience only and should not be read to broaden or limit the scope of any provision. Gender, singular or plural, shall be interpreted as the context requires.

State Law

This instrument is delivered in the state of [State Name], and the laws of [State Name] shall govern all questions as to the validity of this power and the construction of its provisions. The Agent is, notwithstanding anything herein to the contrary, granted the right to exercise any of the rights and powers available under the laws of the State.

IN WITNESS WHEREOF, I have hereunto set my hand and seal this [Day] of [Month], [Year], acknowledging that I have read and understood the powers and rights herein granted and that I voluntarily chose to make the Grant.

Grantor/Principal

—————————————————————

[Your Name]

Witness: Name: _____

          Address: _____

          Signature: _____

[Notary omitted.]

SAMPLE DOCUMENTS TO FORM
LIMITED LIABILITY COMPANY TO OWN AND
LEASE YOUR RENTAL PROPERTY

Note: A limited liability company or LLC is the most popular form of organizing a home-based or other business or rental property. When a business or rental property is held by an LLC, and the formalities of the LLC are respected, a person suing the business or rental property should be limited to suing the LLC that owns that particular business or rental property and not be able to reach your personal assets, such as your home, to satisfy a claim. This is why the manner in which you organize your business and investment activities is critical to the protection of your home. This is a sample form, the actual format will vary by state, to use to set up an LLC. Talk to a lawyer.

CERTIFICATE OF FORMATION
OF
[LLC NAME]

The undersigned, each over the age of majority, and in order to form a limited liability company pursuant to [State Law Reference], under [State Statute Reference] Limited Liability Company Act, hereby certifies as follows:

Note: The name of the LLC must include either Limited Liability Company, or LLC in most states. The name may, but is not required to, include the name of a Manager.

---

a. The name of the LLC shall be: [LLC Name]

Note: The address for the registered office, and registered agent for service of process is governed by state law. This is where service of process in a lawsuit or other matter can be made. The registered office does not have to be the place of business within the state. The registered agent, with prior notice to the LLC, may change the address for the registered agent by filing a certificate with the Secretary of State executed by the Agent.

---

b. The address of the initial registered office of the LLC shall be [Agent Address], and the name of the registered agent of the LLC at that address is [Agent Name].

Note: A one-member LLC is permitted as discussed in Chapter 4. No extra income tax return is required if you are the sole member of the LLC. If for business reasons two or more members are required, amend the form and consult your accountant about filing a partnership tax return each year.

c. The LLC has at least one member.

Note: If the limited liability company is to have perpetual existence, regardless of whether the limited liability company is subject to any dissolution contingencies, then the word "perpetual" should be stated. If the limited liability company is to have a specific date of dissolution, regardless of whether the limited liability company is subject to any dissolution contingencies, the latest date on which the limited liability company is to dissolve should be stated.

d. The LLC shall have perpetual existence.

Note: The purpose of this clause is very broad and the LLC can therefore be used for a variety of activities. It may be advantageous in some situations to provide a more restrictive definition of the activities of the LLC. This may be appropriate when a member wishes to restrict the possible activities to say owning a particular rental property or home business.

e. The LLC may carry on and engage in any lawful business of purposes permitted under state law.

Note: Any other permitted matters may be included in the LLC Certificate of Formation will depend on state law, your attorney's advice, and your objectives. These may include restrictions on transfer or control.

f. Other Permitted Matters (e.g., the LLC shall be a Manager-managed LLC).

g. This Certificate of Formation shall be effective upon the initial filing and recording with the Secretary of State of the State of [State Name].

h. The LLC shall be treated as a separate legal entity.

IN WITNESS WHEREOF, We the undersigned sign, each being an authorized person, sign our names this [Month] [Day], [Year] and affirm under the penalties of perjury in the third degree that the statements in this Certificate are, to the best of our knowledge and belief, true.

_____

[Organizer Name 1]

Note: For a sample operating agreement for your one-person LLC, see www.laweasy.com.

5 LEASING YOUR HOME

There are a host of reasons for leasing or renting your home, or part of it, and many legal, tax, and other consequences of doing so. We discuss a few of the reasons and consequences as examples in this chapter.

Whatever the circumstances of renting a portion or all of your home, the following considerations should always be addressed:

- Verify that your insurance covers the tenant. Review your insurance policy. Some policies may exclude any coverage for commercial use. (See Chapter 4.) Also, inquire of your insurance agent what must be done to extend coverage and get your answer in writing.
- Verify that you are not violating zoning, building, or other ordinances. (See the discussions in Chapter 4.) Many building codes will require reasonable ingress and egress from any area where a tenant lives (e.g., large windows or a direct access door). You can ask the town building department but if there is a problem you will have just brought it to their attention. Worse, you may not have had a problem but the way you presented it might make it appear that you have a violation. Instead, spend the money necessary and have a consultation with a local real estate attorney familiar with such matters. If a realtor helps you find the tenant, the realtor may be familiar with local rules to advise you.
- You may need special fire extinguishers, exit signs, and so on. Speak with the local fire department and building department (after you've consulted with an attorney as suggested in the

preceding paragraph). Your insurance company may have special requirements as well. Even if extra safety measures aren't mandated, it's still worth considering them to minimize the risk of harm, and also the risk of a lawsuit.

When leasing a portion or all of your home or vacation home, you will be a landlord and subject to the laws governing landlords. Although the details will vary by area, you will have to maintain the premises in an appropriate manner. The following note is worth reading.

Note: There is an obligation of a landlord under most state laws to maintain the premises in a fit and habitable form. The duty to operate common areas properly can subject the landlord to liability for harm to tenants arising from the condition of the premises. However, this should not be interpreted to require a landlord to protect a tenant from criminal activity. However, where a landlord increases the risk of loss from criminal activity, the landlord is under a duty to protect its tenants against the foreseeable risk of harm arising from his actions. The moral—play it safe, take precautions before renting.

Report the rental income for tax purposes and claim depreciation on the rental portion of your home. This is discussed at length next. Most rentals will be reported for tax purposes on Schedule E of your IRS Form 1040. It is always worth a consultation with your accountant before you rent a portion of your home. There can be a host of steps to take of which you may not be aware.

If you sell your home, the portion rented will not qualify for the benefits of excluding gain on sale from that portion of the home. (See Chapter 6.)

EXTRA INCOME FROM A BASEMENT OR OTHER SEPARATE AREA

A common rental situation is for you to rent out a spare room or unused basement. In addition to the general planning issues noted earlier, consider the following: The area you are renting, if it was never rented before, is likely to need modifications to make it suitable for rental. If your home has been transferred to a qualified personal residence trust (see Chapter 7), renting out an excessive percentage of it may cause you to lose tax benefits. See your estate tax planner. Be certain to have a written lease with the tenant. Often for a small apartment or room rental, homeowners don't bother. At minimum at least purchase a standard room lease from a stationery store so that you have some documentation and whatever limited protection the standard form provides. If the amount of rent is sufficient, have a lawyer prepare a form you can use for each successive tenant by just filling in the blanks. Review Chapter 6 for the impact on excluding home sale gain.

DUPLEX RENTING

Unlike many of the other rental situations discussed here, a duplex is built with the intent that each of the two units be lived in by separate families. Thus, zoning, and other legal issues are less likely to arise (but they sometime do). For tax purposes, the rental portion is treated as property separate from the portion in which you live. Insurance may be simpler to handle because insurance companies can more readily deal with a defined and common situation than something more novel. Just be certain that the policy you have is expressly written for the duplex, rental and personal, or that if necessary you purchase two policies, one for your home portion and one for the rental. If the tenant is to pay for insurance in addition to rent, be certain to have the insurance agent give you an analysis of the total cost for you to bill the tenant. Some of the common issues that arise in duplex rentals are the use of common areas. If there is only one large basement or attic, specify what portion the tenant can use. What about the porch and backyard? You may also wish to provide a limit on the number of guests, live-in company, noise past a certain hour, and so on. Remember, the tenant is living next to you and his actions will affect you and your quality of life.

LEASE YOUR HOUSE PENDING SELLING IT

If you are going to sell your home, but the real estate market in your area has recently hit a slump, you might prefer to rent the house until the market recovers and then sell. If this seems appropriate, consider the following:

- Most importantly talk to an experienced local real estate broker. Is the market really in a slump? When is recovery anticipated? How much of a recovery is expected? Does it really seem advisable to wait it out?

- Do you personally know the tenant or will you rent to a stranger? Keep in mind that a child with oil crayons can destroy a $5,000 paint job in minutes. A cat can destroy your curtains and carpets. It takes little effort for a bad tenant to turn your dream home into a set for the Adam's Family. The cost of repairing and freshening up the house may be more than the rental payment. How will showing a rundown house affect your chance of sale?

- The lease you use must be short-term and must expressly reserve the right for you to show the house to prospective buyers. You cannot use any standard house lease without making modifications to it. Have a lawyer review or prepare the lease for you.

- Can you structure a lease option arrangement with the tenant to encourage the tenant to buy the house?

Note: See Shenkman and Boroson, *How to Buy a House with No (or Little) Money Down* (John Wiley & Sons, Inc.) for a detailed discussion and sample forms for a lease option arrangement.

- Talk to your accountant about the income tax consequences. Will you taint the house as a rental property and lose the ability to exclude up to $250,000 of gain ($500,000 if married filing jointly). If so, it is unlikely to be worth renting.

RENTING A SECOND OR VACATION HOME

It is common to purchase a vacation home and then rent it out for some portion, or even most, of the year. The tax issues are tricky and are discussed next. This seemingly simple transaction raises a myriad of tax issues.

If the vacation home is a distance from your primary home, consider in advance how you will rent and manage it. Will you need a local real estate professional (e.g., broker) to manage it? To find tenants?

Since it is a separate property from your house, you will undoubtedly need a separate insurance policy. You also should investigate whether the excess personal umbrella liability policy you have (see Chapter 4) will cover the vacation home. Be sure it does. And be sure you get the coverage confirmed in writing after proper disclosure of the time it is rented and any other relevant facts the insurance company requests of you.

RENTING A HOME YOU OWN WITH A PARTNER

Another common residential real estate transaction is when you and a friend or investor jointly purchase a house to rent. One of the simplest real estate investments for many new real estate investors is a summer or vacation home, or a small one, two, or multifamily rental property in a neighboring community. Often these investments are made with a friend or a relative as tenants-in-common.

Note: If you are going to make this type of investment, take the steps below before you sign a contract to purchase the house (yes, before, not after!).

If you first purchase the house (take title) in your individual names, you will then individually be listed in the ownership history (chain of title) for the property. If there is a lawsuit, you may be named and sued personally (i.e., your home and other personal assets, not just the rental property, may be reached by a claimant). This may occur even if you take the correct planning steps later. Further, if you buy the house in your name and then seek to transfer it to an entity, you will have to change the title insurance, casualty insurance, tenant lease, mortgage. You will have to obtain the lender's approval, which may be impossible.

Set Up an Entity to Buy the Property

See a business, real estate, or corporate lawyer (ask when you call if a significant portion of the attorney's time is spent in these areas). Ask the lawyer what form of entity you and your partner should set up to purchase and own the property. The best answer in most cases will be a limited liability company (LLC) as discussed in Chapter 4. However, it may be preferable for a different type of entity to be used. The answer will require legal help and will depend on:

- Your specific facts and circumstances: Will one or all partners participate in management? Will either of you make gifts of interests in the property to children? How valuable is the property involved?
- The laws in your state: Which type of entity under the laws of your state has the legal and tax attributes most appropriate for your circumstances and what is the income tax consequences of each entity in your state?

Ask a lender in advance if there will be a difference in the rates for a mortgage if you sign personally or if instead you have an entity such as an LLC purchase the property. The difference to the lender is that if you sign personally you will have full personal liability (i.e., your home and personal assets will be reachable by the lender if you don't repay the loan and the house involved is not worth enough to satisfy the lender's claim for repayment). If you and your partner/co-investor use an LLC to buy the property, you will not, without further steps, have any personal liability. You can often, but not always, satisfy the lender by signing a personal guarantee of repayment of the loan. (See the sample guarantee document on page 110.) This approach can give you the best of both situations: You have the limited liability the LLC offers from tenant claims and through a personal guarantee you are able to secure the best mortgage rate from the lender.

Planning Tip: The legal nuance above is important to understand. A guarantee will enable the bank to reach your personal assets to get its loan repaid. This is a finite and quantifiable risk. You know how much the mortgage is. You know the value of the rental property you are buying and the down payment you are making. It is unlikely you will feel great concern over the bank needing to reach much of your personal assets for repayment if the house declines in value. However, the use of the LLC, if properly done and respected by the courts, will prevent a tenant or guest on the property from suing you personally over an injury claim. The amount of such a claim could be unlimited. The personal guarantee to the bank only exposes you to the financial claim for the mortgage. Nothing more.

Have an Agreement in Writing with All Co-Owners

Complete a contract to govern the relationship between the co-investors. Many of the form documents available are too long or have been prepared with more substantial commercial investments in mind. A simpler tenants-in-common (see Chapter 1) agreement (if you purchase the property without an entity), or a simple operating agreement (if you purchase the property through a limited liability company) or a simple partnership agreement (if you purchase the property through a partnership) specifically drafted for a small residential real estate investment, should be used in these common real estate transactions.

See a lawyer and have an agreement with your co-owners prepared in advance. Address important issues like the following:

- Who pays if there is a cash shortfall.
- What if there is an emergency (the roof leaks, the boiler breaks down, etc.). Can any co-owner pay and make the repair decision?
- If someone doesn't kick in their fair share, what happens? Does their ownership interest get reduced?
- What happens if you rent to a friend or relative of a co-owner or a co-owner wants to live in the property?
- When can you sell? Does everyone have to agree?

Don't make the mistake of assuming that since you get along fine with your co-owners you don't need an agreement. Most partners get along fine in the beginning. The issues arise later when new circumstances create friction. Get an agreement in place when there is no friction.

Note: For a sample annotated tenants-in-common agreement (when you buy a house without an entity), see the web site www.laweasy.com, real estate forms section.

TAX TIPS FOR LEASING YOUR HOME OR VACATION HOME

Any time an asset can be primarily a personal use asset, such as your home or vacation home, the IRS is rightfully skeptical when you try to claim business deductions relating to that asset. It is just too easy for taxpayers to abuse the system. When this happens, Congress responds by enacting restrictions and rules to limit the abuse. The result is complexity. If you rent a portion of your home or vacation home, you will have to wade through this complexity to determine your tax consequences. Be certain to seek the advice of an accountant. It's too easy to make a mistake and the rules are tough.

Determining the Number of Days You Personally Used the Home or Vacation Home

It is important to know how many days you used your rental home or vacation home because personal use can sometimes limit the expenses you can deduct on the property. You are considered to use your vacation home personally for an entire day if at any time during that day you (i.e., the taxpayer claiming deductions for the expenses paid on the property) use the property as a dwelling unit. If a co-owner or your family uses the vacation home for any part of a day, it counts as if you used it the whole day.

You can't use a rental pool to do an end run around the tough tax limitations. A rental pool is where you enter into an arrangement where a rental pool member whose home is used for a day is entitled to use another rental pool member's home for a day. It can be a great way to see the country without hotel bills. You will be considered to have used your vacation home personally any day a member of the rental pool you belong to uses it. Time share arrangements can result in similar tax situations.

Tax Options for Your Rental Home or Vacation Home

If you rent your vacation home, an important determination must be made with the help of your accountant:

- Will the vacation home be classified for income tax purposes as a second residence so that mortgage interest and property taxes may be deductible?

- Will it be characterized as a rental property (i.e, treated like a business) for income tax purposes? If so, then the income or loss it generates may be subject to the complex passive loss limitation tax rules.

Minimal Rental Use Is Ignored.   If you rent your home or vacation home for less than 15 days during the year, you cannot deduct any expenses related to the rental and you don't have to report the rental income. It's tax free! You can deduct mortgage interest and property taxes under the general home ownership rules described in Chapter 2 (mortgage interest) and Chapter 3 (property taxes, casualty losses, and other home related expenses). While this seems like a freebie, and is, the reason is simple. The rules described next for other situations become so complicated that even the IRS wanted to spare you, and itself, the pain of dealing with them.

Example: Your home abuts a famous golf course. The Masters Tournament is schedule to be there. You rent your home out for what you believe to be an astronomical sum of $15,000 for 12 days. You can pocket the money and not report it for tax purposes. If you paid a broker $5,000 for arranging the lease and $2,000 to clean your house and repair it afterwards, you cannot deduct these expenses. Your home mortgage interest and property tax deductions are not affected.

How to Determine How Your Vacation Home Will Be Taxed.   To qualify as a second residence and the favorable home mortgage interest deduction rules, you must use the property for personal purposes for more than 14 days during the year (or more than 10 percent of the days the house is rented, if greater). This classification has two results. First, any mortgage interest on the property, and allocable to the time the vacation home is used personally, may qualify for the home mortgage interest deduction rules. These rules let you deduct on your tax return interest on mortgages on your principal residence and any second or vacation home, up to $1.1 million. (See Chapter 2.) Without this special treatment, the mortgage interest on your vacation home that is allocable to the days the vacation home is used personally won't be deductible.

The drawback to having the house characterized as a second residence is that the deductions on the property can't exceed the income from renting the property, reduced by allocable mortgage interest and property taxes. This is explained in more detail next.

If you use the vacation home personally for fewer than 15 personal days (or 10% or less of the rental days) during the year, complex limitations will apply to determining what you can deduct. You will need an accountant to help you decipher and plan for the rules. Even if you prepare your own return, at least have a consultation with an accountant the first time you deal with this issue. The rental income or losses from the house will be treated as a rental activity subject to the passive loss limitation rules. The deductions attributable to the rental period of the house will not be treated as a personal residence subject to the mortgage interest and property tax deduction rules discussed in Chapters 2 and 3. These rules are discussed next. You will have to make the allocations of income and expense as between rental and personal use.

Tax Consequences of Your Rented Vacation Home Being Treated as a Personal Residence.   One tax result affected by the number of personal days that you use the vacation home is its effect on the deductions allowable from renting the property. If the days the property is personally used exceed 14 days (or if greater, 10 percent of the number of days the property is rented), than the deductions on the vacation home will be limited.

Here's how this limitation generally works. The deductions that can be claimed for the property can't exceed the income from the property, after that income is reduced by the mortgage interest and property taxes allocable to the rental of the property. Simply, you can't get a tax loss out of the property.

Example: Vicky Vacationer rents her vacation home for 6 months at $2,200 per month. Property taxes run $1,400 per year. Using the same method to allocate property taxes as was used to allocate mortgage interest, $700 of mortgage interest would be allocable to the rental use of the home. Thus, other deductions (depreciation, utilities, management fees, etc.) for the rental home would be limited to the following amount:

Rental income ($2,200/mo. × 6 mo.)	$13,200
Mortgage interest	− 7,750
Property taxes ($14 × 6/12 months)	− 700
Limitation	$ 4,750

Vicky can't deduct any expenses greater than the $4,750 limit. Fortunately, Vicky can use the excess losses in later tax years. For example, if utilities, repairs, and other deductions allocable to the rental use of the vacation home were $6,500, only $4,750 could be used. The remaining $1,750 could be used by Vicky next year (subject to the same limitations).

Tax Consequences of Your Vacation Home Being Treated as a Rental Property. When your vacation home is classified as a rental property under the 14 day/10 percent rules, the following tax consequences apply.

Expenses must be allocated. If you use a vacation home for both personal and rental use, mortgage interest and property tax expenses must be allocated between the time you use the house personally and the time you rent it. The following example illustrates this.

Example: Vicky Vacationer has a vacation home that she uses for two weeks during the year for personal vacations. Assume that her vacation home is not a qualified second residence. She rents the vacation home, at a fair rental price, for six months during the year. She pays $15,500 in interest on the vacation home's mortgage for the year. Her mortgage interest can be allocated to the rental use as follows:

Rental Use = 6 months ÷ 12 months × $15,500 = $7,750

The $7,750 in interest expense not allocated to the rental use will be subject to the limitations on deducting personal interest expense since it doesn't qualify as a second home. Since only a small portion of personal interest expense is tax deductible, Vicky won't get much tax benefit. If, however, the vacation home qualified as a second residence and the totals of all of the mortgages on Vicky's main home and this vacation home were less than $1.1 million, Vicky could probably deduct all of the interest allocable to her personal use.

The IRS says you should allocate interest to the rental use based on a ratio of the number of months rented to the total number of months the vacation home is used. In the example, Vicky used her vacation home two weeks and rented it out six months. The IRS would calculate interest this way: 6 months rented/ 8 months total use × $15,500 = $11,625. Several courts have disagreed with the IRS and have held that you can allocate mortgage interest and property taxes based on the number of days in a year. Because of this disagreement and complexity, have an accountant help you determine your deductions.

Overview of the Passive Loss Rules and How They Affect Your Vacation Home

Once you've made the allocations of expenses as to personal use and rental use, the rental expenses and rental income must be analyzed in light of special limitations.

The passive loss rules arose out of concern that many wealthy taxpayers were sheltering too much of their income from taxation by investments in real estate and other tax shelters. The general approach is to segregate the perceived culprits, tax shelter and rental real estate investments, and to then limit your use of the tax losses from such investments to offset the tax on your other income. The income or loss from these suspect investments is labeled passive. The other major categories are active (e.g., wages) and portfolio (e.g., dividends and interest). More specifically, passive investments (activities) are those which involve (1) the active conduct of a trade or business in which you do not materially participate, or (2) rental activities when you are not a full-time real estate investor.

Limited partnership interests are usually considered passive. Material participation requires you to be involved on a regular, continuous, and substantial basis in the particular activity. Some of the rules for determining whether you materially participate are based on the hours you work in a particular activity.

Losses from passive activities can generally only be used to offset income from passive activities. Losses that aren't used currently are suspended until the earlier of: (1) your realizing passive income to offset such losses, or (2) your selling your entire interest in the activity. When you sell your entire interest, suspended losses from that activity can be used without limitation.

The key concept of the passive loss limitation rules is that losses from the passive category (including tax losses on net leased real estate when you are not an active real estate professional) cannot be used to offset income in the other two categories (e.g., wages from your job and interest and dividends on your securities investments). The actual application of the rules is far more complex.

Tax Losses That Cannot Be Deducted Currently

If the passive loss limitation applies so that tax losses you have incurred cannot be deducted, these losses are generally deferred until a later tax year when they can be used to offset passive income. If you have income or gains in the passive income category in the next tax year, for example, your unused passive loss carries forward from unused loss years (or certain income tax credits earned) realized in the prior tax years. You can apply those losses against the current income to obtain a tax savings. To the extent that you are not able to use up your passive loss carry forwards from prior years before you sell your investment, you can use these losses to offset the gain that you would otherwise have to recognize on the sale.

Special Exceptions from the Passive Loss Rules

If your livelihood is real estate, you may avoid the passive loss rules on your vacation or other rental property. Losses on certain real estate activities may be characterized as active income for certain real estate professionals. Where you meet the following requirements, your interests in rental real estate investments will not necessarily be characterized as passive for the particular tax year:

- You are a real estate professional and spend more than half of your time involved in real property trades or businesses. Real property trades or businesses include construction, development, reconstruction, leasing, brokerage, development, redevelopment, conversion, rental, operation, and management.
- You spend at least 750 hours per year performing such services. Your involvement in different business can be aggregated for determining both the 750-hour test and the "more than half of your time test." The rules do not appear to exclude a real estate professional whose only real estate involvement is owning and renting real estate.

- You are a material participant in the real estate rental trade or business investments being considered. The rules for determining whether you are a material participant are the same as those described in the previous general discussion. Thus, where you invest as a limited partner in a limited partnership and are not involved in the operations of the partnership, income from the partnership cannot qualify for this special exception.

These definitions focus on the phrase "real property trade or business." Alternatively, the term *activity* could be broader than "real property trades or businesses" since a single activity could conceivably include several real property trades or businesses. It is not clear how the IRS will interpret this terminology.

The intent of the new rule was to ease the burden of the passive loss rules for active real estate professionals.

Certain losses from active real estate rentals can be used without limitation. This exception is the one most likely to apply to you when you are renting out a vacation home or other property. Review the rules carefully if tax losses will be realized because you probably will not be able to deduct such losses if you don't meet this exception from the passive loss rules.

Earnings or losses on an interest in real estate rental activities are not considered to be from an active business, except for real estate professionals. This means that losses from real estate investments will generally only be available to offset income from other passive investments (e.g., from limited partnership interests). Real estate losses generally will not be available to offset wage or active business income. An important exception exists to this rule that enables many investors to treat some real estate rental losses as deductible without limitation by the passive activity rules. These losses can be used to offset income from wages or active businesses in which you materially participate.

This exception is intended to enable moderate income taxpayers who hold real estate to provide for their financial security (the investment serves significant nontax purposes) and to deduct losses against other income and receive the tax benefits.

To qualify for this real estate loss exception, you must meet both an income and a participation test. You must have modified adjusted gross income less than $150,000. The modifications to your adjusted gross income include adjustments for individual retirement account contributions, alimony payments, and taxable Social Security benefits. The $25,000 allowance is allowed in full for taxpayers with modified adjusted gross income up to $100,000. For adjusted gross income above this amount, the $25,000 allowance is phased out at the rate of 50 cents for each additional dollar of income.

Note: A stockbroker with adjusted gross income of $120,000 has $32,000 of passive losses (in excess of any other passive income) that would qualify for the special allowance. How much can he use? First, the loss in excess of $25,000 is clearly in excess of the allowance. Thus, $7,000 [$32,000 − $25,000] can immediately be treated as a loss carryover (suspended loss) to future years.

Next, a portion of his allowance will have to be reduced because his income exceeds the $100,000 mark. The $20,000 excess will reduce his allowance at a rate of 50 cents for each dollar, or $10,000. Thus, he can use only $15,000 of his passive real estate losses to offset income from his wages as a stockbroker.

The second requirement to qualify for this allowance is that you must actively participate in the real estate rental activity. To actively participate you must meet the following requirements:

- You must own at least 10 percent of the value of the activity (there cannot be more than 10 investors).
- The tax losses cannot be subject to any other limitations under different tax provisions.
- You must make management decisions or arrange for others to provide services (such as repairs) in a significant and bona fide sense. For example, you could approve new tenants, decide on rental terms, or approve repairs or large capital improvements. You do not have to do these directly. You can hire a rental agent and repair person. This standard is less than the material participation standard discussed earlier. It is not necessary for you to be regularly, continuously, and substantially involved to meet this active participation test.
- The management decisions you make must not be contrived to meet this active participation test. For example, if the promoter of the investment really takes care of all the management decisions and sends you reports for you to acknowledge, this will not be enough.

CHAPTER SUMMARY

Renting a portion of your home, a vacation home or an investment property raises a host of legal, tax, insurance, and other issues. This chapter provided an overview of the tax issues and highlighted many tax planning techniques. It also reviewed a number of the legal issues you should address. If you have a co-owner, get an agreement in writing. If the property is solely used for investment/rental, talk to a lawyer about using an entity to limit your liability exposure. The following section provides samples of documents referred to in the chapter along with additional planning points.

FOR YOUR NOTEBOOK

SAMPLE HOME LEASE FORM

Note: Leasing a house is a very common transaction. It should never be done without a written lease, reviewed by an accountant for income tax issues, and verified for appropriate insurance coverage. This form is illustrative of some of the issues you may wish to address with your attorney.

a. Date of Lease

Note: A lease can be signed on one date, but the lease term and effective date can be at a later time.

This Lease is effective the [Day] of [Month], [Year], and the lease shall be effective on the date listed in the section entitled "TERM."

b. Landlord and Tenant

Note: Before signing a lease with yourself listed as a landlord, talk to an attorney about the advantages of using an LLC or other entity to own the property (unless it's your residence).

This Lease is made between [Tenant Name-1] and [Tenant Name-2] JOINTLY AND SEVERALLY, who presently reside at [Tenant Perm-Address] (the Tenant), and [Landlord Name], of [Landlord Address] (the Landlord).

c. Lease and the Leased House

The Landlord has agreed to lease and does hereby lease to the Tenant, and gives possession and use of to the Tenant, and the Tenant hereby leases from the Landlord, for the term and upon the terms and conditions contained in this Lease, the lower level only of the [Describe Property] two family house, located at [Prop Address], described more fully in Exhibit A annexed hereto (the House).

> **Note:** Talk to an attorney about restrictions you can place on a tenant to protect the property. If you live in the same building, you may want to add a number of details to this in order to assure that the tenant won't unreasonably disturb your use of the property.

The Tenant shall not use the House for any purpose other than as a residence for Tenant and Tenant's immediate family which shall only include the following persons: [Authorized Users] and *NO OTHER PERSONS.* No business of any nature shall be conducted at the House. Tenant may be permitted an occasional visitor (i.e., One) where none shall stay for more than ten (10) days in any forty (40) day period. Any violation of the provisions of this paragraph shall immediately be deemed a violation of Tenant's obligations under this Lease and Landlord, in Landlord's absolute discretion may immediately terminate this Lease, and Tenant shall upon Notice from Landlord quit and vacate the House within forty-eight (48) hours of such Notice.

d. Term of Lease

> **Note:** How long should the lease last? If you are renting a house pending sale, it should be short, say six months or even less.

The Landlord leases the House to the Tenant for an initial term of [Lease Term] years ([Number of] months) commencing on [Commence Date] and terminating on [End Date], unless sooner terminated as a result of tenant's violation of any of the terms or provisions herein.

e. Rent

> **Note:** If the tenant and landlord are related, be certain to get independent corroboration (e.g., a broker's letter) as to the fair rent to charge. Be certain that the lease is clear as to any expenses the tenant must pay in addition to base rent (e.g., utilities).

1. The Tenant covenants and agrees to pay to the Landlord a fixed monthly rent in the amount of [Dollars per Month] Dollars ($[Rent]) per month payable in advance on the [Due Date] day of each month during the term hereof. Tenant shall pay all utilities, including electric, gas, heat, (but not water) direct to the utilities providing same.

2. The Tenant shall pay as additional rent to the Landlord any amounts due under this Lease, any costs paid by Landlord on Tenant's behalf which are required to be reimbursed to the Landlord under this Lease. Additional rent shall also include reasonable attorney fees incurred by the Landlord as a result of the Tenant violating any provision of this Lease. Any additional rent due shall be due on the same date as the next monthly rent payment is due. The Landlord has the same rights to enforce the payment of additional rent as the Landlord does to enforce the payment of rent under this Lease.

3. The Tenant shall pay the rent herein reserved, such payments to be made to the Landlord at the address listed above, or at such other place as the Landlord may designate by notice to the Tenant, without notice or demand.

Note: The following paragraph is unfair and a tenant may not be willing to pay a full month's rent if they don't have use of the area for a full month.

---

4. Even if the Lease term shall commence on a date other than the first day of the month, the rent for the first month shall not be apportioned based on the number of days remaining in said month.

Note: The following paragraph is very important for landlords. If the tenant has a claim that you are not doing something you are supposed to do, you don't want the tenant to be able to simply reduce rent payments.

---

5. The rent reserved herein shall be paid without abatement, deduction, counterclaim or set-off, except as may be specifically set forth in this Lease.

Note: If the tenant is to pay utilities, is there a separate meter for the portion of the house the tenant will use? If not, ask the utility company if separate metering is possible and what it will cost. If not, work out a detailed and objectively quantifiable arrangement for determining the utilities the tenant will pay.

---

6. In addition to any payments provided for in the preceding sections the Tenant shall pay all utilities (including but not limited to heat, electricity, gas and telephone) to the third party providers. Such

payments shall be made directly and upon the request of the Landlord, the Tenant shall, within [Days] days of such request provide proof of any bill and payment of that bill. Tenant shall be liable for any interest, penalties and other charges assessed against the House by any person providing heat, electricity, gas, and telephone.

f. Landlord's Liability

The Landlord shall not be liable for any loss, injury, or damage to any person or any property unless the loss, injury, or damage is due to Landlord's negligence or misconduct. Tenant shall hold Landlord harmless from and against all cost, expense, and liability arising out of or based upon any and all claims, accidents, injuries, and damages.

g. Insurance

Note: Both tenant and landlord should verify with their respective insurance agents the coverage they have. On many smaller properties, owners often erroneously assume that their homeowners or personal excess liability insurance will cover a rental and they may not. Tenants too often assume landlord insurance will cover them when it doesn't.

Tenant shall obtain, and keep in full force and effect throughout the term of this Lease and any extensions, tenants' insurance against loss or damage by fire, with customary extended coverage, including vandalism and malicious mischief including liability not less than [Coverage Minimum] Dollars [$] per incident, and property damage insurance in an amount not less than [Coverage Minimum] Dollars [$] (and shall name Landlord as an additional insured). The insurance, shall be carried with loss payable to Landlord and Tenant as their interests appear. Such insurance shall be maintained with a reputable insurance company rated A or better by Bests. Tenant shall furnish Landlord a copy of such insurance policy and with evidence satisfactory to the Landlord that such insurance has been obtained and is in effect. The Tenant shall procure renewals of such insurance at least [Days Before] days before the expiration of any policy.

h. Security Deposit

Note: Landlords should always try to secure a security deposit large enough to protect them against any damage by the tenant. Be sure the lease is clear as to whether the tenant can use the security deposit as the last month's rent. If the tenant can, what will you have left for damages?

Ask a local landlord/tenant attorney if there are any rules concerning the security deposit. State law may require a separate interest bearing account, and so on.

The Tenant has paid to the Landlord One (1) month's security deposit of [Amount of Security] Dollars [$] which shall continue to be held by the Landlord as a security deposit in a commercial bank in the State of [State Name]. The Landlord shall not be required to pay any interest earned on such account to the Tenant. At the termination of this Lease, the Landlord shall return the remaining security deposit to the Tenant, after reduction for any unpaid rent, the costs of repairing any damage to the House, or any other obligation which the Tenant has to the Landlord under this Lease. The Tenant specifically acknowledges that Landlord may apply this security deposit to repair any damage done to the premises for which the Tenant is liable for repairs, or to reimburse Landlord for any amounts due to the Landlord under this Lease.

i. Representations and Warranties of the Tenant

Note: Is there anything important that you as the homeowner want to have the tenant attest to in the lease?

Tenant represents and warrants:

1. It shall during the term of this lease and any extensions hereunder, maintain and operate the House as a personal residence for the Tenant and the Tenant's immediate family (as defined above), in a lawful manner in compliance with all local, state, federal or other laws, regulations, statutes, ordinances, and the like.

2. It shall not at any time use, or permit others to use the House for any business or non-residential purpose.

Note: Be certain to clearly address the pet issue, not just verbally with the tenant, but in the lease.

---

3. It shall not permit a pet to occupy the house.

4. It assumes total and complete responsibility for any and all liabilities, suits, actions and the like arising as a direct or indirect result of its use of the House.

5. No improvements, including but not limited to painting, wallpapering, or other changes, shall be made to the House without Landlord's prior written consent.

Note: Be sure the smoke detectors and other safety equipment meet your obligations under the law.

---

6. It shall maintain all smoke detectors in the House, shall replace the batteries if necessary, and shall in no way interfere with the proper operation of the smoke detectors.

7. It shall take full care and assume responsibility for maintaining the exterior of the House, including all regular maintenance. This shall include, by way of example and not limitation, mowing the lawn, raking leaves, removing any debris, shoveling any snow and salting any ice. Tenant assumes all responsibility for any damage or injury arising for its failure to maintain the House as required in this Agreement.

8. It shall take any actions requested by Landlord's counsel to effect the purposes of this Agreement.

j. Repairs and Alterations

Note: Even if the tenant agrees in the lease to make repairs, don't count on it. It's your house and if something is broken, you want to be sure to fix it before more expensive and serious problems result. If it becomes necessary to make such a repair, bill the tenant. The amount billed becomes due as additional rent.

---

1. Tenant covenants throughout the term of this Lease, and any extension hereof, at its sole cost and expense, to maintain in good order and condition the House, including all shrubbery, appliances, and systems. Promptly at Tenant's own cost and expense, to make all repairs, ordinary or extraordinary, structural or non-structural, foreseen or unforeseen. Repairs shall include replacements or renewals.

2. Tenant shall not commit or suffer, and shall use all reasonable precaution to prevent waste, damage or injury to the House or anything contained in the House.

3. The Tenant shall not make any alterations, additions to the House except with the prior written consent of the Landlord which may be withheld for any reason. The Tenant shall pay all costs, expenses

and charges for any alterations approved by the Landlord, and shall save Landlord harmless on account of any claims of mechanics, materialmen or any other liens or liabilities arising out of alterations or additions to the House. Any buildings, improvements, alterations or additions shall become the property of the Landlord, unless the Landlord directs the Tenant, in writing, to remove such improvements. Any costs of removal shall be borne by the tenant.

4. The Tenant shall pay all maintenance costs (including but not limited to any costs necessary to maintain the proper appearance of the House such as lawn mowing, weed and refuse removal, extermination to keep the premises free of rodents, insects and other pests, cleaning of chimney and furnace), and any expenses necessary to maintain the House in a safe condition and in accordance with the rules, regulations and ordinances of any local government. The Tenant shall be responsible for all utility costs, including but not limited to electricity, sewer, oil, heat, and telephone.

k. Government Regulations, Ordinances

The Tenant shall comply with all ordinances, orders, judgments, statutes, laws, rules, regulations, decrees, injunctions, and other requirements of any federal, state, county, or local government, or any company insuring the House, which now or at any time during the term of this Lease apply to the House ("Law"). The Tenant shall not have the right to contest any such Law. The Tenant shall give the Landlord prompt written notice of any notices received from any government body or insurance company.

l. Assignment and Sublet, Encumbrances

Note: In almost all cases, you want, as the homeowner, the lease to expressly prohibit the tenant from subletting or assigning the lease. You don't want someone you haven't met or investigated in your home.

The Tenant shall not have the right to assign or sublet the House, or to place any mortgage or other encumbrance on the House. The Landlord shall not be liable for any mechanic's or other lien for any labor or materials due to work initiated by the Tenant. The Tenant shall promptly discharge by payment, bond or otherwise any such lien. The Tenant shall not sell, transfer, mortgage, pledge, lease, license or encumber the House or this Lease without obtaining the prior written consent of the Landlord, which consent shall be in the sole discretion of the Landlord and which may be withheld for any reason.

m. Subordination

Any mortgage placed on the House by Landlord shall not be subject to or subordinate to this Lease. The Tenant's possession of the House under this Lease shall be subject to and subordinate to any such mortgage. Tenant shall take all actions, and execute any documents, reasonably requested by Landlord's lawyer to confirm the provisions of this Section.

n. Inspection

Note: The 24-hour notice period is fair to a tenant, but is it appropriate for you? There should be an exception for emergencies. Also, if you plan to show the house to sell it, add a clause permitting you to show the house on reasonable notice, say 36 hours.

The Landlord shall have the right to inspect the House for any reason, and to show the House to any prospective purchaser or tenant at any reasonable time after 24-hours notice.

o. Taxes and Assessments

The Landlord shall pay all real property taxes and levies on the House. The Tenant shall promptly deliver to the Landlord all bills, notices or assessments for taxes which it shall receive.

p. Fire and Casualty

1. In the event of any damage or loss to the House by fire or other casualty during the Lease term, the Tenant shall give prompt notice thereof to the Landlord. If the fire or other casualty is caused by the Tenant's act or neglect the Tenant shall pay for the entire cost of repairing the House and shall continue to pay rent during the period during which repairs are completed. If the House is partially damaged by fire or other casualty due to no fault of the Tenant, the rent due by the Tenant shall be prorated to reflect the portion of the House that remains usable.

2. If the House if completely destroyed, this Lease shall terminate and rent shall be paid through the day prior to the destruction.

3. If the costs to repair damage due to fire or other casualty exceeds [Amount] Dollars, or will reasonably require more than [Repair Time] days to repair, the Landlord may cancel this lease by giving [Number] days Notice to the Tenant. Should the Landlord cancel the Lease pursuant to this section, the Tenant shall not be relieved

of any liability for the costs to repair the House if the fire or casualty was due to Tenant's act or neglect.

q. Bankruptcy

If the Tenant files a voluntary petition in bankruptcy, is adjudicated a bankruptor, claims benefit under any insolvency act, or if a receiver is appointed for the Tenant's assets, or makes an assignment for the benefit of creditors, the Landlord may cancel this lease with no further obligation to the Tenant.

r. Quiet Enjoyment

So long as the Tenant pays the rent and complies with all other requirements of this Lease, the Tenant shall peaceably and quietly have the right to occupy and enjoy the House.

s. Default by Tenant

Note: Be sure that the lease clearly defines your rights as homeowner/landlord to remove the tenant if there is a default under the lease. Default should include not caring for the property, abusing the use restrictions (e.g., no noise after 12 midnight), and so on. The default provisions should not only address the tenant's failure to pay rent.

---

(1) Each of the following shall constitute a default under this Lease by the Tenant:

    (a) Failure of the Tenant to pay any installment of Rent within [Default Days] days of when due, without notice or demand.

    (b) Failure to pay any additional Rent costs or expenses herein agreed to be paid by Tenant, within [Default Days] days after written notice.

    (c) Failure of the Tenant to observe or perform any of the terms of this Lease and the failure continues for five (5) days after Notice by the Landlord specifying the failure and demanding correction. The only exception to this five (5) day period shall be where the failure requires acts to be done which cannot reasonably be done within such five (5) day period. In this case no default shall exist so long as the Tenant shall have commenced correcting the failure within this period and shall diligently and continuously correcting the failure to completion.

(2) If any Event of Default shall occur and shall not be corrected within the time specified above, the Landlord, at any time thereafter, may

at its option give written notice to the Tenant stating that this Lease shall end on the date contained in the Notice (which shall be no earlier than fifteen (15) days after the mailing of the notice). On that date this Lease and all of the Tenant's rights shall terminate and the Tenant shall quit and surrender the House. The Landlord may also evict the tenant for any cause provided for by law. If this occurs, the Landlord may, without notice, re-enter and re-possess the House, using such force for that purpose as may be necessary without being liable to indictment, prosecution or damages. Tenant expressly waives: (i) the service of any notice of the Landlord's intention to re-enter provided for in any statute; (ii) the instituting of legal proceeding; and (iii) any right of redemption provided by any law presently in force or hereafter enacted, for re-entry or repossession or to restore the operation of this Lease.

(3) Each right and remedy of Landlord provided for in this Lease shall be cumulative and shall be in addition to every other right or remedy provided for in this Lease, at law, or in equity.

t. Condemnation

If there is a condemnation of any part or all of the House, then either the Tenant or the Landlord shall have the right to terminate this Lease, and the Tenant's obligation to pay rent and taxes shall end as of the date the Tenant is required to vacate the House. Rent and other charges payable by the Tenant shall be apportioned. Any condemnation award shall be paid to the Landlord.

u. Surrender

Upon the termination of this Lease, any improvements made by the Tenant shall become the property of the Landlord. This clause, however, shall not be interpreted to provide the Tenant with any right to make any improvements of any nature without first obtaining the Landlord's approval, which can be withheld by the Landlord for any reason, in the Landlord's sole discretion. The Landlord, however, shall have the right to require the Tenant, by giving written notice at least three (3) days prior to the termination of this Lease, to remove any improvement. The Tenant shall, on or before the last day of this Lease, or on the earlier termination thereof, peaceably and quietly leave the House and surrender to the Landlord the House, broom clean and in the same condition in which the House was at the commencement of this Lease, ordinary wear and tear excepted. The Tenant indemnifies the Landlord against any damage or loss which the Landlord shall suffer by reason of any delay in the Tenant's surrender of the House, or failure to deliver the House free of changes or additions. The provisions of this Section shall survive the termination of this lease.

v. Waiver

The Landlord's failure to insist on the observance of any term of this Lease shall not be deemed to be waiver of any provisions of the Lease. No failure on the part of the Landlord to enforce any term of this Lease, and no waiver of any right under this Lease by the Landlord, unless in writing, shall constitute a waiver as to any future right of the Landlord. The Landlord's receipt or acceptance of any rent or any other money from the Tenant shall not reinstate or extend this Lease.

w. Notice

Any notice under this Lease shall be in writing and shall be sent by registered or certified mail, or by hand delivery addressed to the addresses set forth above, or to such other address or person as either party may designate by notice. Any notice, demand or request given hereunder shall be deemed given four (4) days after the date the notice is properly mailed, or on the date the notice is delivered by hand.

x. Tenant's Estoppel Letter

The Tenant shall within ten (10) days after a written request by the Landlord, certify by written instrument, duly executed, acknowledged and delivered, to any Mortgagee, assignee of any mortgage or purchaser, or any proposed Mortgagee, assignee of any mortgage or purchaser, or any other person, firm or corporation specified by Landlord, whether this Lease has been modified, whether or not this lease is in full force and effect and whether or not there are then existing any set-offs or defenses against the provisions of this Lease.

y. Interpretation; Construction

If any term or provision of this Lease is found invalid or unenforceable the remainder of this Lease shall not be affected. The captions in this Lease are inserted only for convenience and in no way limit or affect the interpretation of any section of this Lease. This Lease constitutes the only agreement between the Landlord and Tenant concerning the lease of the House and all other matters discussed in this Lease. There are no oral agreements or understandings other than those contained in this

Lease. This Lease shall be governed by and construed in accordance with the laws of [State Name].

z. Miscellaneous

This Lease may not be changed except by a writing signed by the party against whom enforcement of any such change is to be enforced. The covenants and agreements contained in this Lease apply to, enure to the benefit of, and are binding upon, the Landlord and Tenant and their successors and assigns. The parties intend to create a landlord and tenant relationship, and no other relationship whatsoever, and nothing in this Lease shall be construed to make parties hereto partners or joint ventures, or to render either party hereto liable for any of the debts or obligations for the other party. The parties hereto waive the right to trial by jury in any issue involving this Lease. Tenant, for itself and all persons claiming under it, waives all present and future rights permitting it to redeem the House from Landlord after Tenant is disposed or ejected. Each Tenant hereunder shall be jointly and severally liable for the performance of each and every covenant under this Lease.

aa. Recording of Memorandum

The Tenant shall not record this Lease or any memorandum of this Lease.

IN WITNESS WHEREOF, the parties hereto have duly executed this lease the day and year first above written.

Note: Check with a local attorney. It may be necessary or advisable to have signatures witnessed, notarized, or both.

LANDLORD:

_____   Date:
[Landlord Name]

_____   Date:
[Landlord Name]

TENANT:

_____   Date:
[Tenant Name]

_____   Date:
[Tenant Name]

SAMPLE RENT COLLECTION LETTER
TO DISCUSS WITH YOUR ATTORNEY

[Your Name]

[Your Address]

Via Certified Mail Return Receipt Requested.

[Tenant Name]

[Tenant Address]

RE: Rent due for [House Address].

Dear [Tenant Name]:
This notice is made this [Month, Day, Year] under the provisions of Section [Lease Paragraph] of the lease between you as tenant, and me as landlord (the Lease) for the premises located at [House Address] (Premises).

You are delinquent in the payment of rent for the Premises and demand is hereby made for payment of such rent and the late payment charge due under [Lease Paragraph] of [Dollars]. If said rent and late charge are not received forthwith further action as permitted under said Lease. Such action may include the appropriate legal action necessary to evict you from the Premises and have all my costs and expenses, including legal fees, paid by you.

Sincerely yours,

[Your Name], Landlord

6 SELLING YOUR HOME

Selling your home, like your earlier decision to buy it, is a major legal, financial, emotional, and investment decision. The process itself is time consuming, preparing the home for sale, obtaining an appraisal or estimates from various brokers, deciding whether to choose a broker or go it alone, making a deal with the broker you choose, showing the home to an endless stream of potential buyers, and finally the closing (the meeting where all the sale papers are signed and the checks handed out). There are a host of legal issues to deal with when you sell a home: Contracts with brokers, agreements with lawyers, and contracts and ancillary documents with buyers. This chapter guides you through the legal and tax issues of this process.

USING A REAL ESTATE BROKER

There is much published on selling your home without a broker. The decision to use a broker or not is beyond the scope of this book. We'll assume you've made the decision to hire a broker. This raises a number of legal issues, starting with the contract you sign with the broker. Hiring the right broker is extremely important. Even with the best possible broker, you will need to carefully review the brokerage contract.

Who Is the Right Broker?

A good broker can take much of the work off your hands, writing advertisements, screening buyers, suggesting tips to improve the marketability of your home, acting as a buffer between you and the buyer (and sometimes between you and your lawyer). As an interested, but reasonably objective participant in the deal, an experienced broker can defuse potentially destructive confrontations between the buyer and the seller, and can suggest solutions to objective problems. Since brokers get paid for deals that close, putting a good broker on your team will help you reach your objective—selling the house for a good price in a reasonable amount of time.

Before you hire a broker:

- Interview a number of brokers. What will the broker do for you? Exactly what services will be provided? What is offered that is unique compared with other brokers? How often does the broker plan to advertise your house? How? What sort of access does he want to your house, and how many brokers will have access to the keys? How long has the broker and the particular office been in business? What sort of volume does the broker do? You want a busy broker in a busy office that closes deals.
- Ask your friends for referrals, who to hire or who to avoid. But make sure those giving advice have some basis for their opinions.
- Research brokers on the Web.

Brokerage Agreement

Once you've made a decision on which broker you will hire, get a copy of the standard contract from the broker's firm. The following discussion will guide you through the process of reading this document. Get everything in writing. In many states, agreements with brokers must be in writing to be enforceable. Whether or not your state requires it, make a written agreement your own requirement.

Forms are not standard. Nothing preprinted should be assumed to be fair or standard. The only thing standard about a broker's preprinted form is that it is that broker's standard policy to give all customers that contract. You must carefully read the contract, and preferably have it reviewed by your lawyer. Significant changes may not be necessary; however, there are a number of important legal matters that you should understand. There are a number of blank spaces that have to be filled in, and these should be filled in to best accomplish your objectives. Remember the brokerage agreement was written by brokers primarily to protect brokers (and to meet certain disclosure requirements the law requires the broker to make to you). It wasn't written for your protection.

Most good brokers are going to be reluctant to sign anything different from their standard agreement. Everyone else signs it, why shouldn't you? While you should make sure the brokerage agreement you finally sign protects your interests, you don't want to alienate the broker, and you don't want to hire the only broker willing to sign the agreement you want. Approach the whole process in a positive way. You know the broker is the most important person in the sales process. You want to protect yourself because of the large amounts involved. An honest broker shouldn't object to reasonable requests you make.

Letter Agreements to Modify the Standard Contract. Since the brokerage agreement will generally be a preprinted form, the easiest approach may be to sign the form and add to the bottom (above the signature lines) the following phrase: "See attached letter agreement." Be certain that the broker signing the form initials this change. Then have a short letter typed that includes in simple language any of the changes or additions you need. This can be far easier and less intimidating than trying to rewrite the broker's standard form. A simple and understandable letter doesn't look particularly ominous and is probably the easiest way to get a broker to accept your changes. If properly done, it should protect your rights. Always have the letter agreement reviewed by your attorney before signing.

Practically speaking, you may have to sign a form agreement to get your property listed in the multiple listing services. A separate letter agreement is probably the best approach to use since it will result in the least number of changes to the multiple listing agreement and facilitate getting your house listed with the least number of problems or delays.

The first provision in your letter agreement should make it clear that this attachment is modifying the brokerage agreement. Your lawyer will include language similar to the following:

This letter agreement is attached to and made part of [insert exact title on the top of the brokerage agreement] between Sam and Susan Seller, and Barbara Broker, dated [insert date of brokerage agreement]. If any provision of this letter agreement conflicts with any provision of the brokerage agreement, the provisions of this letter agreement shall take precedence.

This last sentence makes it clear that the changes made in the letter agreement are what count.

Consult with your lawyer concerning the appropriate language to add to the letter agreement. The terms must be fair and reasonable. Remember, your objective is to get the broker to do the things necessary to sell your house. You're not trying to antagonize or sue the broker. The following sample language indicates some of the terms your lawyer might want to consider:

If the broker doesn't perform as promised in this letter agreement, the seller can give the broker written notice of the specific step which the broker has failed to perform. Within seven (7) business days of the broker's receiving the notice, the broker has the right to perform. If the broker does not do so, the seller's sole remedy shall be to cancel the listing agreement. Any notice may be sent by certified mail return receipt requested, express mail, or personal delivery. The seven (7) day period begins with the next business day after the day on which the broker has received the notice.

Define the Legal Relationship. All brokerage arrangements aren't the same. There are a number of different types of legal relationships that you can have with a broker. You should understand exactly what type of arrangement you're getting into. How do you know? Read the agreement. Better still, have your lawyer read the agreement as well. The title to the agreement alone will usually indicate what type of agreement you are signing. However, read through the entire agreement and make sure you understand exactly what rights you're giving the broker.

A brokerage agreement is an agency relationship. You grant the broker the legal right to act on your behalf, as your agent, to find a buyer (or seller, or a tenant, etc., depending on the circumstances). This grant to the broker is usually for a specified period of time and subject to specified conditions.

The most common type of arrangement is where you give the broker the exclusive right to sell your house. If anyone buys your house during the period the brokerage agreement is in force, you must pay the commission to the broker. It may not seem fair that if your cousin brings a friend to buy your house you have to pay the broker a commission. One of the reasons brokers want to have an exclusive listing is that it reduces the potential for confusion and lawsuits. If an agent is actively showing your house, it can be very difficult, if not impossible, to determine where the buyer came from. Your cousin may have seen an advertisement the broker paid for. Should the broker get the commission or not? To avoid these questions, agents generally prefer an exclusive listing. No agent wants to have to go to court to decide who was responsible for introducing the buyer to you. Going to court is expensive, time consuming, and not a great deal of fun. If the matter drags on long enough, the legal fees you and the broker incur could end up exceeding the commission that was in question.

If you want to sell your house, you want to do everything possible to encourage the broker to sell your house. If an exclusive right to sell is what it takes, that might be the best choice. Also, if the agent lists your house, the agent will put up a sign, work with you to get your house in the best condition for sale, help you price the house, and a host of other steps that will help you sell. Because you will benefit from this assistance and expertise, you should be willing to pay for it.

There are two ways to deal with the short list of potential buyers you know before hiring a broker. You could pursue your contacts before signing up with a broker. Alternatively, make a list of all buyers you've already prospected with before consulting a broker. Most sellers speak with neighbors and family about selling their house before going to a broker. Make a list of the names and addresses of all these prospects and attach it to the brokerage agreement. Be sure to add a sentence in the brokerage agreement stating that a sale to anyone on this list is excluded.

Alternatively, you could use an exclusive agency or open listing arrangement. In an exclusive agency arrangement, you will pay the agent if the agent sells the house. If you sell the house to a buyer who came to you directly and not through the broker, you won't owe a commission. In an open listing arrangement, you agree to pay whichever broker brings you the buyer. If you find your own buyer, you don't have to pay. This type of arrangement is not common.

Make certain that your listing broker agrees to list your house with the multiple listing services and to share any commission with another broker who sells the property. The brokerage agreement should contain a clause stating that "Broker agrees to list the house with the [insert name of multiple listing service] and to pay the selling or sub-agent [insert customary percentage] of the commission earned." If you interview a few brokers, you'll quickly find out the expected percentage for your area.

Another type of broker arrangement is called a nonexclusive relationship. With this approach you can use any number of brokers and you only pay the broker that finds the buyer. This is not likely to be a great choice. The broker is unlikely to be comfortable with such a "free-for-all" environment. You want the broker to work hard to sell your house, especially in a buyers' market, so carefully consider using the exclusive right to sell arrangement instead.

In the typical brokerage agreement, you agree to pay the broker a commission if you sell, rent, or exchange your house. It's only fair that the broker be protected in case some other arrangement is made with a buyer the broker introduces to you. But the agreement should also protect you by specifying the minimum price you are willing to accept, or that you have the right to turn down an offer you don't like without being liable for the commission.

Is a Key Box Best for You? A key box provides a mechanism for agents to gain access to your home when you're not there. The key box is a small metal safe attached to the outside of your house. Your house keys are kept inside. The key box itself is locked and only brokers (generally those participating in the multiple listing service through which your house is listed) are provided keys to the key box. If your schedule is rigid, or you want to be as accommodating as possible to get your house shown to prospective buyers, this is one step you might like to take. If you agree to a key box, you should remove all small valuables from your house. Don't be surprised that the brokerage agreement contains a provision where you agree not to hold the listing broker or the multiple listing service liable if a theft or other problem occurs as a result of the key box. While any broker will use its best efforts not to permit a theft or other problem to occur, you can't expect them to agree to be responsible for any problems.

An alternative to using a key box is to entrust your real estate agent only to hold the keys. All brokers wishing to show the house in your absence will have to clear the appointments through your agent. If your agent agrees to taking on this extra responsibility and burden, don't make your next question "Will you accept less than the standard commission?"

If a key box sounds appropriate, think carefully through the potential for problems. If you use it, take every precaution in advance. Be certain that the agreement with the broker includes the details of what you have agreed to.

Services the Broker Has Committed to Provide. The brokerage agreement or the attached letter agreement should expressly list the services the broker has agreed to perform as a minimum. The list could include some of the following:

- Weekly advertising until your house is sold.
- Distribution within 48 hours of the listing information to brokers participating in the multiple listing service (thousands of agents).
- Distribution within 72 hours to agents participating in another multiple listing service.
- Immediate installation of a "For Sale" sign and free replacement if the sign is damaged or stolen.
- An open house within seven days for all real estate agents.
- Display in the realtors' brochure and Web site which is distributed to companies participating in whatever programs apply or that the brokerage firm has, as well as to various real estate agents and potential home buyers.
- The realtor's agents agreement to present your home "with the highest degree" of professional standards.
- If you've agreed to have a key box installed, it will be in place within 24 hours.
- A fact sheet will be displayed in your home within seven days.
- If you sign up for the realtor's buyer's protection plan, brochures explaining the program to potential buyers will be displayed in your home within seven days.
- Make a floor plan of your house (if you don't have one). This can be an indispensable sales tool.

- The broker should represent that it will use its best efforts to sell your house and that there are no obligations, commitments, or impediments that could hamper the broker's ability to properly render its services.

- All persons working with the broker, and the broker himself, are properly licensed.

- Provide you with a biweekly or monthly activity report of all steps taken, all prospects shown your house, all appointments made, and so on.

- Conduct a minimum number of open houses where your house is advertised and a broker is present throughout the advertised hours.

- The realtor agrees to present every offer they get to you as soon as possible (generally within 24 hours).

- The realtor will assist you and your attorney in the delivery of any documents and will expeditiously process the transaction.

- The realtor will notify you of any inspections which are necessary.

Some brokers may insist that if they are to commit to provide you with a minimum level of service that you need to agree to some terms as well. The broker may insist that you keep your home listed with them for at least a minimum number of months to warrant the commitments they are making to you. You also can't price your house for sale at more than 10 percent above its fair market value. These are all reasonable requests. A brokerage company should be entitled to know that it will have a reasonable time to earn the commission and to get the going commission rate, if it's going to invest effort and money on your behalf. But look at what they are agreeing to do. Every agent you interview may look at this list and say that they'll do that much and more. Fine. Put it in writing.

The Agreement Must Set the Broker's Commission.   Commission rates are generally established by local custom. Most brokers (except certain discount and other types of brokers discussed elsewhere in this book) will charge the going rate for the area you're in and for the type of property involved. This does not mean that this is the rate you must pay the broker. Brokerage agreements are contracts and *every* term of a contract can be negotiated. It is illegal for brokers to set commissions at any specific rate. The problem is that many if not most brokers are unwilling to vary much, if any, from the commission rates generally paid in the area. The only way you will know is to ask and shop. Just remember, whatever you agree to in the contract will be what you'll have to pay.

Does it always make sense to pay the commission rate typically paid in the area? Generally it will, but there are certainly exceptions.

If the market is slow, you might consider offering an incentive commission to the broker under certain conditions. If the house is priced right, and you push hard while the house is still new on the market, the extra commission could prove to be very cheap by comparison to having your house sit on the market for a year or longer awaiting a sale.

One of the problems with paying the full commission rate typically requested by the broker is what happens when the house is sold for considerably less than the amount the broker appraised the house for.

Example: Sell It Quick Brokers, Inc. appraises your house at no charge. They set the value at $220,000. You're pleased with the way they handled the appraisal and all the promotional work they promised so you sign an agreement giving them the exclusive right to sell your house for a six-month period, and at a 6 percent commission. Three months later, after getting a number of offers around $170,000, you finally agree to sell the house for $173,000. Is it fair that Sell It Quick Brokers, Inc. should get its full 6 percent commission? They've sold the house for about 25 percent less than they said it should be sold for. Have they really kept their end of the bargain? Sure the broker will be getting a smaller commission, but you're getting a lot less than expected.

If the broker is the one giving you the appraisal, they should be able to sell your house for something in the range of the amount they appraised it for. Since no appraisal can be exact, you can't expect the broker to get exactly what they've appraised it for. In many markets, coming as close as 10 to 15 percent may be more than reasonable. But in the above example, the substantial difference makes it look like the broker may have sold you on an inflated appraisal to get you to sign up with them. Unless something substantial happened in the economy or local market to cause such a drop, the broker really couldn't have done an acceptable appraisal job. So instead of agreeing to a standard flat commission, discuss with the broker what will happen if the house is sold for substantially less than what they've appraised it for. It is certainly a fair question. Even if you can't get a broker to agree to a scaled commission (e.g., 6 percent if the house sells within 15 percent of the broker's appraisal, and 5 percent if lower), you will certainly get good insight into how comfortable the broker is with the appraisal.

Consider a commission structure to help move the house. Assume that the going rate is 6 percent. If the house is sold within 60 days for at least 95 percent of the value the broker appraised it for, you'll pay a 7 percent commission. If the house is sold for more than the appraised value, you'll give the broker a bonus of 20 percent of the excess. For example, if the house is appraised for $150,000 and sells for $163,000, the broker gets an extra $2,600 [20 percent × (163,000 − $150,000)]. If the house sells for less than 80 percent of the appraised value, the broker gets only a 5 percent commission. In all other cases, the broker gets the standard 6 percent commission.

If you agree to pay a bonus commission, you might want to limit that bonus commission to the selling agent. The agent who listed your house might not be the agent selling it. The listing work is completed as soon as the listing is done. It is the selling agent you want to inspire. So instead of offering a 7 percent commission in a 6 percent area, consider using the standard arrangement with a 1 percent bonus commission to the selling agent.

Brokers are in business to make commissions. This approach makes it clear that you're willing to pay the broker the regular commission and a potentially significant bonus if they can really push your house. You've also given the broker a number of incentives to avoid inflating the appraisal of your house. When you combine the carrot and stick, you're much more likely to get a more favorable response. Again, the key point is that everything in the brokerage agreement is legally negotiable. Whether or not the terms of the brokerage agreement can practically be negotiated will depend on the brokers you interview.

If the market is tight and you really want to sell, try offering an incentive commission package. It has rarely been done in the past, but it's hard to see why a good broker would turn down a potentially lucrative bonus commission. Where the market is tight, this extra cost to you might just be the extra edge to distinguish your house from the dozens of others for sale in your neighborhood.

Whatever deal you strike, make certain it is clearly set forth in the brokerage agreement and any multiple listing service agreement.

How Long Should the Brokerage Agreement Last?   The first point is to make sure the agreement you sign has the date you sign on it as well as the date the agreement expires. The best approach is to state a specific date, such as June 13, 2004, for an expiration date.

The tougher problem is when the termination date should be. There's two sides to the issue. You want to give a good broker a long enough period to have the listing so that there will be an incentive to give a 100 percent effort to selling your house. On the other hand, you want to keep a fairly short rein on a bad performing broker so that the listing will expire and you can switch to a better broker. Some experts suggest a listing of three months. This may or may not accomplish both objectives. The time period will be affected by how the local housing market is doing, the time of the year, how difficult the house is to sell, and a host of other factors. You should discuss the issue openly with the broker and express your concerns for getting locked in should things not work out, making it clear that you're sensitive to the agent's need to have a long enough listing period to warrant investing time and money in selling your house.

One partial solution to the problem is to use a letter agreement specifying the minimum steps the agent will take to sell your house. If the agent will list the steps it guarantees it will take and if you reserve the right to cancel the contract if the agent doesn't keep his end of the bargain, you've achieved much of the same protection which a shorter listing period would provide. If the agent wants a longer listing, the agent should be willing to give you the right to cancel if the agent isn't actively selling your house. Don't expect the agent to agree to "actively sell" your house since nobody knows what "actively sell" means. Instead rely on specific actions like in the examples of services listed in a preceding section.

What happens if one week after the listing agreement expires a buyer introduced to you by the broker signs a contract to buy the house? Most likely, the broker will be entitled to a commission. Court cases in many states interpret how far this goes. But rather than face this uncertainty, the brokerage agreement should include a cut-off date. For example, if there is no contract signed within 60 days with anyone the broker introduced you to, then no commission should be due.

Most brokerage agreements are written for the broker's benefit, not for the home-seller's benefit. They typically won't provide for any way out of the brokerage agreement. You should insist on an exception to the agreement if the broker doesn't perform the minimum services that have been agreed to. But there are other important exceptions you might want to include in the letter agreement as well.

What if you're moving only because your employer transferred you and then your employer changes his mind? Can you get out of the brokerage agreement? Possibly not. You should ask the broker to agree to language similar to this: "Seller is selling the house because seller has received a transfer by seller's employer [name of employer] to [name of city where relocating]. Should seller's employer provide seller with written cancellation of the transfer, at no fault and due to no action of seller, then seller may cancel this brokerage agreement upon providing 48 hours written notice to the broker."

What happens if there is a serious or unexpected illness or injury, or perhaps even a death, that forces you to delay your plans to move? You should have the right to cancel the brokerage agreement in these cases with no further obligation. Death, injury, or illness is not something you could plan or anticipate and you should not be held to a brokerage agreement if a tragic or unforeseen event occurs.

There are a number of cases where the payment of the commission, or some other amount might not be appropriate. But if the brokerage agreement doesn't clearly state when you can avoid paying a commission or other compensation, it's likely you'll have to pay.

Who Pays the Expenses of Selling Your Home?   Are you responsible for any of the expenses your broker incurs in selling (or trying to sell) your house? If you don't think you should be (and you shouldn't), the letter agreement should say: "The commission is the only payment the seller may have to make to the broker. The seller shall not be responsible for reimbursing the broker for any costs."

What Must Be Done for the Commission to Become Payable? You really don't want to pay a commission unless the house is sold. Simply because the broker brings you a buyer willing and able to buy your house on the terms contained in the brokerage agreement should not obligate you to pay the commission. You don't want to pay unless the contract is signed, the closing of title occurs, and you have your money from the sale. Be absolutely certain that the brokerage agreement says this.

If the brokerage agreement isn't clear, have your lawyer add a provision, similar to the following:

> Notwithstanding anything in the brokerage agreement or this letter agreement to the contrary, the broker shall not be entitled to a commission, or any other form of compensation, unless and until a contract of sale is signed by both buyer and seller, and if, and when, the closing of title to the house occurs pursuant to the contract of sale, and the buyer performs all obligations with respect to the payment of the purchase price as contained in the contract of sale. The broker shall not be entitled to a commission or any other form of compensation if the seller for any reason does not sign a contract of sale, or for any reason either the seller or buyer default under the contract of sale, whether willfully or otherwise.

This should not negotiable. You must insist that the brokerage agreement clearly state (i.e., to the satisfaction of your lawyer) that you won't have to pay if the sale doesn't go through for any reason whatsoever. If the broker won't agree, go elsewhere.

Brokerage agreements might contain other forms of compensation for the broker. For example, if you discontinue the arrangement, the brokerage agreement may require you to make certain payments to the broker. If there is a provision for this, make sure that there are ample opportunities for you to cancel the agreement under the appropriate circumstances. The theory behind this type of payment is that a broker spends money on advertising and a sign, and perhaps other items used to sell your house. The broker then expects a reasonable amount of time to try to sell the house to earn a commission. If you cancel the contract, a required payment compensates the broker for his or her expenses. If you are willing to agree to such a payment, make sure it's reasonable when compared to the real out-of-pocket costs the broker incurred. Make sure you have legal rights to cancel the contract in reasonable situations.

Settling Disputes with Your Broker.   What happens if you and the broker have a dispute about the brokerage agreement, whether the commission is due, whether the broker is performing properly, or some other matter? Either party can sue, but as noted earlier, this tends to be very expensive and time consuming. One alternative is to provide for an alternative dispute resolution mechanism in the brokerage agreement. The most common alternative approach is to provide for arbitration. In arbitration, you and the broker present your arguments to a third person whose decision will generally be binding. It is generally much cheaper and quicker than commencing a lawsuit and going to court. But arbitration can have a number of drawbacks. You may not have any recourse to sue further. Arbitrators are often chosen for their expertise in a certain area. Would you want the question of whether your broker is entitled to a fee to be heard by a retired broker? While your lawyer is the best person to discuss whether you should agree to an arbitration clause, you must also be careful in applying your lawyer's advice. Your lawyer may have a vested interest in your not using arbitration if he or she would anticipate handling the lawsuit for you. So listen to what the broker has to say, discuss it with your lawyer and then make the best informed decision you can.

SELL YOUR HOUSE AT AUCTION

You might be able to sell your house through an auction. Because this is not a common approach, exercise caution and consult with an experienced real estate attorney and broker before choosing an auction. One of the biggest advantages is that the auction process offers a definitive time table. This just isn't the case when you attempt to sell your property through the common listing approach. By designating a time, date, and place for the auction, and by setting a minimum bid on a property, prospective buyers or real estate investors have a barometer of your motivation to sell. Consult with an experienced real estate broker about how to handle the details connected with the auction. You will have to handle many things differently. For example, you will probably have to have a complete home inspection report, engineer's report, environmental report, and other documentation prepared and copied in packages for the broker to make available to prospective bidders.

HIRING A LAWYER TO HELP YOU SELL YOUR HOUSE

When hiring a lawyer to represent you selling your home, choose a lawyer whose references indicate sufficient competence to handle the transaction, and whose price seems reasonable. You need an astute attorney to protect your interests. So it's important not only to hire the right lawyer, but to use that lawyer for better protection of your interests.

How do you know whether a lawyer is good? Ask people who have worked with lawyers extensively (not merely someone who had a lawyer assist them with a house purchase a few years ago). This can include your broker, banker, business associates, and a few selected friends. The *Martindale-Hubbell* directory provides an independent rating of many lawyers. The ratings are compiled by an independent staff and are based on peer reviews and other procedures. If other lawyers state that a particular lawyer is good, it's a pretty good sign. The highest rating is "av." A description of the ratings is available in the front of the book. The book should be available in most law offices and at many local libraries and on the Internet. You can always ask a lawyer if and how well he or she was rated.

You should always ask the lawyer as to how extensive his or her experience is in real estate matters, how many house closings they've completed, what other real estate work they do, how long they've been practicing, and whether they have lectured or published articles on related topics. Since much of the paper work in a house closing is fairly standard, most lawyers have secretaries or paralegals prepare the documents for their review. That's fine so long as the lawyer you're hiring properly reviews and supervises everything, is available for questions and to deal with problems, and attends the closing. Ask about other procedures if you're concerned.

Lawyers have very different personality types. A lawyer who is combative or tough may be perfect for suing a recalcitrant creditor, or for negotiating a tough business deal. This personality type is generally far less appropriate for selling a house. A lawyer with an abrasive personality may be a major impediment to getting a sale through. You simply can't afford to be (or to appear through your lawyer to be) intransigent or difficult. The buyer may just pick-up and go elsewhere. So it's important that your lawyer either be easy going, generally, or act that way on your instructions.

How can you be sure of the type of lawyer you're getting? You may inquire as to what types of work the lawyer does. A lawyer that spends 80 percent of his or her time on litigation and 20 percent on real estate closing may not be for you. You might prefer a lawyer who spends less time on litigation and more time on other legal matters. Unfortunately, this isn't really a sufficient answer, since a lawyer with litigation experience may be the best equipped to protect you should problems arise. The truth is you really can't be sure. But, you can certainly use your own impressions after an initial telephone call or meeting as a guide. If a lawyer is abrupt with you, a prospective client, it's not a good sign.

Fees

Fees are always an important issue, and unfortunately, too often a sensitive issue between clients and lawyers. If your lawyer is uncomfortable discussing fees before being retained, you can expect problems later. Although many if not most lawyers bill their time by the hour, many charge a flat fee for a house closing. There may be different fees depending on whether the lawyer is representing a buyer or seller, and depending on the circumstances. In most cases, competition for house closing work has kept prices rather low by comparison to the hourly rates lawyers charge for most work. Should you take the lowest priced lawyer? Maybe and maybe not. While it's often true that you get what you pay for, sometimes you don't. The fee for a house closing is negligible by comparison to the value of the house being sold. It's far more important to get the house sold and to get everything wrapped up without problems, than to save a few hundred dollars on legal fees. The problem is that the more expensive lawyer may or may not be the better lawyer for the job. The only practical solution is to evaluate all factors discussed in this chapter, and try to choose the lawyer who you think will do the best job as long as the fee is in the same range as other fees you're being quoted. This way, you'll focus on the most important factor—getting the job done right, even if problems arise. Most house closings are generally straightforward and don't encounter a great deal of problems. Unfortunately, some do run into difficulties. Whatever the source of the problems, you're unlikely to switch lawyers midstream. This is why you have to pick the lawyer upfront who has the skills you need. You don't want to be one of the minority closing with problems and find that you've hired an inexperienced lawyer to save $200.

Have a Written Agreement with Your Lawyer

Once you've chosen the lawyer you want to hire, ask for a written agreement, referred to as a "retainer agreement." This is analogous to what most accountants call an engagement letter. It sets forth what services the lawyer will provide, how much they will bill you, under what circumstances they can increase the bill, what out-of-pocket costs you'll have to reimburse them for, and other matters. Read the letter or agreement, ask questions if you aren't clear as to what's involved. The retainer agreement is for your protection as well as your lawyer's. If services you expect aren't listed, or provisions don't make sense, ask. If the lawyer is not willing to discuss your concerns, go elsewhere. You're entitled to know in advance what the arrangement is supposed to be.

Most retainer agreements contain open ended or vague language concerning cost reimbursements or additional charges. The reason is that it is impossible for anyone to know in advance what charges or problems will be encountered. However, there should be some reasonable parameters. For example, most lawyers will ask you to reimburse them for the cost of messenger services, overnight mail shipments, long distance phone calls, and so forth. Some lawyers charge their actual out-of-pocket costs. Some charge a small administrative mark-up. Some lawyers charge substantially more than their out-of-pocket costs and make a profit on these reimbursements. You're entitled to know how and what the lawyer expects to bill you for.

Should you object to paying such reimbursements? No, as long as the lawyer only incurs costs absolutely necessary to serve your interests, doesn't mark them up to make a profit (isn't that what the legal fee is for?), and gives you sufficient detail so that you can determine that you've been fairly charged. You shouldn't have to pay for Federal Express charges your lawyer incurred because he or she was too slow in getting the work out. On the other hand, if it's important to get a number of documents out quick to keep the deal rolling and to make critical deadlines, you wouldn't want the lawyer economizing. So the bottom line is you should be willing to pay reasonable out-of-pocket costs, but nothing more. To protect yourself, you should ask the lawyer to estimate the expenses, and to put the estimate in the retainer agreement. The lawyer should also agree to notify you before that amount is exceeded.

Caution: Is your lawyer giving you a deal or the business? Some lawyers advertise ridiculously low prices for representing you on a house closing. But watch the fine print. You must be provided with a Form HUD-1 RESPA statement that itemizes all charges. If that bargain basement price is being handsomely supplemented with mark-ups on overnight courier charges, doubling or tripling of recording fees, additional review fees which everyone would assume included in any house closing? Don't be shy to question fees. Most lawyers charge for out-of-pocket costs and additional services. But these should really be for costs (not profits) and additional services, not what you were told was included. Safest bet: Get a clear retainer agreement before deciding which lawyer to use.

As for charges for extra work, your lawyer needs a safety valve to bill more if major problems occur. But you also need protection. What is extra work and how much should you pay for it? Discuss the issue with your lawyer. There are many approaches to dealing with this, but the common difficulty is no one can anticipate what may happen, and in most cases, nothing extra comes up. One approach is for the retainer agreement to require the lawyer to notify you if he or she believes extra work will be involved. The lawyer should be required to notify you before any extra time or expenses are accumulated. Then you can discuss the extra work, determine if in fact it is extra and what is a fair additional charge. You don't want the lawyer to start building up extra time or work without your agreement.

LEGAL TRAPS TO WATCH FOR WHEN SHOWING YOUR HOME

Hiring a good broker and attorney won't solve all of the legal issues when selling your home. You still have responsibilities that the law will hold you accountable for. When showing your home, be careful to properly respond to any questions posed by prospective buyers. There is an important difference between selling and misrepresenting facts about your home. The old adage of "caveat emptor," or "buyer beware" has been eroded by laws and court cases. The home seller in the following example learned the hard way.

Example: Sellers represented that walls of their home were made of masonite when in fact it was later discovered after title closed that the walls were made of asbestos board. The purchasers brought an action claiming fraud based on the sellers' willful failure to disclose a latent hazardous defect. The purchasers proved that the sellers misrepresented and concealed a material fact, with the intent to deceive, and upon which purchasers justifiably relied. The court found an inference of knowledge on the part of the sellers based on the seller's prior repairs to, and maintenance of, the walls.

Example: In another case, a court went even further. A home seller, even though not in the business of building and selling homes for profit, was still held to be a builder-vendor and thus liable for an implied warranty of habitability.

The moral of these examples is quite simple. Selling a home is not as simple a matter as you might think. If you were thinking of doing it alone, without a professional broker, consider the problems the homeowners in the examples got themselves into. A trained real estate broker would have known better. Saving commissions is great, but the legal costs for the homeowners in the examples, not to mention the grief, far outweighed the savings.

PREPARING FOR THE CLOSING OF YOUR HOUSE SALE

The closing is the transaction at which you are paid and the buyer takes over ownership (title) of your home. You have to do your homework.

If you were required to clear any problems with title, or complete any repairs, be certain that everything is done in advance of the closing.

Get a written confirmation from your bank as to the principal balance remaining outstanding on your mortgage. Also have the bank notify you of the amount of interest that accrues (becomes due) each day. This is important because if the final payment is mailed to the bank, additional interest should be paid to cover the day or two the mail will take to reach the bank.

Be certain that your lawyer has estimated all of the closing adjustments and discussed these with the buyer's lawyer so that any questions or disagreements can be resolved before the closing.

Review the contract and make certain that any items upon which the closing is contingent have been properly dealt with.

Confirm by telephone a few days before the closing that everyone who must attend the closing will in fact be there, and has the correct address, time, and directions.

File a change of address form with the post office and the IRS. Call for water, electric, gas and other utility company final meter readings to make the adjustments at the closing. Advise the utility to send the final bills to you at your new address. If the utilities are a lien on the house being sold, some of your money may be held in escrow pending payments of the bills. In this case, the utilities should be directed to send their final bills to the escrow agent.

Obtain a flood hazard or other necessary certificate.

TAX ISSUES AFFECTING THE SALE OF YOUR HOME

Analysis of the New Exclusion on House Sale Gain

The key tax issue on selling your home is whether you qualify for the valuable exclusion of gain on selling your home. The maximum gain that can be excluded is $250,000 or $500,000 if you are married and are filing a joint income tax return. These rules replaced the prior rules that had provided the ability of homeowners to rollover gain on a sale if they reinvest, and older taxpayers were able to exclude up to $125,000 of gain.

To qualify, for this valuable home sale exclusion, a number of requirements must be met. These are analyzed next.

Use as Principal Residence.   The house sold must have qualified as your principal residence for at least two of the five years prior to the sale. To add some flexibility, if you don't meet the full two-year test, you may qualify to benefit from a portion of the

$250,000 maximum exclusion if you had to move because of a job change, health problem, or other qualifying reason.

If the residence was partially used for personal purposes as a principal residence and partially used for business purposes (rental or house office), the full exclusion may not be available. To the extent that depreciation was claimed on the property after May 6, 1997, the exclusion will not be available. This means that depreciation prior to such date will not have an adverse impact. This is an important point to consider when you plan on renting your home, as noted in Chapter 4.

Maximum Exclusion.   The maximum gain that can be excluded is $250,000 for a single person, or $500,000 for a married couple filing a joint tax return. These recent changes, however, are not always favorable. If your gain on the sale of your house exceeds $250,000 ($500,000 on a joint return), then a significant capital gains tax cost could be incurred (albeit, at a lower capital gains rate than under prior law).

To use the higher $500,000 exclusion, one of the spouses had to have owned the house for at least two of the preceding five years. Both spouses had to have used the house as a principal residence during at least two of five years preceding the sale.

Not More Than Once in Each Two Years.   This exclusion can be used once every two years. Therefore, if you sold a prior house and used this exclusion, less than two years prior to the sale of your current house, the gain on the sale of the current house will be taxable. To qualify for the house sale exclusion, you could not have excluded gain under this provision within the two-year period preceding the sale intended to qualify. There are some exceptions.

There is some leniency embodied in the new rules in the event you fail some of the requirements for reasons beyond your control. If you fail the two of five-year ownership and use rule, or the once-every-two-year sale rule, as a result of a change in your employment, health, or certain circumstances to be specified in future regulations, you may qualify for a partial exclusion. The exclusion is the lesser of:

- One-half multiplied by the time you owned and used the house as a principal residence during the prior five years; or

- One-half multiplied by the period of time elapsing from the last time you sold your house and claimed the exclusion until the date of the current sale.

Expect Tax Audits

With such a tremendous tax exclusion involved, the IRS may pay more attention to the facts and circumstances necessary to support the treatment of any property as a qualifying principal residence (since for most clients the record keeping that was of primary importance under prior law is no longer critical). Filing an income tax return using the address of your vacation house and periodic visits will alone be unlikely to meet the qualifications. Thus, you will do well to ignore the advice of many newspaper articles that you can forget about record keeping. It is still advantageous to keep records of capital improvements to prove your tax basis if you have a taxable sale.

The Mobile House.   The new $250,000/$500,000 tax exclusion is available every two years. From a pure tax planning strategy, what this means is that any time you are coming close to realizing the $500,000 of gain, you could sell your house, claim the exclusion, and then purchase a new house. Rather than owning one house for 20 years, because a modest annual inflation alone could push your gain beyond that permitted, sell and reinvest. In effect, live in a mobile house, moving as the tax cost becomes a likelihood.

Recordkeeping Still Can Be Important.   Capital gains are eliminated for most house sales. Many commentators have concluded from this that record keeping can be ignored. This could be a huge and costly trap. What if your gains exceed the new $250,000 or $500,000 limits?

If you paid $400,000 for your house. That amount may not be your tax basis in the house. If you had rolled over gains from prior house sales (under the rollover provisions of prior law), your income tax basis may be substantially lower. Under prior law, gain not recognized on the sale of your house because it was reinvested in a new house was applied to reduce your tax basis. Thus, if you have a valuable house, you may still have to maintain records and perform the complicated calculations required under prior law.

Renting Your House Pending Sale.   A common planning technique can become quite costly if you don't maintain records. What if you wish to sell your principal residence and buy a new residence tax free, but unfortunately the market where your old house is located is soft and you want to wait a while to sell it? You might rent the house for a period of time pending the recovery of the local housing market. Can you sell it as a personal residence which qualifies for the exclusion after this rental period?

Under the old law, you could have, within reasonable limits, pursued this temporary rental followed by a sale. You could have temporarily rented your old house to help cover the carrying costs while you waited for selling conditions to improve to maximize your selling price. You could have then sold the house and rolled over the gain tax-free into your new house. If, however, you had not occupied the house for too lengthy a period of time before the sale, the IRS may have argued that you abandoned it as your principal residence and the tax-free rollover rules should not apply.

Take this planning scenario one step further. What if you convert a personal residence to rental use? If so, you will have to determine your tax basis in the property to calculate gain or loss on a sale, or depreciation if you rent it. Your tax basis will be the lesser of the fair market value on the date of the conversion or your adjusted tax basis. Thus, records of your tax basis should be kept.

To qualify for the home sale exclusion, the house you sell must be used as your principal residence. The potential risk with renting your old house before the sale is that, if improperly handled, it could change its character from being a principal residence to being a rental property. The IRS might claim that you abandoned the house as your principal residence if you rented it for an extended period. A rental property cannot qualify for the home sale exclusion. However, the courts have permitted (under prior law cases) persons to temporarily rent a house while trying to sell it. But what is temporary? The following list of suggestions will help you to structure the transaction to support your argument that the house should still qualify for the tax benefits:

- Rent for as short a lease term as possible. The shorter the better.

- Reserve the right in the lease for you to show the house to prospective buyers.

- Continually advertise the house for sale throughout the entire rental period.

- Include a realistic arm's-length option in the lease to confirm your efforts to sell the house.

- Consummate the sale of the old house within two years of moving out of the old principal residence subject to the lease option.

Vacation Houses.   Planning for the new house sale exclusion can also, with a bit of planning, extend to vacation houses. Assume that you own two residences. You could sell the first house and avoid gain, then move into the vacation house making it your personal residence for two years. Thereafter, you could sell this second residence and exclude up to $250,000 ($500,000 on a joint return) of gain on it as well. This may be particularly useful for seniors looking to downsize to a smaller house or move from their primary residence.

House Equity Is Liquid.   These home sale exclusion rules governing house sales will enable you to reside in your house and still free up the investment equity in it by selling, without incurring tax cost. Seniors can scale down house ownership since they will no longer be required to reinvest to avoid tax. These funds can be used to cover other costs of retirement. Even if a gain has to be incurred because profits exceed more than the $250,000 or $500,000 limits, the capital gains tax cost will be lower still, facilitating senior clients cashing out their house investments.

Special Rules for Separated and Divorced Spouses.   If you are involved in a divorce, a host of further complications will affect planning. If one spouse is granted exclusive use of the residence pursuant to a separation agreement, divorce decree, or other instrument, that use will be credited to the second spouse for purposes of meeting the use and ownership requirements. For many homeowners, this may be of little practical benefit if the children of the marriage are so young that the five-year time period is insuffi-cient. For other taxpayers, this won't be an issue.

Caution should be exercised to be certain that the usage is man-dated by a qualifying agreement. If not, it will not be credited to the spouse not residing in the house. The timing of each spouse's use and ownership should be considered to assure the maximum qualification for the exclusion.

It may be advantageous to delay the divorce or the common fil-ing of separate tax returns, to assure that the full $500,000 exclu-sion is available. In the context of a divorce settlement, if the house is transferred to one spouse, that transferee spouse may treat the house as if he or she had owned it during the period it was owned by the transferor spouse.

Special Rules for Estates

The 2001 Tax Act extended the home sale exclusion rules in a man-ner that makes them easier for your estate or heirs, following your death, to take advantage of the home sale exclusion. An estate (when you die your assets are owned by your estate) or trust may qualify to exclude the gain realized on the sale of the decedent's personal residence. Your estate could qualify for this benefit, an heir who inherited the property from you (e.g., your child) could qualify, and a special trust referred to as a qualified revocable liv-ing trust could qualify. Your heirs can also add (tack) the period you owned the house before you died (i.e., the decedents holding period) to the time that they use the house to meet the require-ments for the home sale exclusion.

Home Office or Partial Rental Impact on Sale Tax Consequences. It is not unusual for people to lease out a portion of their house (see Chapter 5) or use part of their house for an office (see Chapter 3). When selling a house that has partially been used for an office or rental, you will not be able to qualify that portion for the home sale exclusion of $250,000/$500,000. The home office or rental por-tion is a business use of the property, not a principal residence use.

When you sell a house that has been used for another purpose, analyze the situation as if you were selling two separate properties:

(1) Your house, which may qualify as a personal residence and for the home sale exclusion of $250,000/$500,000 (or under prior law the tax-free roll over rules or $125,000 exclusion); and (2) a home office, which is a separate business property that cannot qualify for the tax-free roll over of a principal residence. Allocate the price you will receive for the sale of the old house between the residential portion of the house and the business/rental portion of the house. The ratio to make this allocation should be the same ratio that your accountant has used to allocate various house-related expenses between your home office/rental expenses (often reported on Schedule C with respect to a home-based business or Schedule E for a rental) and personal itemized deductions (reported on Schedule A). Form 8829, "Expenses for Business Use of Your Home," which your accountant will prepare for filing with your tax return should reflect the calculation of the appropriate percentage.

The tax consequences for each property can then be separately determined. In most instances, practitioners should have the calculations made, or at least reviewed, by your accountant.

Planning Tip: There are limited opportunities to avoid gain on the business/rental portion when you sell a house that is both a personal residence and a business property (either a home office or a rental). It may be possible to arrange a transaction where you roll over the gain on the residential portion and separately roll over the gain on the business portion under rules that permit a tax-free (deferred) exchange of property used in your trade or business or held for investment. This is a complex planning technique that will only work if the amounts involved are substantial. You will need professional advice from a tax specialist.

WEB SITES TO HELP YOU SELL YOUR HOME

There are a host of web sites that are useful for buying and selling homes. Given the rapid changes in web sites, you should always engage in a search of current sites through online search engines. Here are a few sites that might be of interest:

- http://www.forsalebyowner.com includes the following features: buy a home, sell a home, service directory, mortgages, neighborhood research, moving and relocation, insurance, appraisals, and more.

- http://www.homegain.com endeavors to provide an informative resource to help homeowners navigate the home selling and buying process. HomeGain focuses on three primary areas: finding out what your current or future home is worth; preparing your home for sale; and finding the right real estate agent. The site includes home searches (for buying), a mortgage center, moving help and advice, home improvement resources (tools, projects, contractors) and more.

CHAPTER SUMMARY

Selling your home involves a host of legal and tax issues. You have legal issues to review in hiring a broker and lawyer, and when showing your home. There are significant legal issues when you prepare for the closing of the sale. Tax issues further complicate the sale. The home sale exclusion rules are broad and can enable many taxpayers to avoid any taxable gain on selling their homes. However, you must fit within the requirements. This chapter helps you navigate these many issues.

FOR YOUR NOTEBOOK

SAMPLE SALE CONTRACT RIDER (ADDITIONAL TERMS) FORM TO DISCUSS WITH YOUR REAL ESTATE BROKER AND ATTORNEY

Note: Home sale contracts address many issues which you, now wearing the shoes of the home seller, have to address. However, many standard contracts don't provide all the protection you need as a seller as they try to be somewhat impartial between the buyer and seller. Thus, it is common for sellers to have to add additional terms to the standard contract to protect your interests. These additional provisions are usually attached as a separate document, called a *rider*. The main contract, above the signature lines, must indicate that a rider is attached. The actual rider will vary considerably depending on the terms of the form contract that is being modified, and the deal involved. This example rider will help you as a seller identify some of the issues to address with your lawyer. You should also review the annotated contract in Chapter 1 that provides comments for both buyers and sellers.

RIDER TO CONTRACT FORM FOR SALE OF REAL ESTATE
BETWEEN [SELLER NAME]
AS SELLER AND
[PURCHASER NAME] AS BUYER
DATED [MONTH, DAY, YEAR]

Note: The rider should reference the exact contract to which it is attached.

This 2nd Rider is attached to and made a part of the [Contract Form] "Contract For Sale of Real Estate" between the above parties.

a. Legal Construction

Note: Every rider should include provisions to clarify how the terms in the rider, which will always differ from the contract, should be interpreted.

1. In the event of any inconsistency between this 2nd Rider and the "Contract For Sale of Real Estate," inclusive of the Rider and addendum and "ADDITIONAL CLAUSES" attached thereto, and "Schedule A—Description" attached to the Contract, the provisions of this Rider shall control. The Contract For Sale of Real Estate and this 2nd Rider are collectively referred to as the "Contract."

2. The invalidity or unenforceability of part or all of any provision of this Agreement or any Exhibit, shall not affect the other provisions or portions thereof, and this Agreement, and any of the Exhibits attached hereto, shall be construed in all respects as if any such invalid or unenforceable provisions or portions thereof were omitted.

b. Additional Contract Clauses

Note: Lawyers will have many different approaches to drafting riders. The following is but one example. The next paragraph indicates contract paragraphs which are to be deleted by number. The problem with this approach is that it is easy to make a mistake. It is probably better to list the paragraphs by name.

---

1. The following additional contract clauses attached to the Rider to Contract are hereby deleted in their entirety: 1.; 2.; 6.; 8.; 9.; and 10.

2. The following additional contract clauses added to the Contract are hereby deleted in their entirety: 28.

3. The following additional contract clauses attached to or on the Contract are hereby modified as provided in this 2nd Rider: 3. and 7.

c. Deposit Monies

Note: An issue that affects you as a seller is the deposit. If the deal falls through who should get the buyer's deposit? You, the buyer or a division between you depending on the facts? Should it be an interest-bearing account? While in theory an interest-bearing account sounds worthwhile, it is often not worth the cost and paperwork.

Section 5 of the Contract is hereby amended to provide that:

Where this Contract is legally and rightfully canceled, the Buyer shall receive the payments provided in the Contract and the parties shall be free of liability to each other, except as provided in Section 20 of the Contract. The deposit monies shall be held in a non-interest bearing account. All parties hereto hereby authorize any deposits presently held by either Broker to be transferred to Sellers' attorney's trust account.

d. Mortgage Contingency

Note: If you agree to give the buyer a mortgage contingency (i.e., if the buyer cannot get a loan, they can get out of the deal) at least try to modify the contract so that the buyer has to make reasonable efforts to get a mortgage. If not, why should you tie up the sale of your house for that particular nonserious buyer? (See Chapters 2 and 6.)

Section 6 of the contract for sale of real estate is hereby amended to provide that:

Buyer shall:

a. Make prompt application to an institutional lender or licensed mortgage broker (Lender) for such mortgage loan;

b. Promptly furnish accurate and complete information when requested by the Lender;

c. Pay all fees, points, and charges required in connection with such application and loan to the extent not in excess of those set forth in the contract, Section 6;

d. Pursue such application with diligence; and

e. Comply with all requirements of a commitment if one is received.

Buyer shall promptly forward any commitment received to the attorney for seller. If the buyer has followed the requirements of this section and is unable to secure a commitment at the terms listed, either party may cancel this contract.

e. Closing

Section 7. of the Contract is amended to provide that:

Note: Specify where the closing should take place and when. This is usually a matter of convenience for all.

The closing shall take place at the office of the Buyer's or Seller's attorney, in [Any Town], [Some State] or at the place designated by

Buyer's mortgagee in [A County] County or such other place as shall be mutually agreeable to the parties (the Closing).

The date of Closing shall be September 4, 2004.

f. Personal Property and Fixtures

Section 10 (a) of the Contract is amended by:

Note: You can commit to repair any damage from your removing your property. For example, if you remove a bookcase, you should patch the wall it was unscrewed from. If the contract is too broad, it could have you making other types of repairs or even incurring costs for things you would consider improvements. You may have to limit this in the rider.

Repairs and replacements: Sellers shall repair any damage resulting from their removal of any personal property in, on or attached to the Property. Where light fixtures are removed they shall be replaced by working light fixtures. These repairs and replacements shall be completed at Sellers sole cost and expense and prior to closing.

g. Termite, Radon, Structural, and Other Inspections

Note: Most contracts give the buyer carte blanche to walk out of the deal if there is a termite, radon, or other type of problem. The issue for you with these clauses is that if the cost of repairing or correcting the problem is modest, you would probably rather make the correction than lose the sale. Therefore, if you are given a form contract with these open-ended ways out, restrict them in a reasonable manner so you can fix inconsequential problems and keep the buyer to the deal.

Sections 11 and 12 of the Contract are amended as follows:

Termite

The Buyers are permitted to have the Property inspected by a reputable termite inspection company, at their cost and expense, to determine if there is any damage or infestation caused by termites or other wood-destroying insects. Said inspection shall be ordered and completed, and the Seller shall be given Notice of the results of such inspection, within fifteen (15) days of the Contract Date. If the inspection reveals infestation or damage which can be repaired, treated and corrected for not more than Five Hundred Dollars ($500.00) then Seller shall make such repairs, treatments, and corrections prior to Closing at Buyer's sole cost and expense. If the cost to repair, treat and correct is more than Five Hundred Dollars ($500.00) and the Buyer is unwilling to be responsible for such additional costs to repair, treat and correct the condition, Seller may elect to proceed to Closing with Seller being responsible for the excess over Five Hundred Dollars ($500.00) of such costs. If Seller is not so agreeable, then this Contract shall be void and Buyers shall receive an immediate refund of all monies deposited.

Home Inspection

Buyers shall have the option to arrange for, and complete, a home inspection, by a reputable home inspection company, or individual, at Buyers' expense, within Fifteen (15) days of the Contract Date. If said home inspection report reveals any defects then the Buyers shall, prior to the expiration of such Fifteen day period provide the Sellers Notice of said written report. If the defect can be repaired or corrected for not more than Five Hundred Dollars ($500.00) then Seller shall make such repair or correction prior to Closing at Buyer's sole cost and expense. If the cost to repair or correct is more than Five Hundred Dollars ($500.00) and the Buyer is unwilling to be responsible for such additional costs to repair or correct the defect, then Sellers may elect to proceed to Closing with Seller being responsible for the excess over Five Hundred Dollars ($500.00) of such costs. If Seller is not so agreeable, then this Contract shall be void and Buyers shall receive an immediate refund of all monies deposited.

Radon

a. Buyers may have conducted, at their expense, a radon inspection to commence within Fifteen (15) days of the Contract Date. If such report reveals particles in excess of 4.0 pico curies per liter, then Buyers must give the Seller Notice, within Five (5) days of Buyers receipt of the radon test results, of the radon test results and if the Radon level can be corrected for not more than Five Hundred Dollars ($500.00) then Seller shall make such repair or correction prior to Closing at Buyer's sole cost and expense. If the cost to correct such radon problem is more than Five Hundred Dollars ($500.00) and the Buyer is unwilling to be responsible for such additional costs to correct the radon problem, then Sellers may elect to proceed to Closing with Seller being responsible for the excess over Five Hundred Dollars ($500.00) of such costs. If Seller is not so agreeable, then this Contract shall be void and Buyers shall receive an immediate refund of all monies deposited.

b. Seller acknowledges that tests must be conducted in closed conditions. All doors, windows, and other openings should be closed 12 hours prior to beginning the test and through the completion of the test. Seller shall endeavor not to open any window or door, turn on a fan, or perform any other similar acts during the testing. Seller shall not permit the use of cleaning sprays in the basement area during the testing period. Seller shall not have or permit others any direct or indirect contact with any testing materials or equipment during the testing period. Buyer shall provide Seller with verbal notice of the testing period.

h. Certificate of Occupancy

Section 13 of the Contract is amended as follows:

Note: As explained in Chapters 1, 4, and 6, each town may have different issues with a certificate of occupancy. Speak to the real estate attorney and broker you hire before you begin to show your house. There may be modest repairs you can make to bring your house up to code before you even show it to buyers (e.g., adding a few smoke detectors). Determine what are appropriate steps to take in advance and then address with the attorney what you should be willing to commit to in a contract. You may not want to agree to pay for unlimited repairs to bring the house up to code or to get a certificate of occupancy. This is the type of issue for which you need a good real estate attorney familiar with the local rules.

Seller shall deliver to Buyer, at Seller's sole expense, a certificate of occupancy. Seller shall make any repairs or other changes necessary to obtain the certificate of occupancy at Seller's sole expense. If the repairs or other changes can be completed for not more than Five Hundred Dollars ($500.00) then Seller shall make such changes prior to Closing at Seller's sole cost and expense. If the cost to repair or correct is more than Five Hundred Dollars ($500.00) and the Buyer is unwilling to be responsible for such additional costs to repair or change, then Sellers may elect to proceed to Closing with Seller being responsible for the excess over Five Hundred Dollars ($500.00) of such costs. If Seller is not so agreeable, then this Contract shall be void and Buyers shall receive an immediate refund of all monies deposited.

The provisions of Rider 7. are hereby amended as follows: Sellers shall reasonably endeavor to assign to Buyer, to the extent legally and practically possible, any New Home Warranty which Sellers have and any guarantees and warranties in effect with respect to any improvements or repairs or equipment. Any costs required to do so shall be paid for solely by Buyers.

i. Fire; Risk of Loss

Section 19 of the Contract is amended by adding the following:

Note: The clauses in many contracts concerning fire or casualty are not reasonable. As with termites and radon, you don't want to lose a buyer on a $450,000 sale because of a $5,000 casualty loss. Be sure the contract rider corrects the contract so you have the option to make a minor repair, or reduce the contract price, and keep the buyer in the deal.

---

1. The risk of loss or damage to the premises by fire or any other casualty until the delivery of the deed is assumed by the Seller. Seller shall repair, if feasible, all damage to the Property (inclusive of any personal property to be transferred as part of the Contract) to Buyers' reasonable satisfaction prior to the Closing, or by any reasonable extension of the Closing date agreed to in writing by Buyers in Buyers sole discretion. Should such damage occur within thirty (30) days prior to Closing, Seller may extend the Closing for up to the lesser of the days reasonably necessary to complete the repairs, or thirty (30) days. If such repair is not feasible, Buyer may reduce the Purchase Price by the costs reasonably necessary to repair the damage.

2. If there is a fire or other casualty to the Property prior to the Closing and at least fifteen percent (15%) of the Property (in terms of square footage) is destroyed or damaged, or the costs of restoration are at least fifteen percent (15%) of the total purchase price, the Buyer may cancel this contract and receive an immediate refund of all the monies deposited, without reduction.

j. Complete Agreement

Section 24 of the Contract is amended by providing that only the party to be charged with a change must sign a writing consenting to such change.

k. Notice

Section 26 of the Contract is amended by adding the following language:

Notice may also be given by facsimile or overnight courier. In the case of Notice to the Buyer, a copy of such notice shall be sent by an authorized method to: [Buyer's Lawyer].

In the case of Notice to the Seller, a copy of such notice shall be sent by an authorized method to: [Seller's Lawyer].

l. Assessments

Section 21 of the Contract is amended by adding the following language:

Seller has no knowledge of any assessment which has or may be levied against the Property.

m. Condemnation

The Contract is amended by adding the following:

This sale also includes any right of the Seller to any unpaid award by reason of any taking by condemnation of the property. The Seller shall deliver, at no additional cost to the Buyer, at the closing, or after the closing, on demand, any document which the Buyer may require to collect any such award. However, if there is any condemnation or other public taking of the Property prior to the Closing the Buyers may, in their sole discretion, elect to cancel this Contract and receive an immediate refund of all monies deposited, without reduction, and inclusive of interest.

n. Brokers

The Contract is amended by adding the following:

Sellers and Buyers each represent and warrant to the other that they dealt with no brokers concerning the subject matter of this Contract other than [Realtor 1 Name], [Realtor 1 Address] and [Realtor 2 Name], [Realtor 2 Address]. Each shall hold the other harmless against any violation of this representation. These representations shall survive the Closing and delivery of deed.

o. Contract Date

The date upon which the Contract and this Rider are executed by both Buyer and Seller shall be referred to as the Contract Date. No time period provided in this Contract shall run, and the Contract Date shall not have occurred, until both parties (or their respective attorneys) have signed a copy of this Contract, inclusive of this 2nd Rider, and have received a copy of this Contract and Rider 2nd signed by the other party.

p. Tax Reporting

Seller's Social Security number is: [Social Security No.].

Buyer's Social Security number is: [Social Security No.].

The Parties agree to comply with Internal Revenue Code of 1986 Sections 897 and 1445 and related provisions (FIRPTA), as amended. Seller represents and warrants that it is not a foreign person as defined by the above Code sections, and agrees to furnish at or prior to Closing a Certificate of non-foreign status in accordance with FIRPTA, unless the transaction is exempt from such requirements. If Seller shall fail to deliver such certification by Closing, Purchaser shall deduct and withhold from the purchase price such sum required by law, and remit such amount to the Internal Revenue Service. The Parties shall execute and deliver such instruments, and take such other actions as may be reasonably necessary to comply with the reporting requirements of Section 6045 of the Internal Revenue Code, and the regulations issued pursuant thereto. This obligation shall survive the Closing.

q. Broom Clean

At time of closing, house and grounds will be in broom-clean condition and free of all garbage and debris. The property, premises, grounds and all systems are to be properly maintained by the Seller until closing of title, and are to be in working order.

IN WITNESS WHEREOF, this Rider to the Contract has been executed by the parties as of the date first above written:

[Signature lines and notary forms omitted.]

SAMPLE INSTALLMENT LAND CONTRACT FORM
TO DISCUSS WITH YOUR ATTORNEY

Note: You might choose to finance the sale of your house over time by having the buyer pay you. This form illustrates the type of document your lawyer will have to prepare for you.

---

a. Agreement made this [Month, Day, Year] between [Seller Name] residing at [Seller Address] (the Seller), and [Purchaser Name], residing at [Purchaser Address] (the Purchaser).

b. Witnesseth, the seller agrees to sell and the purchaser agrees to buy the following described property: [Insert Description].

c. The purchaser will pay for the property and the settler will agree to the purchase price therefore the sum of [Amount] to be paid as follows:

Note: Set the interest rate in consultation with the real estate broker and lawyer. The broker can advise you what is appropriate in your area and the lawyer can verify that the rate doesn't violate laws that may restrict the rate of interest which you can charge (called usury laws), when interest should be paid, when it is compounded, and so on. All key terms should be addressed in the contract.

---

d. [Amount] on the signing and conveyance of this contract, the receipt of which is acknowledged; the sum of [Amount] on the [Day] of [Month], [Year] and a similar sum on the [Day] of each month thereafter. The payments are to be applied, first, to the payment of interest owing on unpaid balances of the purchase price at the rate of [Percent] per year and, second, to the reduction of the purchase price. Together with the monthly payments, the purchaser shall pay an amount equal to one-twelfth of the yearly taxes, assessments, and water rents taxed or assessed upon or levied against the said premises and an amount equal to one-twelfth of the yearly insurance premiums as hereafter provided.

e. The installment payments by the purchaser shall continue until the whole purchase price is completely paid or when the purchaser shall have paid a total of [Amount] at which time the whole unpaid balance of the purchase price shall become due and payable. When either of the above events occurs, the seller shall convey to the purchaser a bargain and sale deed with covenant against the grantor's acts in proper form for recording, duly executed and acknowledged by the seller, including revenue tax stamps, if any, so as to transmit to the purchaser the fee simple of the said premises, free of all encumbrances, and the rest of the purchase price shall be paid by the purchaser executing, acknowledging, and conveying to the seller a purchase money note and mortgage in a sum equal to said balance. The notice shall be paid in equal monthly payments of [Amount] beginning one month after the making thereof and a similar sum monthly thereafter until said note has been completely paid at the same time with interest thereon at the rate of [Percent] per year from the date of said note, to be paid monthly at the same time with the payments of principal.

f. The mortgage shall be formulated upon the standard form used by title companies for first mortgages.

Note: When you are selling your house, you will use a mortgage on the property to secure your interest and a note to evidence that the buyer is personally obligated to pay you. (See Chapter 1.)

---

g. The purchase money note and mortgage are to be formulated by the attorney for the seller at the purchaser's cost. The purchaser shall pay the mortgage tax, recording fees, and stamps on the said bond, if any, at the time of the conveyance of the deed and execution of the said bond and mortgage.

h. Taxes, water rates, rentals, and insurance premiums are to be distributed proportionately as of the date the seller conveys the deed to the purchaser.

i. Notwithstanding the fact that the deed to the aforesaid property will not be conveyed to the purchaser until the purchase price and interest thereon has been completely paid, the purchaser and his agents and employees may enter upon the premises for the purpose of taking soil samples, making surveys, removing underbrush and other vegetation, and for general inspections of the property, assuming that such activities cause no long-lasting damage to adjoining property or to the premises themselves in case title does not close due to the purchaser's default, then the seller, in addition to other solutions which he may have, including the right to keep or recover liquidated damages, shall be entitled to be indemnified and held free of blame by the purchaser for any long-lasting damage caused to the premises or adjoining property by reason of the purchaser's entry upon the premises.

Note: What steps must you take if the buyer is late in a payment? What is your recourse? Be sure to review with your lawyer the protection you have and the steps you must take to avoid your inadvertently failing to meet the terms of the contract.

---

   j. If the purchaser defaults in making any of the installment payments and the seller, as a consequence, wishes to exercise his option to end this agreement as heretofore provided, this agreement shall not end unless the seller first notifies the purchaser of the default and conclusion, in writing by certified mail, return receipt requested, addressed to the purchaser at the location set forth above. The purchaser may remedy the said default by payment of all amounts in arrears by cash or certified check conveyed to and received by the seller no later than [Days] business days following receipt of the aforesaid notice by the purchaser.

In witness whereof, the parties hereto have set their hands and seals the day and year first above written.

_____

Borrower:

_____

Seller:

7 GIVING/BEQUEATHING YOUR HOME

Since your home is likely to be an important asset, you need to plan how you will give it to your surviving spouse, children, or other heirs when you die. Alternatively, if your estate is so large that there could be an estate tax at your death, you might choose to gift away some or all of your home while you are still alive to save gift and estate taxes. This chapter shows you how.

Note: For a more detailed discussion of estate taxes and the use of trusts for your home, see *The Complete Book of Trusts* (John Wiley & Sons, Inc.).

HOW TO GIVE YOUR HOME TO YOUR HEIRS WHILE YOU'RE STILL ALIVE

To understand some of the planning ideas that follow, you need a quick overview of gift and estate taxes. While the rules are extremely complex, this discussion will simplify them dramatically.

- You can give away up to $11,000 per year per person without limit. Most tax advisers, even if they don't think the taxpayer is likely to be subject to estate tax will recommend planning gifts within this amount to avoid using up the $1 million you can give away free of tax (see below). If circumstances change before your death, you will have preserved the maximum estate tax exclusion. What this means in practical terms is that if you wish to gift interests in a home or vacation home to children while you are alive, you may have to issue small percentages each year to each to fall within the $11,000 limit. The $11,000 limit is inflation indexed.

- You can give away up to $1 million (2002) while you are alive with no gift tax. While this sounds like a tremendous amount, consider the planning point above. If you can easily plan to come within the $11,000 annual gift exclusion amount, why use up any of your lifetime exclusion? On the other hand, if you wish to give away a house, for the vast majority of Americans the $1 million figure assures they will never pay a tax. So, you can give away a vacation home located out of state one day before you die and avoid any probate proceeding in that state.

- On death, you can give away up to $1 million (2002) without any estate tax. Note, that any of the $1 million gift exclusion you used up will reduce the amount you can bequeath tax free at death.

Example: If you gave away $450,000 while you were alive, at death you can only give away $550,000 more before tax will be charged.

This $1 million amount is scheduled to gradually increase to $3.5 million, but check with your lawyer or accountant as changes in the law may occur.

OUTRIGHT GIFTS OF INTERESTS IN THE HOUSE

It might be beneficial to transfer ownership of your house to another relative to remove the value of the house from your estate or the reach of medical care providers. For example, this could be done by simply giving away undivided interests in the house each year through a deed using the annual $11,000 (indexed) per donee gift tax exclusion amounts. Alternatively, if you will never be subject to an estate tax, you can simply give away the entire property at one time.

If you are considering a gift of your house to avoid medical care costs, consider a deed with a reserved life estate. (See Chapter 4.)

Why might you give away a house now?

- Your heirs may need a home and you want to help.

- You anticipate that the home may increase in value and you wish to remove that appreciation, before it happens, from your estate to avoid an estate tax problem.

- The house is located in a state other than the state in which you reside and you wish to avoid ancillary probate (the legal process of transferring the ownership of the house in that state after your death).

- You are concerned about qualifying for state aid or Medicaid and wish your house to be protected.

- You no longer wish the responsibility.

GIFT YOUR HOME NOW AND RENT IT BACK

You might wish to continue to use your house for a period of time after you give it away. The solution is to give it away and then enter into a lease with your heirs (or the other persons to whom you have given it, called *donees*). (See Chapter 5 concerning leases.) If you wish to protect your house from medical costs, see the discussion of a deed with a retained life estate in Chapter 4.

QUALIFIED PERSONAL RESIDENCE TRUST

If your estate is larger and you are concerned about minimizing estate and gift taxes, a more sophisticated approach may be appropriate for you. This is to gift your house to your heirs using a qualified personal residence trust (QPRT) to remove the value of the house from your estate at a discounted rate. When using this technique, you transfer the entire ownership of the family house, by gift, to a special trust while retaining the right to live in the house for a term of years (say 10 years). At the end of the specified number of years, the ownership of the house would be transferred to the beneficiaries of the trust, generally your children. The term of years is basically a gamble on the likely duration of your life. The longer the term, the lower the value of the gift of the future interest in the house to the children (or other heirs) for gift tax purposes. However, the longer the term of years, the greater the likelihood that you may not survive the term of the trust, thus causing the entire value of the house to be included in your estate.

Planning Tip:　The QPRT is a great technique, but it is complicated. Be certain to hire an attorney who specializes in estate planning, not just a general practitioner, to help you.

The QPRT technique can be especially useful if your estate is large enough to be subject to an estate tax on your death, and your house is a valuable part of your estate. It is also a great tool when you want to leave a vacation property to your family.

The key benefits of the QPRT technique include:

- You leverage the use of the your $1 million gift exclusion amount (as a result of the time value of money discount feature of the QPRT calculation).
- Future appreciation (postdate the gift of the house to the QPRT) will never be taxed to your estate, and it won't use any of your gift exclusion.

Following the termination of the QPRT term, the house will be retitled (i.e., the name on the deed changes) from the QPRT to your children (or whomever else you listed in the QPRT to receive the house). If you still want to live in the house, as is likely, you must rent it from your children (or whomever else then owns it). This means that you must sign a written, arm's-length lease with the children and rent the house from them. While this may seem uncomfortable, if you didn't trust your children, why try to save tax and assure that your house goes to them?

GIVE YOUR HOME TO CHARITY

You can donate your house to charity. This can be done in one of two ways:

1. If you no longer wish to live in your home, you can simply give it to a charity. To do this, your lawyer will prepare a special

deed called a gift deed. The charity will have to investigate the house to assure that there are no environmental or other issues. However, this is not always a wise step because any gain on the sale of your house may avoid tax under the home exclusion rules discussed in Chapter 6. You may be better off selling your home, pocketing the proceeds tax free (if you meet the requirements), and instead giving securities to the charity. You can give appreciated securities, claim a charitable contribution deduction for the fair value of the securities, and avoid the capital gains. If you instead sold your securities, you could not use any exclusion (i.e., like you can with your house). Finally, a gift to a charity of marketable securities is far simpler, won't require a formal appraisal, and is far less likely to be challenged by the IRS. The moral: Think twice before giving your house to charity. It's a great thing to do, but make sure that there are no better options.

2. If you want to continue to live in your house, you can gift a remainder interest in a personal residence or farm and qualify for an immediate charitable contribution deduction. This is a special rule only available for homes. You would make a gift today of a future interest in your house or farm, obtain a current income tax deduction, and still be able to live in your house or farm for the rest of your life, or for some specified number of years. In addition, you can accomplish all of this without having to go through the legal complications, and expense, of setting up a trust. To accomplish these benefits with any asset other than your house, you would have to hire an estate attorney to draft a complex trust document. To qualify for these benefits, the gift must be irrevocable (no "backsies").

HOW TO OWN YOUR HOME FOR ESTATE TAX BENEFIT

If your house is a valuable part of your estate, there may be planning steps to take while you are alive to minimize estate taxes. This planning is based on taking maximum advantage of the exclusion amount that you and your spouse can give away free of estate tax. This amount is $1,000,000 (2002) and is scheduled to increase.

The key to this planning is that your will, and your spouse's will, should include a special trust called a bypass or exclusion trust. The concept, in very simplified terms, is this: If you give all your assets to your wife on your death, on her death the entire family fortune may exceed the exclusion amount that can be given away tax free. So instead, on your death your will transfers all of your assets, up to the exclusion amount, into a special trust. Your wife, as the survivor, will have substantial access to this trust, but not absolute control. The result is that your wife is protected financially, but the value of those assets are not included in her estate. This means that you can double, for a married couple, the amount of assets you can bequeath without an estate tax.

So what does all this have to do with your house? Potentially everything. For many homeowners, their house is one of the primary assets (other then pension assets) available to fund a sizeable portion of an applicable exclusion (bypass) trust under the will of the first spouse to die. You can't merely have an estate attorney draft a will including the magic trust language. You must also make sure that you and your wife each have approximately half of the family wealth in each of your names alone. This way, whichever one of you dies first, you will have significant assets for your will to transfer to the bypass or exclusion trust. How you own your assets is as important to the planning as having the right language in your will.

To achieve this funding, in many situations the title to your house may have to be changed. Typically, a house is owned as "husband and wife" (joint tenants or tenants by the entirety) will pass outside of either your estate or your wife's estate, by operation of law, to the surviving spouse. The value of the house will thus not be available (absent a successful disclaimer—the survivor takes legal action to avoid receiving the property) to fund any portion of an applicable exclusion trust.

Thus, a common transaction for estate planning for homeowners is to change the ownership ("re-titling") your house from joint tenants or tenants by the entirety to tenants in common. This can be a relatively simply procedure of deeding the house from you and your wife, as joint tenants, to you and your wife as tenants in common. In some situations, the house may be placed solely in the name of one spouse to equalize assets available to fund the maximum applicable exclusion amount no matter which spouse should die first.

Planning Tip: At the end of this chapter, a sample balance sheet is shown to help you identify, with your estate planner, how you should own your house. Always get professional advice because the simplified discussion just given does not address a myriad related issues.

HOW TO BEQUEATH YOUR HOME TO YOUR HEIRS UNDER YOUR WILL

The simplest way to bequeath a home is not to address it at all in your will. Let the executor deal with it. The problem with bequeathing a home to a specific person is that all sorts of issues can arise:

- What if the home is sold or given away before your death? What happens to the clause in your will bequeathing your home? If you do include a specific clause, make sure that you address what happens if the house is not owned by you at death.

- What if you have several beneficiaries? You might leave a four-family house to your three children. Sounds simple, but what happens if one of the children moves in, refuses to pay rent, and the other children are out the revenue? Even if the children all occupy apartments in the house, or rent the entire house, will they agree on important decisions like building a new roof? If you really want to bequeath a house to several children, consult an experienced estate planner well in advance. What seems like a simple decision can create a legal nightmare when you are gone. All of the decisions for co-owners of a rental property discussed in Chapter 6 need to be addressed.

- What if you're in a second or later marriage, how can you handle the home? Perhaps you can bequeath the home and other assets to a trust, or in limited situations (only an estate planning specialist can help you determine which) you can use a life estate. This is discussed in more detail next.

- If you bequeath your home to a specific heir but all your family has long since moved to another part of the country, what you have bequeathed is a headache. If your heirs have to pay for insurance, repairs and maintenance, brokerage commissions, and so on, have you really accomplished your goal?

Example: You have two children. Your home is worth $600,000 and you have $400,000 in securities. Your son has lived with you and cared for you for many years while your daughter has raised her own family 1,000 miles away. So you have a lawyer prepare a will leaving your son the house and your daughter the securities. What happens if your son then moves 2,000 miles away? What if your house increases in value to $1 million and your securities decline to fifty cents? Is this really the division you want?

- What is the value of the home you are bequeathing?
- If you bequeath specific assets, be wary of who will pay expenses and taxes.

Example: You have three children. You bequeath your house to your eldest daughter, and your remaining estate to your two sons, in equal shares. At the time you write your will, your house is worth $400,000 and the securities, $600,000. Your total estate is $1 million and no tax is due. Your daughter is named executrix. At your death, all assets have doubled in value. Your house is worth $800,000 and the securities, $1.2 million. However, if the house is given to your daughter and your will provided that expenses are paid from the residuary, which is common, your sons' share will be reduced by a large executrix fee to be paid to your daughter. Your sons' share will also bear the burden of all estate expenses (lawyer, accountant, etc.). If your estate of $2 million qualifies for a $1 million exclusion, the tax on the balance could approximate $400,000. So your sons' $1.2 million share could be reduced by $400,000 in tax, and expenses of perhaps $150,000. Is this really the result you want? It might be if you wanted to assure that your sons and daughter never speak again. The moral is you have to carefully plan out a specific bequest of a house to assure that it works. Simple sounding bequests can create havoc with your estate.

What to Put in Your Will

If you wish to specifically address your house in your will, review your goals with an estate planning specialist. You won't get this done if you're buying a $500 will from a general practice attorney. Review the preceding discussion to obtain an indication of the many problems that can arise.

When you meet with an estate specialist, review the following issues in deciding how to bequeath your house:

- What steps must be taken to minimize or eliminate federal estate and gift taxes?
- What should the tax allocation clause of the will state concerning the house (i.e., which heirs should bear the tax cost)?

Caution: If you think the answer after reading the problems discussed in the preceding section is to divide the tax pro rata, that may not be a workable answer either. Why? If you leave a $1 million house to one child and a $1 million money market account to your second child, and provide that the tax is shared equally (after all they are getting equal value) how will the child with the house pay his $250,000 share of the taxes? Mortgage the house or sell the very house you wanted to give him?

- What happens if the house is sold or given away while you are alive?
- Would it be advantageous to give away the house now, while you are alive, to a charity, trust for yourself (e.g., a revocable living trust), a trust for your spouse (e.g., a qualified terminable interest property or marital trust), or a QPRT?
- How will your surviving wife, trusts, and eventually heirs, pay for the upkeep of the house?
- Should your planning be affected by your desire to safeguard assets from medical costs and nursing home fees?
- Are there any unique circumstances or rules that apply to you?

GIVING YOUR HOME TO SPECIAL PEOPLE

Who you bequeath your home to under your will can also create issues. Consider the following, but in all cases consult with an experienced estate planning attorney.

Noncitizen Spouse

There are severe restrictions on how much you can give or bequeath to a noncitizen spouse without triggering tax costs. You can gift at most $110,000 per year. This amount is inflation indexed. For a spouse who is a citizen, there is no limit.

Example: You meet with an estate planner and decide to equalize your estate and your spouse's so that you can each fund a bypass trust under each will no matter who dies first. To do this, you decide to transfer your house worth $450,000 from joint title to your wife's name alone. If you neglect to tell the estate planner that your spouse is not a United States citizen, the transfer is equivalent to your giving your spouse $225,000 (she already owned half the house). Since this exceeds the $110,000 you can gift, you will use up $115,000 of your exclusion. It might have been better to gift the house over several years.

On death, you cannot give assets, such as your house, outright to a surviving wife who is not a citizen since your estate won't qualify for the unlimited estate tax marital deduction. The only way to qualify for a marital deduction when your spouse is not a citizen, is to bequeath assets intended to qualify for the marital deduction to a qualified domestic trust (QDOT). Consult with an estate planning specialist.

Nonmarried Partner

Gifts and bequests to nonmarried partners raise a number of special issues. A nonmarried partner won't qualify for a gift tax marital deduction. Thus, you may want to plan the gift to use annual $11,000 exclusions. You could also consult an estate planner about a special technique called a grantor retained interest trust (GRIT). This is a sophisticated technique that is similar to the QPRT. Consult with an estate planning specialist.

If you give a house, or an interest in a house, to a nonmarried partner while you are alive, consider some type of living together agreement in the event the relationship ends. This would be similar to the co-ownership or partnership agreement discussed in Chapter 6.

Child with Special Needs

If you wish to assure that a special needs child can live in your home, you will have to first determine if the child will need and qualify for state and federal aid programs. If so, your provision of a house may disqualify the child from these benefits. A better alternative in these situations might be to give all your assets to other children or heirs who will help care for the special needs child, and to fund a special needs trust under your will. This is a restrictive trust that can only make distributions that benefit the child for matters which state and federal and other programs do not provide. Hence the name "special needs" since only special needs are paid for, generally not basic needs such as shelter, food, and clothing.

CHAPTER SUMMARY

If your house is one of your largest assets, it will also be critical to your estate planning. Unfortunately, there are a host of legal, tax, and related complexities. This chapter identified many of these problems and provided you with specific practical guidance.

FOR YOUR NOTEBOOK

SAMPLE LIFE ESTATE CLAUSE TO
INCLUDE IN YOUR WILL

Note: The following are excerpts from a sample will illustrating a life estate. This can be used, when appropriate, instead of a trust, to hold a house. For example, if you are in a second marriage, you could grant your second wife a life estate in your house, and thereafter provide that it will be distributed to your children from your first marriage. Before opting for this approach, review any divorce and prenuptial agreement for requirements that may affect planning for your home. Next, consult with an estate planning specialist and review the benefits of using a special marital trust, such as a qualified terminable interest property (QPRT) trust instead. If you decide to use a QPRT instead of a life estate, still review this sample form since you may want to address the same issues in the language your lawyer prepares for the trust.

Debts and Administrative Expenses

Note: This illustrative provision assumes that the property is a cooperative apartment. The language can be adjusted by your attorney for any property.

. . . Notwithstanding the foregoing I direct my Executor to pay any mortgage or other loan secured by my cooperative apartment (equity, shares or lease) located at [Property Address] ([City Name] Co-op), if any exists at the time of my death, as soon as possible after my death and if I shall own the [City Name] Co-op at the time of my death. This provision is intended to affect a loan on my apartment only and not any financing on the building itself.

Specific Bequest of Contents of [City Name]
Cooperative Apartment

If my close friend, [Partner Name] survives me, I specifically give and bequeath my tangible personal property located in the [City Name] Co-op, as provided in this provision:

Note: Any time you bequeath your house, be sure to address separately who gets the furniture. This is because a general clause in your will may distribute this property differently if you don't address it. Do you want the person having the house to have the furniture, too? If you're using a life estate or trust, should the personal property be held in trust or given outright to the person (e.g., your second husband)? If it is given outright you will have no control over where it is eventually given.

1. With respect to such tangible personal property, including the household furnishings and art work contained in said [City Name] Co-op, I hereby specifically give and bequeath the following:

2. Within sixty (60) days of my death, my Executor shall compile a list of all of my tangible personal property in the [City Name] Co-op List. My Executor shall mail a copy of the [City Name] Co-op List to my children, [Child 1] and [Child 2].

3. Within twenty (20) days of receiving such notice, [Children] may request distribution of any item on the [City Name] Co-op List by notifying my Executor.

4. At the end of the twenty (20) day period, my Executor shall give [Partner Name] notice of the items requested by [Children] from the [City Name] Co-op List. If [Partner Name] objects to the distribution of an item on the basis that such item was her property, then the issue must be submitted to arbitration by any independent person selected by my Executor.

Note: The following provision assumes that you have a revocable living trust in place owning the property.

5. All of the remaining tangible personal property, including the household furnishings contained in said [City Name] Co-op, I give, devise and bequeath to the Trustee of Trust for Children and Issue in GST-Exempt Trust established under this Will or under a certain Trust Agreement entitled [Your Name] Revocable Living Trust, made [Month, Day, Year], between myself and [Trustee Name] as Fiduciary.

If [Partner Name] does not survive me, I bequeath all of my tangible personal property located in the [City Name] Co-op in accordance with the provision entitled "As Adult Children Shall Agree [not reflected in this excerpt]."

[Partner Name]'s Interest

1. This provision shall be referred to as "[Partner Name]'s Interest."

Note: What should the life tenant be responsible to pay for? Does he have the funds to do so?

---

2. If [Partner Name] survives me, the Trustees shall allow her to live in my [City Name] Co-op, should I own such property at the time of my death, and make use of any of my furniture, furnishings, art work and household effects located therein which are not previously distributed pursuant to prior provisions of my Will to my Children (as hereinafter defined), without the necessity of paying rent or furnishing bond or other security therefor, but subject to and upon the condition that [Partner Name] (the Co-op Beneficiary) pays all property and similar taxes, and assessments (by government authorities or the cooperative corporation) on the [City Name] Co-op and the underlying building, all principal and interest payments on the underlying building allocated to the [City Name] Co-op, carrying charges (including fire and extended coverage insurance premiums for the full insurable value thereof), and normal costs of maintenance and repairs, in respect thereof (collectively Carrying Costs). However, the Co-op Beneficiary shall not be responsible for payment of any mortgage on such [City Name] Co-op which exists at the time of my death, such responsibility being solely an obligation of my estate.

The Co-op Beneficiary shall have reasonable responsibility and liability for waste, and shall have a reasonable duty to account to any remaindermen.

The Co-op Beneficiary shall have no authority to sell, mortgage or in any manner encumber such property.

Note: Address specifically when the surviving husband or partner's interest ends. Simple forms may say on death. But after reviewing the following, it will be clear that there are many other circumstances that would warrant ending the interest. If this is not done, your ultimate heirs (e.g., children from a first marriage) will have to wait until the life tenant dies to sell the property.

[Partner Name]'s Interest shall terminate on the earliest of the following events occurring:

1. On the Co-op Beneficiary's death.

2. On the Co-op Beneficiary's renunciation or disclaimer of the interest in said property.

3. On the Co-op Beneficiary's long-term or permanent disability which prevents her from occupying and maintaining the [City Name] Co-op. A written statement from two doctors properly licensed to practice that [Partner Name] is unlikely in their reasonable professional judgment, to be able to occupy and reside in the [City Name] Co-op for a period of at least Eighteen (18) months shall be conclusive proof upon which any fiduciary may rely for determining [Partner Name]'s permanent disability, Upon receipt of such notices the fiduciary may immediately terminate [Partner Name]'s Interest and sell or transfer the [City Name] Co-op in accordance with the provisions hereof.

4. If the Co-op Beneficiary is in default in the fulfillment of her obligations to pay the Carrying Costs or any other expenses of the [City Name] Co-op which are her obligations hereunder for Two (2) consecutive months, the Trustees shall give her written notice of such default and four (4) months to cure same. If she fails to cure the default within four (4) months of the date of such notice being sent, [Partner Name]'s Interest shall terminate.

At the termination of [Partner Name]'s Interest, the [City Name] Co-op shall be added to and administered as part of the GST-Exempt Trust.

Note: What happens if the cooperative board won't let your surviving spouse or partner reside in the apartment?

If the Board of the [City Name] Co-op does not allow [Partner Name] to live in the [City Name] Co-op as described above, or permit the transfer of the Co-op to the trusts under my Will, then I give, devise and bequeath an amount equal to the present value of the fair market rental value of the [City Name] Co-op multiplied by [Partner Name]'s life expectancy, as determined under the Internal Revenue Service's life expectancy tables to [Partner Name], if she survives me. This amount shall be determined by my Executor obtaining a written estimate of the monthly fair rental value of the Co-op, unfurnished and in the condition it is then in, and multiplying such amount by the estimated number of whole months in the life expectancy of [Partner Name]. The figure so obtained shall be discounted to a present value figure by the attorney or accountant preparing the Federal Estate Tax Return for my estate and such figures shall be conclusive and binding on all persons herein.

The GST-Exempt Trust shall terminate upon the first to occur of the following events:

1. Upon the youngest of my Grandchildren living upon my death reaching the age of thirty-five (35) years, or

2. Upon the death of my youngest Grandchild living at any time if my other Grandchildren living shall all have then reached the age of thirty-five (35) years, or

3. Upon the death of the last to die of all my Grandchildren if none of them shall reach the age of thirty-five (35) years.

Upon the termination of the GST-Exempt Trust, the Trustee shall transfer, convey, and pay over the principal of the trust to my then living Grandchildren in equal shares (per capita and not per stirpes), provided, however, that if a Grandchild is not then living but has then living issue the share to which such deceased Grandchild would have been entitled had such Grandchild then been living shall be paid to the issue of such Grandchild, per stirpes, outright and free of trust for any of my Grandchildren or more remote descendants who are then over age Thirty Five (35), or in trust for any of my Grandchildren or more remote descendants who are then under age thirty-five (35) in accordance with the provision below "Bequests and Devises to Persons Under Age Thirty-Five (35)."

My Children are [Child 1] and [Child 2].

The Trustee is authorized, but not required, to combine this trust with any similar trust formed under any Trust Agreement created by me during my lifetime.

SAMPLE TEMPLATE FOR DETERMINING
THE ESTATE IMPLICATIONS OF YOUR HOME
AND OTHER ASSETS TO DISCUSS WITH YOUR
ESTATE AND FINANCIAL PLANNERS

The template that follows will help you organize a balance sheet. This provides an overview of your current financial picture. It is vitally important to have such a perspective to properly begin to identify planning opportunities, or to update an estate plan, which includes determining how your house and other real estate should be owned. This balance sheet will help you and your estate planner use the values of your house, investments, and other assets to analyze your overall estate tax picture and identify appropriate estate planning techniques to minimize tax. For real estate assets you may wish to note in the margin if they are located outside the state where you reside (this highlights the issue of ancillary probate, which may warrant planning to minimize or eliminate).

If you have too many different accounts and assets, your advisers may recommend that you consolidate assets to simplify planning to make your estate more manageable in the event of your disability, and to minimize probate fees. If you consolidate, watch out for transfer costs triggering taxable income or capital gains on having to sell certain funds or assets which the institutions you are consolidating to won't handle.

If you are married, you may wish to take advantage of the $1 million in 2002 (increasing thereafter to $3.5 million) available to each of you and your spouse (after 2009 the estate tax is to be repealed and modified carry over basis rules will apply, but the estate tax is scheduled to be reinstated in 2011). Ownership of assets, and especially large assets such as your home or other real estate, will have to be divided between you and your spouse so that each estate can fund an applicable exclusion trust. This is a trust designed to benefit your surviving spouse (and often other heirs) while assuring that the assets in that trust are not taxed in his/her estate. This trust is also called a "Bypass Trust" since the assets bypass taxation in the surviving spouse's estate. Joint ownership of assets defeats this planning opportunity because on death joint assets pass automatically to the joint owner and cannot pass through a will (or revocable living trust) to the Bypass Trust. It may be possible to use disclaimers (a formal process of refusing an inheritance so the assets pass as if you were not alive) to salvage this type of planning. Disclaimers, however, are complex and should generally not be counted on except as a last resort.

Post-etate tax repeal, assets will have to be divided to take maximum advantage of the modified carry over basis rules.

Joint ownership, the most common ownership of a home by a husband and wife, can supersede the distributions provided in your will since such assets pass to the joint owner on death, and not as your will (or revocable living trust) directs. You have to coordinate the ownership of assets with your documents and plan. For many people, most of their estate may pass outside of their will (i.e., outside probate). Insurance may be paid to a named beneficiary, IRA accounts will be paid to the designated beneficiaries of those plans, a house may be owned as tenants by the entirety (a special form of joint ownership) and your vacation home may be owned jointly with a sibling or other person, and so forth. This must be evaluated to be certain that your goals are met. Discussion with your financial and estate planners how assets have to be restructured to better fund the Bypass Trusts, take advantage of the modified basis step-up rules after 2009, consider asset protection planning, and so forth. This may often require changing assets from one spouse to another.

Caution: In doing so, be careful. If the recipient spouse is not a United States citizen there is no unlimited marital deduction, thus, a tax could be incurred on the transfers. A transfer could trigger an acceleration clause in a mortgage making it immediately due.

If you have substantial security, nonpersonal real estate, and/or business holdings, your advisers may recommend that you consolidate some of these assets into a family limited partnership (FLP) or a limited liability company (LLC) to facilitate making annual gifts, to try to secure discounts, to somewhat protect these assets from claims, or to use these entities to fund complex tax-oriented trusts such as Grantor Retained Annuity Trusts (GRATs). These are trusts to which you transfer assets but retain an annual (or more frequent) annuity payment. After a specified number of years, your heirs (not grandchildren) will own the assets. This technique can help leverage the value of large gifts you make.

If you have a valuable house, your adviser may recommend that you consider using a Qualified Personal Residence Trust (QPRT) to transfer the value of a primary residence, and/or vacation home, to your children (not grandchildren) in a tax advantaged manner. You would retain the right to live in the residence for a specified number of years, after which your children would own the house and you would rent it. Your advisers may indicate QPRT in the "Planning Comments" column if this technique warrants further consideration.

Does the spouse or partner with the greatest risk (e.g., malpractice, business) own too many assets? Your advisers may circle certain assets and draw arrows to the spouse in whose name they should be transferred. Consider costs, legal constraints, and so forth of any such transfers.

Consider the cost or tax basis for assets. This can affect income and estate tax planning. It is often not possible to note this level of detail on the balance sheet. However, generally, if you have an asset which has appreciated substantially over what you paid for it, dying holding that asset will usually eliminate all pre-death capital gains. If you gift that asset to heirs, they will continue to have your low purchase price as their tax "basis." If they sell the asset, the excess of what they receive over this basis figure will generally be taxable.

Do you have adequate property and casualty insurance for all real estate and other assets. A common error is not purchasing business liability insurance and assuming your homeowner's policy covers it. Don't assume. Get written confirmation from your agent. If you don't have adequate personal excess liability (also called "umbrella") insurance, your planner may note in the "Planning Comments" column "umbrella" to remind you to pursue this with your property and casualty insurance agent. You should consider periodically having your insurance agent provide you with a summary of all your coverage and review its adequacy.

Estate Planning Balance Sheet

Asset Category	Owned by You	Owned by Spouse/ Partner	Jointly Owned with Spouse/ Partner	Pension/ Retirement Assets	Total by Category	Planning Comments
Cash	$	$	$	$	$	
CDs						
Marketable securities						
Mutual funds						
House net of mortgage						
Vacation home net of mortgage						
Other real estate investments net						
Annuities						
IRAs						
Other pension/ retirement						
Closely held business net						
Possible inheritances						
Possible claims/ losses						
Liabilities						
Life insurance: [ ] Death values; [ ] CSV						
Total estimated net worth	$	$	$	$		

DEED FOR CHARITABLE
REMAINDER INTEREST IN RESIDENCE

Note: The following sample deed illustrates the gift of your home in a manner preserving the use for you during your life, and then a transfer to a charity of residence on your death (a life estate).

THIS INDENTURE, made this [Month] [Day], [Year], between [Your Name], residing at [Your Address], and [Charity Name], a corporation existing under the laws of the State of [State Name], and doing business at [Charity Address].

WITNESSETH, that [Your Name] transfers to [Charity Name], its successors and assigns forever.

ALL the land, with the buildings and improvements thereon, at [Home Address], (hereinafter "premises").

Note: Do not transfer tangible personal property along with a personal residence when a life estate is retained. If the real property is subject to a mortgage, the gift will be considered a "bargain sale."

TOGETHER with all right, title and interest, if any, of [Your Name] in and to any roads abutting the premises to its center lines.

TOGETHER with the appurtenances and all the estate and rights of [Your Name] in the premises.

TO HAVE AND TO HOLD in fee simple remainder the premises at the expiration of the following life estate:

An estate in the premises is reserved to [Your Name] for his life.

This deed is accepted by [Charity Name] as a gift from [Your Name], subject to the retained estate for the life of [Your Name].

[Your Name] will be obliged to maintain the premises during his lifetime, and to insure the premises against damage by fire or other hazard.

In donating this remainder in his personal residence to [Charity Name], [Your Name] intends to obtain the full benefit of any income, gift and estate tax charitable contribution deductions to which he (and his estate) may be entitled under the Internal Revenue Code (Code). Accordingly, this deed shall be interpreted consistent with [Your Name]'s intent.

Note: If the charity you are giving your home to, after your death, is not qualified as a charity for tax deduction purposes, the deed can recite an alternate charity as a recipient to preserve your tax benefit. It is essential to omit the reference to Code Section 170(b)(1)(A) if the remainderman is a private foundation or may be a private foundation at the time when the property passes to it.

If [Charity Name] is not an organization described in each of Code Sections 170(b)(1)(A), 170(c), 2055(a) and 2522(a) on the death of [Your Name], then the premises shall pass to [Charity Name 2], if it is then an organization described in each of Code Sections 170(b)(1)(A), 170(c), 2055(a) and 2522(a). If neither [Charity Name] nor [Charity Name 2] is then an organization described in each of Code Sections 170(b)((1)(A), 170(c), 2055(a) and 2522(a), the premises shall pass to [Corporation Name 3].

Note: The following paragraph specifies that if any estate, inheritance, or other death taxes are charged against your estate, none will be charged against the value of the house you've given to charity. A similar provision should be used anytime there is a charitable gift.

No federal estate taxes, state death taxes or any other estate, death or inheritance taxes ("death taxes") with respect to the premises shall be allocated to or recoverable from the premises. [Your Name] imposes an obligation on his estate to pay any death taxes from sources other than the premises and agrees to so provide in his Will or in another way. This provision may be enforced by [Charity Name].

_____ (L.S.)
[Your Name], Grantor

[Charity Name]

By _____
(seal)

[Add appropriate acknowledgements, notary forms, etc. here.]

Glossary

Abstract of title.   A short summary reflecting the history of the ownership and title to a certain parcel of real estate. It should indicate all transfers, judicial proceedings, encumbrances, and so on.

Accelerate expenses.   A common year-end tax planning step is to pay for certain expenses prior to December 31, rather than incur them after December 31. This can give you the tax benefit of a deduction a year earlier than if you had waited until January 1 or later to pay the expense. An example of this is to pay your estimated state taxes by December 31, rather than by the following January 15 when they are often due. Consider the alternative minimum tax before committing to any planning step.

Accelerated cost recovery system.   The rules for calculating depreciation (annual write-offs) for buildings, furniture, and other assets have been called the Accelerated Cost Recovery System (or ACRS) since 1981. Sometimes the depreciation system after 1986 is called the Modified Accelerated Cost Recovery System (or MACRS). Depreciation write-offs are technically called recovery deductions under these rules. The basic approach to calculating depreciation under these rules is to multiply a percentage you look up in charts provided by the IRS by the costs (adjusted basis) of the building, furniture, or other assets you are depreciating.

Acceleration clause.   A provision in a contract or loan agreement that provides that when a specified event occurs all payments due in the future become immediately due and payable. For example, in an installment sale contract, a clause could provide that if the buyer is more than 10 days late on three separate occasions, the seller can make all future payments on the installment note due immediately.

Acquisition costs. When buying a business or property many costs can be incurred which have to be added to (capitalized as part of) your cost (adjusted basis) in the property. For example, the cost of a title insurance report, legal fees, transfer taxes, accounting fees, and so forth may all have to be added to your cost in the property. If the property is an investment property, and not your home, carefully evaluate the acquisition costs to find expenses which you can deduct currently. Plan how you allocate the total acquisition cost between land, building, furniture, and other assets you purchased since land can't be written off (depreciated), buildings and furniture can be written off (depreciated) quickest of all.

Active participation test. Investors who are sufficiently involved with their rental property to meet this test, and have income (see Modified adjusted gross income) less than $150,000 can deduct some or all of the tax losses, up to $25,000, from their rental property against any income including wages (active income) and dividends and interest (portfolio income). The amount of this $25,000 loss allowance that can be used is reduced as your income exceeds $100,000, and is eliminated entirely when income reaches $150,000. To meet the active participation test you must own at least 10 percent of the investment, make management type decisions (approve new tenants, set rental rates, approve major repairs, and so forth). *TIP:* Keep a diary or log of everything you do for the rental property to prove that you were actively involved.

Adjusted basis. Roughly speaking your investment, for tax purposes, in certain property. The cost you pay to buy or build a building (or any other asset), plus costs to improve it. If you have a casualty loss it reduces your adjusted basis. Adjusted basis is used to calculate depreciation (multiply it by the appropriate depreciation or MACRS percentage) and to determine the taxable gain or loss when you sell property (subtract adjusted basis from your net sales proceeds to determine your gain). If you're subject to the alternative minimum tax your assets may have different adjusted basis for the regular tax and the alternative minimum tax. Consider the home sale exclusion.

Affidavit. A written statement sworn to and signed before a notary public or other authorized person. For example, if there is a judgment against a person with the same name as the seller, the seller will give the buyer an affidavit saying the judgment isn't against him.

Allocation.   The purchase price for a business or a rental property must be allocated between different assets acquired, such as intangible rights (customer lists, etc.), land, building, furniture, and fixtures, equipment, inventory, and so forth, in order to determine your depreciation deductions. See Acquisition costs.

Alternative minimum tax.   This is a second parallel tax system which many wealthier taxpayers will have to consider when calculating their tax. The alternative minimum tax (or AMT) is calculated by starting with your taxable income calculated according to the regular tax rules. Add certain tax preference items and adjustments required by the AMT. Only certain itemized deductions are allowed. Next, subtract an exemption amount. The result is multiplied by AMT tax rate for individuals. If the tax due exceeds the tax you owe under the regular tax system than you must pay the larger alternative minimum tax.

Amortization.   The schedule of periodic (generally monthly) payments made to a bank or other lender on a mortgage. The amortization period (e.g., 30 years) is the number of years over which the mortgage principal will be paid off. Where there is a mortgage amortization period which is longer than the maturity date of the mortgage (the date the mortgage is due) a balloon payment will be due when the mortgage matures.

Amount realized.   The money and the fair market value of any property you receive when you sell property. It also includes the amount of any liabilities which the buyer takes responsibility for.

Annual exclusion.   Every person is permitted to give away up to $11,000 per year to any other person without incurring any gift tax. There is no limit on the number of people you can make these gifts to in a year. To qualify for this exclusion the gifts must be of a present interest, meaning that the recipient can enjoy the gift immediately. This can present problems when you make gifts to trusts. This exclusion can be doubled to $22,000 per person, per year, if you're married and your spouse consents to join in making the gift. This is called gift splitting.

Assessed value.   The value of real estate as determined by the tax assessor. Often it is some percentage of fair market value.

Assumption of mortgage.   Where a buyer purchases property and agrees to be personally liable on the mortgage which is on the property. Note, the buyer's assumption of a mortgage will not necessarily relieve the seller of liability on the mortgage the buyer assumed. To accomplish this the seller must obtain a release from the lender. Compare an assumption to the situation where a buyer simply purchases the property subject to any mortgage. In this latter case the buyer acknowledges that the mortgage is a lien on the property, however, the buyer doesn't agree to become personally liable on the mortgage.

Bad debt.   A loan which can't be collected. It may give rise to a deduction for tax purposes in the year in which worthlessness can be established.

Balloon payment.   Where a large balance is due on a note and mortgage at a date which is before the time when regular payments would have amortized (paid off) the loan.

Basis.   Your investment in property for tax purposes. It includes the price you paid to purchase the property, including ancillary costs such as legal fees. It is increased by capital improvements (e.g., a new deck). It is decreased by depreciation (e.g., on a home office or rental unit included in the home).

Beneficiary.   A person who receives the benefits of a trust or of transfers under your will or trust, such as a QPRT. In legal jargon, sometimes referred to as cestui que trust. The grantor is the beneficiary of the QPRT during the term of the QPRT since the grantor preserves the right to use the residence. The remainder beneficiaries (typically, but not always, grantor's children) receive their interest following the termination of the QPRT term.

Bequest.   Property transferred under you will.

Bill of sale.   A written agreement which transfers ownership and title to personal property from the seller to the buyer.

Binder.   Money paid by a buyer as a good faith deposit to encourage the seller to take the property off of the market. A binder is also used in the context of insurance policies where a binder, or temporary policy, is issued, pending issuance of the actual policy.

Capital improvement.   A permanent improvement or addition to real estate which will materially prolong the life of the property, change its use, or enhance its value. For example, patching 5 percent of a roof is a repair. Replacing the entire roof is a capital expenditure.

Capital expenditures even on a rental or business property can't be deducted for tax purposes. They are added to your basis, or investment, in the property.

Capitalize.   When expenses which are not deductible are added to your investment (adjusted basis) in the property they are capitalized.

Cash flow.   The actual cash you receive after paying expenses on your rental property. Depreciation write-offs are an expense for tax purposes which does not require you to pay cash. So when calculating the cash flow from a property you must add back depreciation write-offs to the income (or loss) you report for tax purposes on the property.

Casualty loss.   A loss deduction may be allowed for a loss to your real estate investment property or for a loss on your home resulting from a fire, storm, theft, and so forth. Certain disaster losses may be deducted in the year before they actually occurred. New rules ease the requirements for reinvesting insurance proceeds received as a result of a casualty.

Certificate of occupancy.   Also called "C of O." This is an authorization or document issued by a local government body permitting the use of a property for a certain purpose. In some instances a certificate of occupancy must be obtained for the closing to be completed or for the buyer to move into the house.

Charitable remainder trust.   You donate property or money to a charity, reserving the right to use the property, or to receive income from it for a specified time (a number of years, the duration of your life, or the duration of your life and the life of a second person such as your spouse). When the agreed period is over the property belongs the charitable organization.

Closing.   The final meeting where all checks are paid and the buyer is given title to the house.

Condominium.   A system of separate ownership of individual units in a multiunit real estate project. Each owner of an individual unit is a tenant-in-common in the common areas (halls, athletic facilities, parking, etc.).

Consideration.   Something of value given in return for a promise to perform a certain act or contract. Legal consideration is required in certain instances so that some legal documents might say for "Ten dollars and other good and valuable consideration" or something similar.

Damages.   Money award which a court may give to redress a wrong and make the injured person whole.

Debt.   Money or other valuable rights or property owning from one person to another. A note is where the borrower acknowledges the debt and agrees to personally repay it. A mortgages is the document by which the borrower pledges his real estate as collateral for the repayment of a debt.

Deed of trust.   In many states, particularly those located in the western half of the country, a deed of trust is used instead of a mortgage. Although there still may be differences between a deed of trust and a mortgage, the differences are primarily historical.

Default.   Where a borrower violates a provision of a mortgage loan, or one of the parties to a contract (e.g., the buyer or seller under a sales contract) violates a provision of the contract, a default may be triggered. A default, or failure to perform, will have the consequences that the contract or loan agreement provides when a default occurs. For a loan this could mean acceleration (the entire loan balance becomes due and payable). In a sales contract a default could excuse the other party from having to continue under the contract.

Defect of record.   A lien, encroachment, encumbrance, or other defect in the title to property that is set forth in the public record. This means that the title search completed by the title company or the attorney will identify this defect.

Defective title.   Title which is not marketable.

Demand note.   A loan evidenced by a note which is due immediately upon an agreed upon maturation, for example, where the lender states it is due, without requirement for further demand.

Donor.   A person who makes a gift. The person setting up a trust can be called donor, trustor, grantor, or settlor. In a QPRT the donor gives his or her interest in a qualifying residence to the QPRT and retains the right to use it for the term of the QPRT.

Durable power of attorney.   A durable power of attorney is one which will remain effective when you become disabled. Almost every power should be prepared as a "durable power" so that in the event of your disability it will be effective. In order to be durable the power of attorney must generally include language to the effect that "This power of attorney will remain effective despite the subsequent disability of the grantor." Without language specifically stating that the power remains effective, it may not do so and all your good planning intentions may be for naught.

Earnest money.   A good faith payment which a buyer pays to the seller (often to the real estate broker to hold in escrow on the seller's behalf) to encourage seller to take the property off the market and pursue a sale to that buyer.

Easement.   The right of one person to make lawful use of another's land. For example, a neighbor might have an easement to use your driveway to reach his property. The electric company might have an easement to run wires along the back 10 feet of your property. Distinguish an easement from an encroachment, where, for example, a neighbor illegally, or inadvertently built his fence two feet inside your property line.

Elective expensing.   The cost of furniture and equipment used in a business or rental property must be written off over seven years using the 200 percent declining balance method of depreciation. If certain requirements are met, however, you may be able to write off certain furniture and equipment (personal property) immediately.

Eminent domain.   The right of a government body to take private property for public use.

Encroachment.   To unlawfully intrude on another's land. For example, if your neighbor's tool shed is on the last five feet of your property without your permission. This would be shown in a survey of the property and may be a defect which the buyer demands corrected.

Escrow.   Monies and documents are generally held by an unrelated third party (escrow agent) pending the closing of the sale of the house. If the requirements and conditions to close are met, the monies in the escrow will be given to the seller and the deed conveying title to the property to the buyer.

Estate tax.   On the death of a taxpayer a tax may be due on the transfer of wealth to family and others. Exclusions are provided for transfers to the taxpayer's spouse, charities, and so forth. The tax rate for the estate tax can reach as high as 50 percent (2002, decreasing thereafter). A once in a lifetime credit is permitted that enables you to pass property worth up to $1 million (2002, increasing thereafter) to others without having to pay an estate tax. In a QPRT, if the grantor dies before the termination of the QPRT, the value of the residence will be included in the grantor's estate and may thus be subject to estate tax. For many taxpayers, re-titling their home from joint tenants or tenants by the entirety to tenants in common assures each spouse sufficient assets to take advantage of the credit, fund a Bypass Trust, and eliminate estate tax entirely.

Execute.   To complete a legal agreement. For example, to sign a contract.

Family partnership.   A partnership owned by members of the same family for purposes of transferring some of the value of the business or real estate to the younger generation and possibly involving them in the management of the business as well.

Fee simple.   Absolute ownership interest in land.

Fiduciary.   A person in a position of trust and responsibility, such as your executor or the trustee of a trust. The QPRT will have a trustee and successor trustees who are fiduciaries and as such will owe a fiduciary duty to the QPRT beneficiaries.

Fixture.   Personal property (movable property) which became permanently attached to the real estate. Fixtures will generally be sold automatically with the sale of your house unless you exclude them from the sale. An example is a bookcase which is permanently nailed to the subwall.

General partnership.   A partnership which has only general partners and no limited partners. This is the most common way for a few friends or investors to put their money together to buy a rental property. Ask your attorney about an LLC.

Gift.   Where you transfer property without receiving something of equal value in return the federal government will assess a transfer tax where the value of the gift exceeds the annual exclusion and your unified credit is exhausted. The initial transfer of the residence to the QPRT is a gift subject to gift tax. A current gift tax will be due to the extent that the grantor's unified credit does not offset the tax liability.

Gift tax.   A tax which can be due when you give property or other assets away. You are allowed to give away a maximum of $11,000 per person (to any number of people) in any year without the tax applying. This amount is to be indexed for inflation. Above the $11,000 amount you have a once-in-a-lifetime exclusion which permits you to give away $1 million of property without paying any gift tax.

Grace period. A period of time beyond a due date which a payment or other required action may be completed without penalty. For example, a note may commonly have a five day grace period. Although all payments are due on the first day of each month, any payment received within the first five days of the month will not result in any penalty or acceleration.

Grantor. Where you establish a trust and transfer assets to it you're called the grantor of that trust. Also called trustor, settlor, and, occasionally, donor.

Grantor trust. A trust on which the person who set up the trust is required to report the income on his own tax return. The most common is a revocable living trust to which many people transfer their home, and in particular a vacation home located in a different state, to avoid probate.

Heirs. The persons who receive your assets following your death.

Improvements. Payments for additions or betterment to property which will last more than a year and must thus be added to your investment (capitalized as part of your basis) in the property.

Imputed interest. In most sale transactions, if the seller and buyer don't set a reasonable market interest rate on deferred payments (e.g., an installment sale) the IRS can set a minimum payment and require the calculations to be made as if interest had been paid. This can have a significant effect on the tax results to be realized by the parties.

Installment sale. A sale where taxable gain is recognized over a number of years as the payment for the property sold is received. If you are a dealer in property you can't use the installment method.

Inter vivos trust. A trust created during your life time. Also called a living trust or revocable living trust.

Involuntary conversion. When your property is destroyed (converted) by a casualty loss and you receive an insurance payment you can avoid a current tax cost by reinvesting the money in qualifying replacement property. The tax laws permit reinvestment during a period lasting four years after the close of the tax year in which the conversion occurred.

Irrevocable. Where a trust cannot be changed after you've established it, the trust is irrevocable. This is an essential characteristic to have assets you give to the trust removed from your estate. A QPRT is always irrevocable. A bypass trust under your will is irrevocable after death.

Joint tenancy. Where you and your spouse, or another person, own assets as joint tenants, when one of you dies the property automatically passes to the surviving joint tenant. Too often used as a means of avoiding probate even though it is not necessarily the optimal tax strategy for most people. When structuring a QPRT the title to the residence may be changed to tenants in common so each spouse, where applicable and appropriate, can transfer one-half interest to his or her separate QPRT.

Judgment. A determination of a matter by a court of proper or competent jurisdiction.

Kiddie tax. Unearned income (dividends, rents, interest, etc.) of a child under age 14 will be taxed to the child at the parent's highest tax rate. This tax makes family tax planning much harder.

Land contract. A method of sale which permits the seller to retain title to the property until all amounts due are paid by the buyer. The seller's rights to repossess the property may be limited by local law.

Lien. A charge or claim on another's property as security for a debt due. A mechanic's lien is a lien for work performed and materials furnished to a property. Buyers will generally require that certain liens, such as mechanic's liens, be paid or discharged before closing so that the buyer may obtain marketable title.

Listing broker.   The broker who signs the listing or brokerage contract with you to sell your house.

Marital deduction.   Where you and your spouse are legally married either of you can transfer an unlimited amount of assets to the other without incurring any gift or estate tax cost. This is too often used as a simplistic approach to eliminate the entire estate tax on the death of the first of you or your wife.

Marketable title.   Ownership interest in the real property which a buyer should be willing to take and a court willing to require a buyer to take.

Material participation.   Relates to your ability to deduct losses on a rental property. The passive activity rules create three general types of income: (1) passive (i.e., an investment in a limited partnership); (2) portfolio (i.e., dividends and interest on stocks and bonds); and (3) active income (i.e., wages and earnings from a business in which you are active). For income to qualify as active you must materially participate in the business. This requires that you are involved on a (1) regular; (2) continuous; and (3) substantial basis.

Minor.   Person who is not old enough to be an adult under state law. The age varies by state. When drafting a QPRT consideration should be given to limiting the remainder beneficiaries to solely the adult children of the grantor. If the QPRT had to modified or changed, having only adult children (e.g., excluding the common bequest to issue of a deceased child, or heir), and instead providing that in the event a child died prior to the end of the QPRT term, the deceased child's siblings would inherit.

Mortgage.   Under the lien theory followed in many states a mortgage is the legal document which gives the lender a lien on a house (or other real property) to secure a loan. Under title theory states a deed of trust is used. Under a deed of trust an independent third party (i.e., someone other than the borrower and lender), called the trustee, holds title to the property. When the debt is paid the documents of title are returned to the owner/former borrower. If the borrower defaults the trustee can transfer the documents of title to the lender.

Moving expenses.   If you have to move to a new home in connection with starting work at a new principal place of work you may qualify to deduct, as an itemized deduction, a number of expenses of the move. Deductible expenses may include the costs of moving your household goods. To qualify your new principal place of work must be at least 50 miles farther from your former home than was your former principal place of work.

Note.   A document in which a borrower personally agrees to assume responsibility for the payment of a loan. Distinguish a note from a mortgage which is the document that pledges the house (or other real estate as collateral for repayment of the loan).

Notice.   Information concerning a legal matter actually communicated to the party. Most contracts and agreements have provisions which specify how notice must be given. If you ever have to notify a buyer, for example, of default under a purchase money mortgage, be certain that the requirements for giving the buyer notice, as contained in the sales contract, mortgage and note, and so forth, are followed.

Ordinary and necessary expense.   For payments to be deductible they must be ordinary and necessary expenses of your trade or business. Extravagant or personal expenses will not be deductible.

Ordinary income.   Income or gain from selling property that is not a capital asset. See "Capital Asset." Ordinary income is taxed at maximum rates, which are less favorable then capital gains rates of a maximum 20 percent. There is an advantage for many taxpayers to realizing capital gains rather than ordinary income.

Partnership.   A syndicate, joint venture, group, or other arrangement, in which two or more investors join their money and skills to carry out a business as co-owners and to earn a profit. A partnership is generally treated as a flow-through (conduit) so that the partners each report their share of partnership income or loss on their personal tax returns. The partnership files a Form 1065 as an information report with the IRS but doesn't pay any tax. An election is available to avoid being taxed as a partnership.

Passive income. The passive income and loss rules divide income into three types. (1) active (wages, income from an active business); (2) passive (income earned from rental property or as a limited partner investor); and (3) portfolio (dividends and interest on stocks and bonds). Passive losses (tax losses from rental property or from investments made as a limited partner) can only be applied to offset passive income. If you qualify as actively participating in a real estate rental you may be able to deduct up to $25,000 of you passive tax losses against any income without regard to this limitation.

Passive loss. Passive losses are tax losses from rental real estate properties (e.g., as a result of depreciation write-offs) or from investments as a limited partner. Passive losses can generally only be used to offset passive income.

Personal property. Furniture, equipment, and other moveable property and assets. Buildings and land are not personal property, they are real property. When buying or constructing a building valuable tax benefits can be found by carefully identifying which property is properly treated as personal property instead of real property. This is because personal property can be written off (depreciated) much more quickly than real property.

Qualified domestic trust (Q-DOT). If your spouse is not a United States citizen your estate will not be entitled to claim the benefit of the unlimited marital deduction except to the extent that assets are transferred into this special trust. Where one spouse is not a citizen the gift tax marital deduction is limited to $110,000 per annum. This should be considered in restructuring the title to a residence to fund a bypass trust.

Qualified terminable interest trust (Q-TIP). A trust which qualifies for the unlimited marital tax exclusion. Therefore, there will be no estate tax on the value of the property transferred to your spouse in a Q-TIP trust on your death. Your spouse must receive all income at least annually. The Q-TIP enables your spouse to obtain income and other benefits, your estate avoids tax, and you can designate who will receive the property remaining in the trust on your spouse's death.

Quiet enjoyment.   The unimpaired right to use and enjoy property purchased or leased.

Real property.   Land and anything that is permanently affixed to land (e.g., house, garage, under-lawn sprinkler). Compare to personal property. Generally all items which constitute real property are sold as part of the sale of your house unless the sales contract specifically excludes them.

Remainder beneficiary.   The person who will receive assets of a trust after the interests of persons who are currently receiving income ends. The remainder beneficiaries under a QPRT will receive the residence following the QPRT term.

RESPA.   A form required by the U.S. Housing and Urban Development under the Real Estate Settlement Procedures Act.

Restrictive covenants.   Rules and regulations governing how property can be used. For example, when the subdivision your house is in was formed all of the deeds for the houses might have included restrictions requiring a minimum lot size, and so on.

Sale.   A contract by which one person transfers ownership in certain property to another person.

Second mortgage.   Money loaned on the house which is behind, or second in priority, to the first mortgage in the event of a foreclosure. Purchase money mortgages, loans provided by the seller, are often second mortgages.

Settlor.   Person who sets up a trust. Also called grantor, trustor, and, occasionally, donor.

Take back mortgage.   Purchase money financing. A loan which the seller agrees to extend to the buyer for part of the purchase price.

Tenancy by the entirety.   Where husband and wife are joint tenants, it is a special type of joint tenancy called tenancy by the entirety. It provides limited protection from creditors and malpractice claimants, but has several drawbacks which the use of other types of ownership or a trust can address.

Title.   The right to use and enjoy property.

Transfer taxes.   Taxes or fees (which sometimes are not deductible as taxes) required to be paid when title or ownership in property changes. For example, a cooperative corporation may require the payment of a transfer fee when a current owner sells. This won't qualify as a deductible tax for income tax purposes. A transfer tax paid to a county based on, for example, a percentage of the contract price, may be deductible as a property tax.

Trust.   Property is held and managed by a person (trustee) for the benefit of another (the beneficiary) under a fiduciary relationship. The terms of the trust are generally governed by a contract that you the grantor have prepared when you establish the trust.

Trustee.   The person (fiduciary) who manages and administers a trust you establish.

Trustor.   Person who sets-up a trust. Also called grantor, settlor, and, occasionally, donor.

Uniform gifts (transfers) to minors act (UGMA or UTMA).   A method to hold property for the benefit of another person, such as your child, which is similar to a trust, but which is governed by state law. It is simpler and much cheaper to establish and administer, but is far less flexible.

Unified credit.   Every taxpayer is allowed to exclude from estate and gift tax a total of $1 million (2002, scheduled to increase thereafter) of transfers.

Index